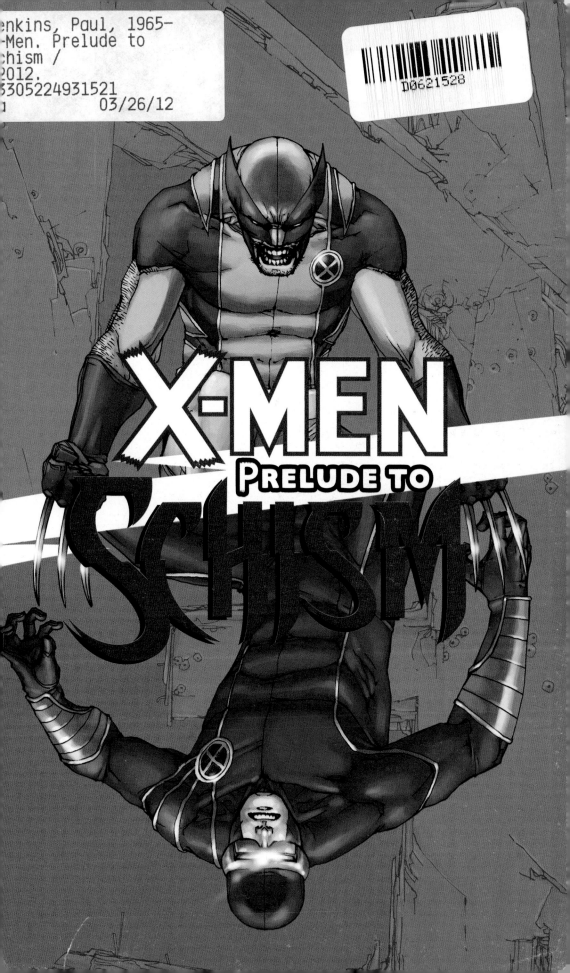

# X-MEN
## PRELUDE TO
# SCHISM

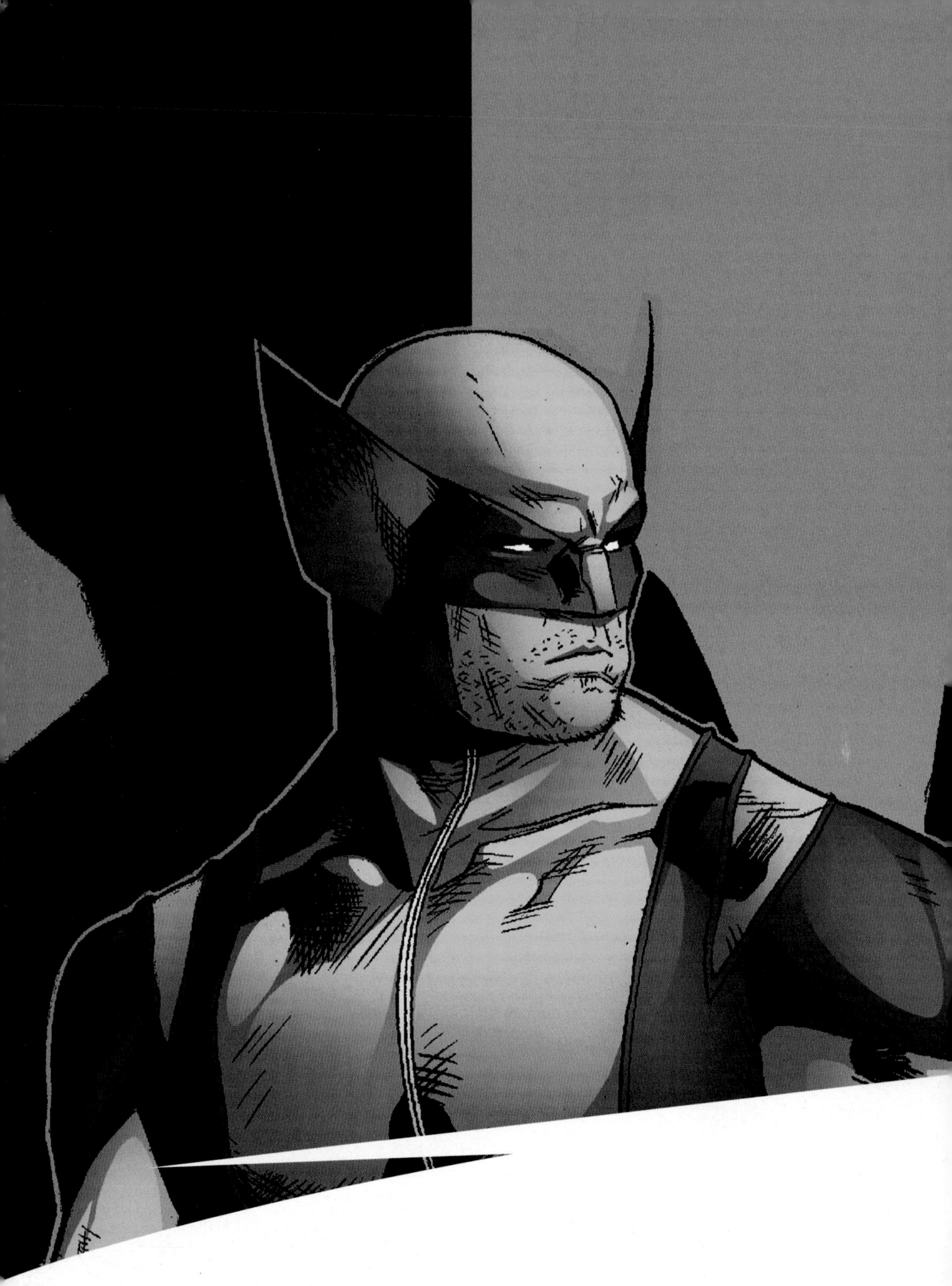

COLLECTION EDITOR: JENNIFER GRÜNWALD • ASSISTANT EDITORS: ALEX STARBUCK & NELSON RIBEIRO
EDITOR, SPECIAL PROJECTS: MARK D. BEAZLEY • SENIOR EDITOR, SPECIAL PROJECTS: JEFF YOUNGQUIST • SENIOR VICE PRESIDENT OF SALES: DAVID GABRIEL
SVP OF BRAND PLANNING & COMMUNICATIONS: MICHAEL PASCIULLO • BOOK DESIGN: JEFF POWELL

EDITOR IN CHIEF: AXEL ALONSO • CHIEF CREATIVE OFFICER: JOE QUESADA • PUBLISHER: DAN BUCKLEY • EXECUTIVE PRODUCER: ALAN FINE

**X-MEN: PRELUDE TO SCHISM.** Contains material originally published in magazine form as X-MEN: PRELUDE TO SCHISM #1-4 and X-MEN FIRST CLASS SPOTLIGHT. First printing 2012. ISBN# 978-0-7851-569 Published by MARVEL WORLDWIDE, INC., a subsidiary of MARVEL ENTERTAINMENT, LLC. OFFICE OF PUBLICATION: 135 West 50th Street, New York, NY 10020.  **Printed in the U.S.A.** ALAN FINE, EVP - Office of the President, Marvel Worldwide, Inc. and EVP & CMO Marvel Characters B.V.; DAN BUC Publisher & President - Print, Animation & Digital Divisions; JOE QUESADA, Chief Creative Officer; DAVID BOGART, SVP of Business Affairs & Talent Management; TOM BREVOORT, SVP of Publishing; C.B. CEBULS of Creator & Content Development; DAVID GABRIEL, SVP of Publishing Sales & Circulation; MICHAEL PASCIULLO, SVP of Brand Planning & Communications; JIM O'KEEFE, VP of Operations & Logistics; DAN CAR ecutive Director of Publishing Technology; SUSAN CRESPI, Editorial Operations Manager; ALEX MORALES, Publishing Operations Manager; STAN LEE, Chairman Emeritus. For information regarding advertising in Comics or on Marvel.com, please contact John Dokes, SVP Integrated Sales and Marketing, at jdokes@marvel.com. For Marvel subscription inquiries, please call 800-217-9158. **Manufactured between 1/25/ and 2/13/2012 by R.R. DONNELLEY, INC., SALEM, VA, USA.**

10 9 8 7 6 5 4 3 2 1

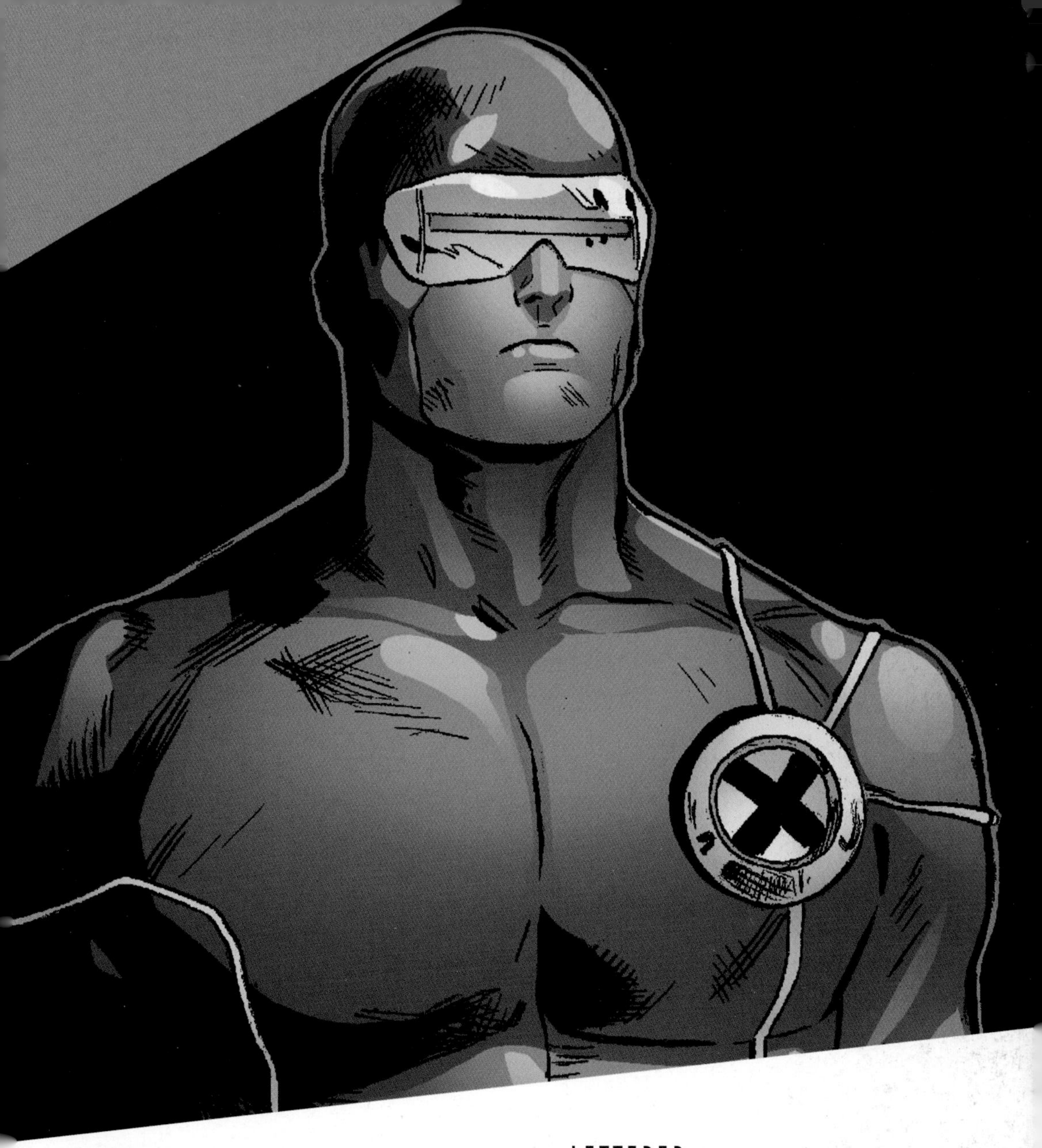


WRITER
**PAUL JENKINS**

ARTISTS, ISSUES #1-3
**ROBERTO DE LA TORRE** (#1)
**ANDREA MUTTI** (#2)
**WILL CONRAD** (#3)

PENCILER, ISSUE #4
**CLAY MANN**

INKERS, ISSUE #4
**JAY LEISTEN & SETH MANN**

COLOR ARTIST
**LEE LOUGHRIDGE**

LETTERER
**ROB STEEN**

COVER ART
**GIUSEPPE CAMUNCOLI & DAN BROWN**

ASSISTANT EDITOR
**SEBASTIAN GIRNER**

ASSOCIATE EDITOR
**DANIEL KETCHUM**

EDITOR
**NICK LOWE**

# PREVIOUSLY

Seeking to escape persecution from those who hate and fear them, the X-Men created a new home for mutantkind just off th
west coast of the United States, on an island they call Utopia. Under the leadership of Scott Summers, a.k.a. Cyclops, the X-Me
safeguard their new sovereign nation against those who would see the mutant species wiped out.

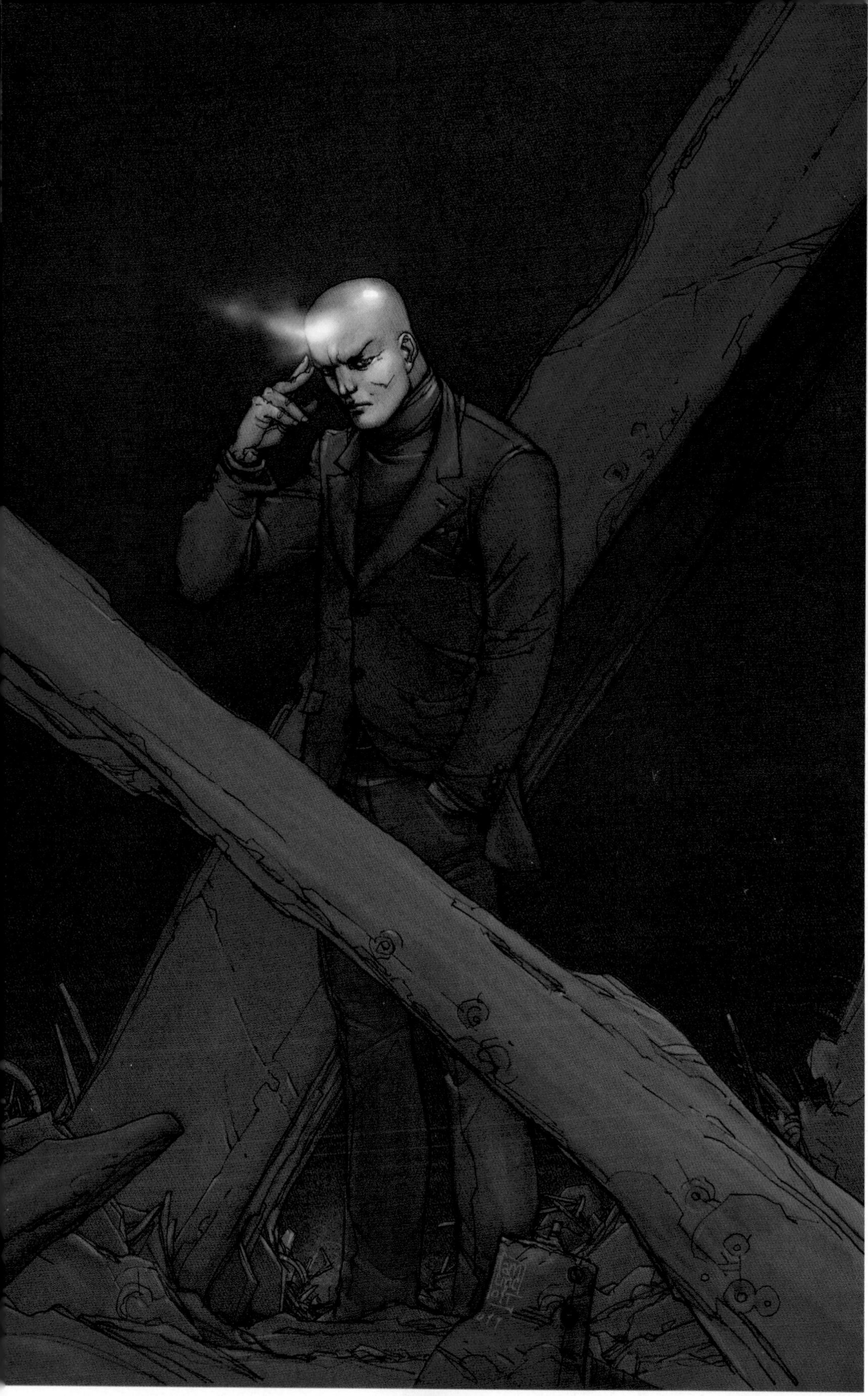

# 1

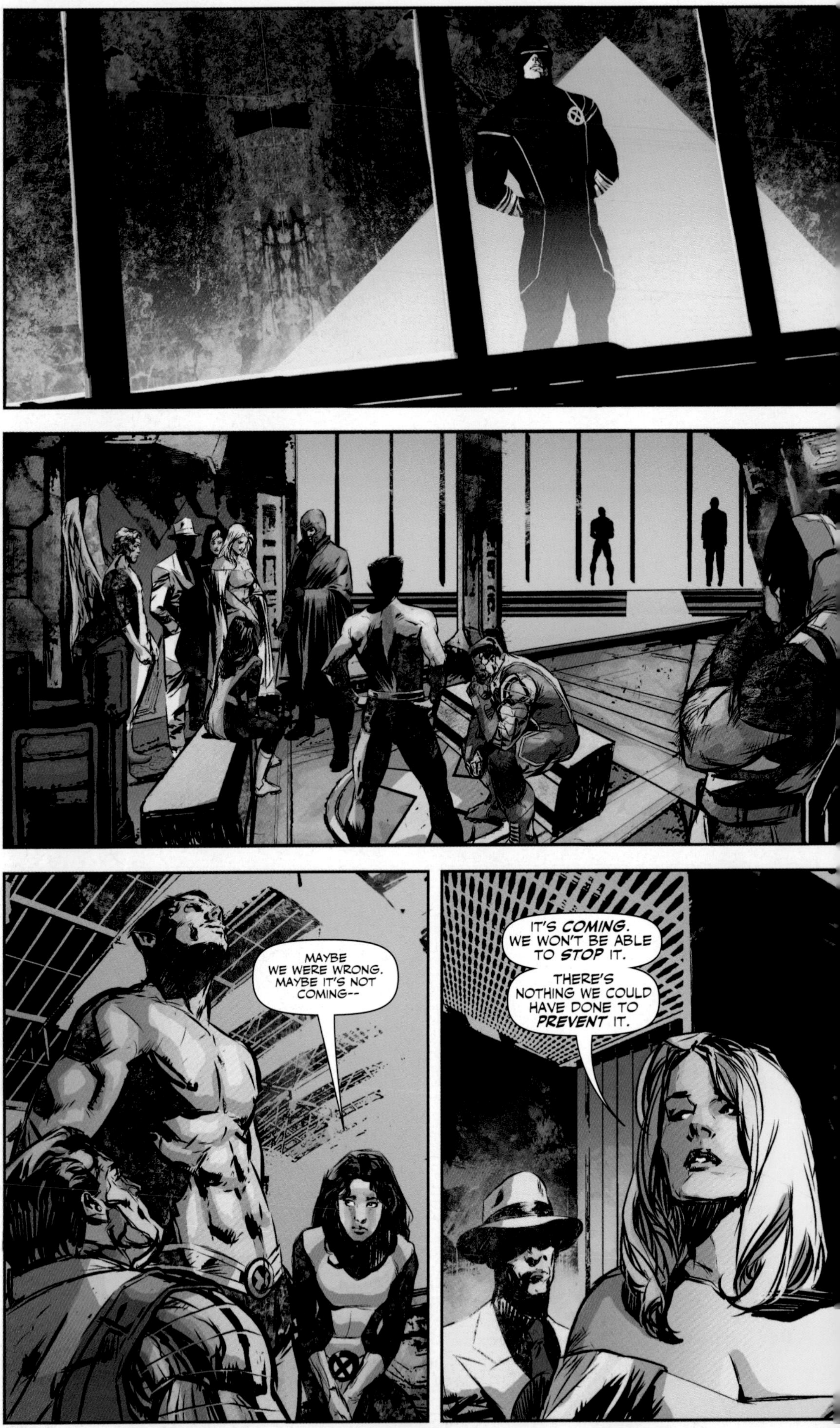
MAYBE WE WERE WRONG. MAYBE IT'S NOT COMING--
IT'S COMING. WE WON'T BE ABLE TO STOP IT.
THERE'S NOTHING WE COULD HAVE DONE TO PREVENT IT.

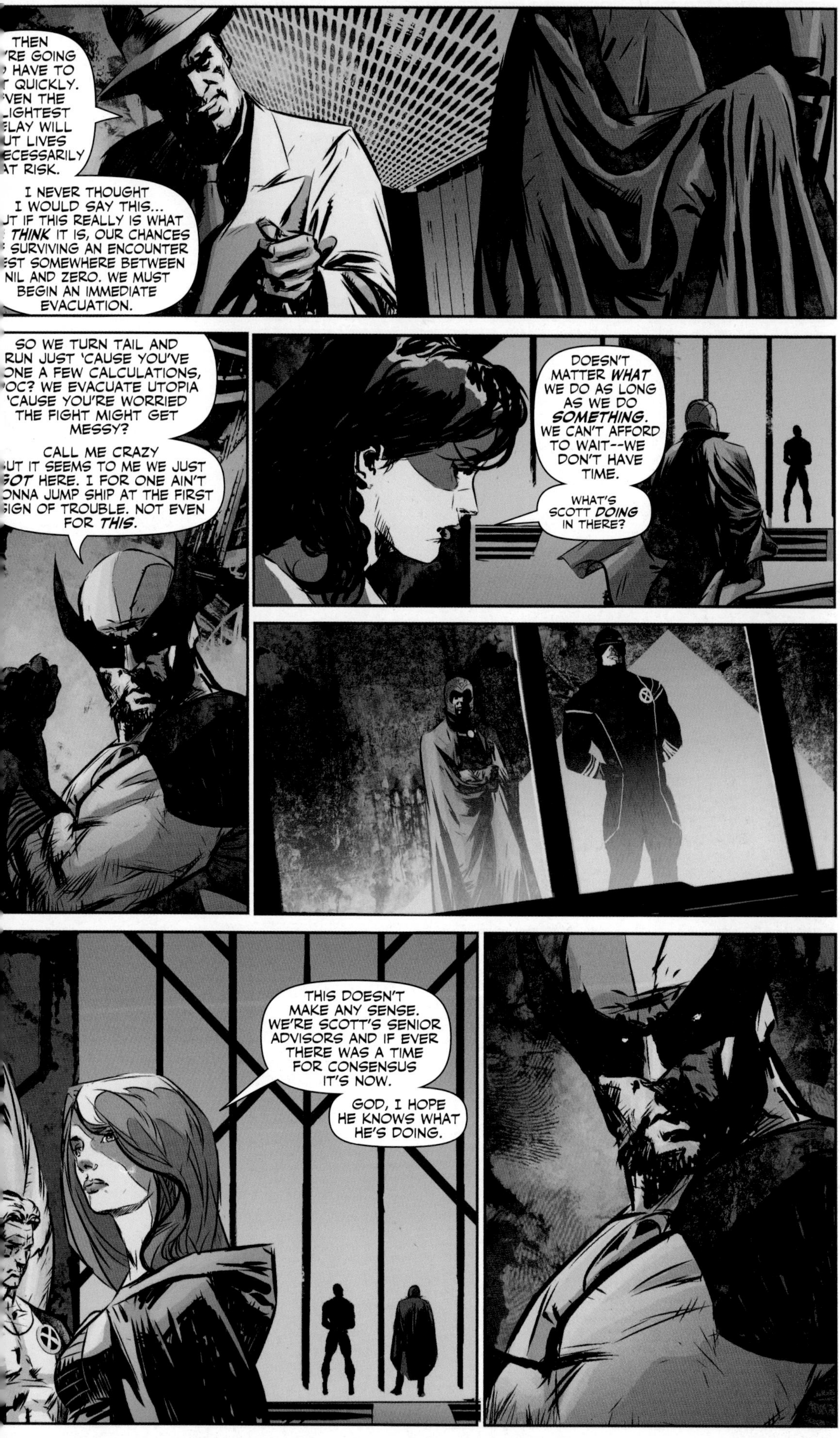
THEN 'RE GOING HAVE TO T QUICKLY. EVEN THE LIGHTEST ELAY WILL UT LIVES ECESSARILY AT RISK.
I NEVER THOUGHT I WOULD SAY THIS... UT IF THIS REALLY IS WHAT THINK IT IS, OUR CHANCES SURVIVING AN ENCOUNTER EST SOMEWHERE BETWEEN NIL AND ZERO. WE MUST BEGIN AN IMMEDIATE EVACUATION.
SO WE TURN TAIL AND RUN JUST 'CAUSE YOU'VE ONE A FEW CALCULATIONS, OC? WE EVACUATE UTOPIA 'CAUSE YOU'RE WORRIED THE FIGHT MIGHT GET MESSY?
CALL ME CRAZY UT IT SEEMS TO ME WE JUST GOT HERE. I FOR ONE AIN'T ONNA JUMP SHIP AT THE FIRST SIGN OF TROUBLE. NOT EVEN FOR THIS.
DOESN'T MATTER WHAT WE DO AS LONG AS WE DO SOMETHING. WE CAN'T AFFORD TO WAIT--WE DON'T HAVE TIME.
WHAT'S SCOTT DOING IN THERE?
THIS DOESN'T MAKE ANY SENSE. WE'RE SCOTT'S SENIOR ADVISORS AND IF EVER THERE WAS A TIME FOR CONSENSUS IT'S NOW.
GOD, I HOPE HE KNOWS WHAT HE'S DOING.

WHAT IF WE DON'T HAVE TO EVACUATE? WE COULD MAKE A STAND HERE. THERE'S ENOUGH OF US TO HOLD BACK THE FIRST WAVE--

WHAT GOOD IS THAT GOING TO DO? HOLDING IT BACK IS JUST DELAYING THE INEVITABLE!

NOTHING IS INEVITABLE, AND NO ONE SAID WE'RE DELAYING ANYTHING. BESIDES, EVEN IF WE COULD TRY TO EVACUATE WE'RE ALREADY PAST THAT POINT.

WE HAVE TO GIVE SCOTT TIME TO MAKE THE BEST DECISION.

SCOTT WILL BE WITH [...] PRESENTLY. HE [...] ME TO APOLOG[...] HIS BEHALF BUT [...] SURE YOU'RE ALL [...] THIS IS A MOM[...] OF MONUMEN[...] GRAVITY.

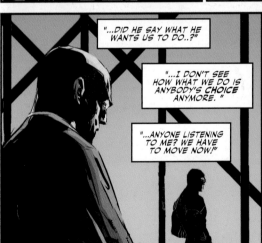

"...DID HE SAY WHAT HE WANTS US TO DO..?"

"...I DON'T SEE HOW WHAT WE DO IS ANYBODY'S CHOICE ANYMORE."

"...ANYONE LISTENING TO ME? WE HAVE TO MOVE NOW!"

WHEN I THINK OF YOU NOW...

...I THINK OF A FIELD OF BARLEY.

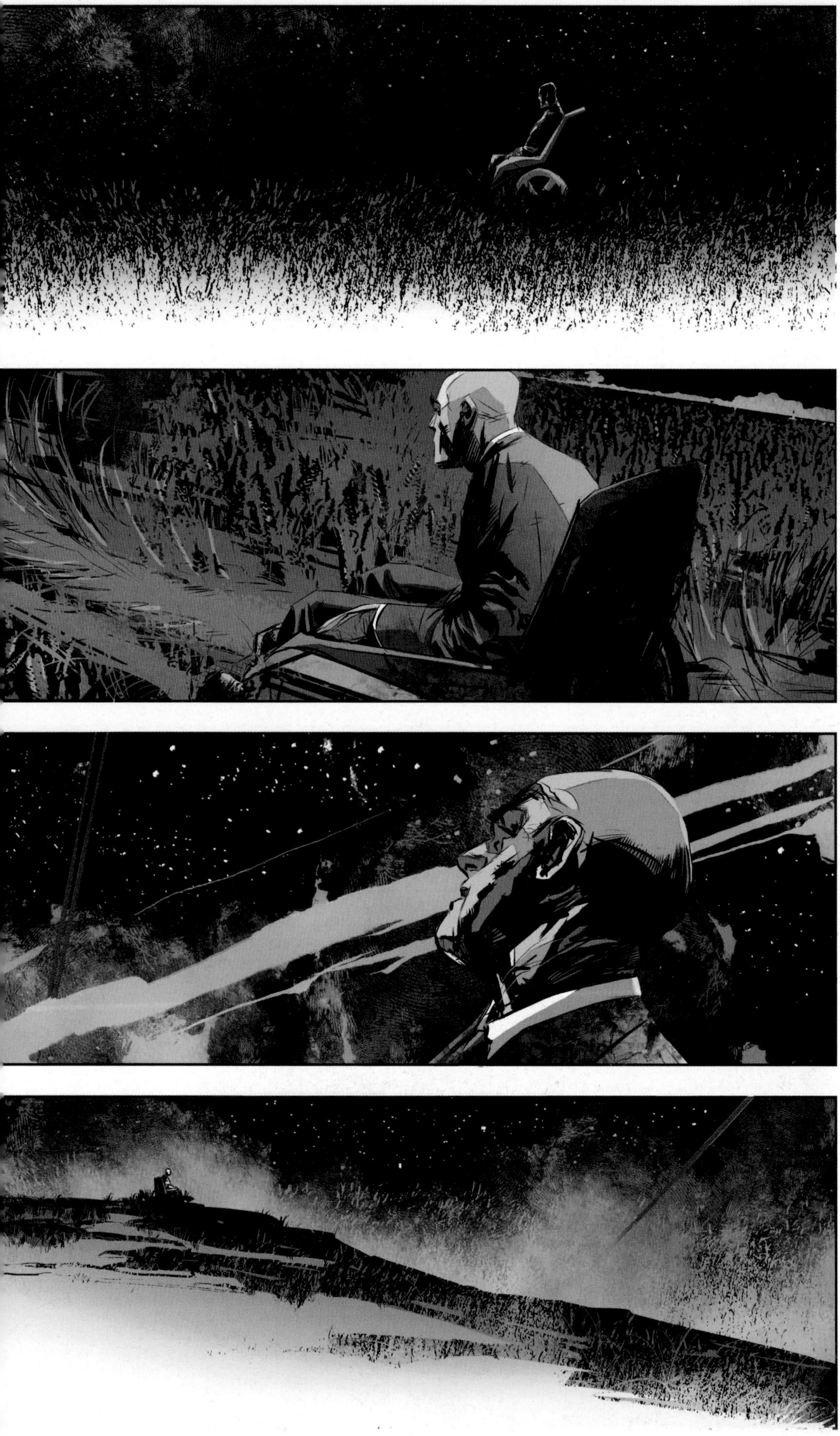

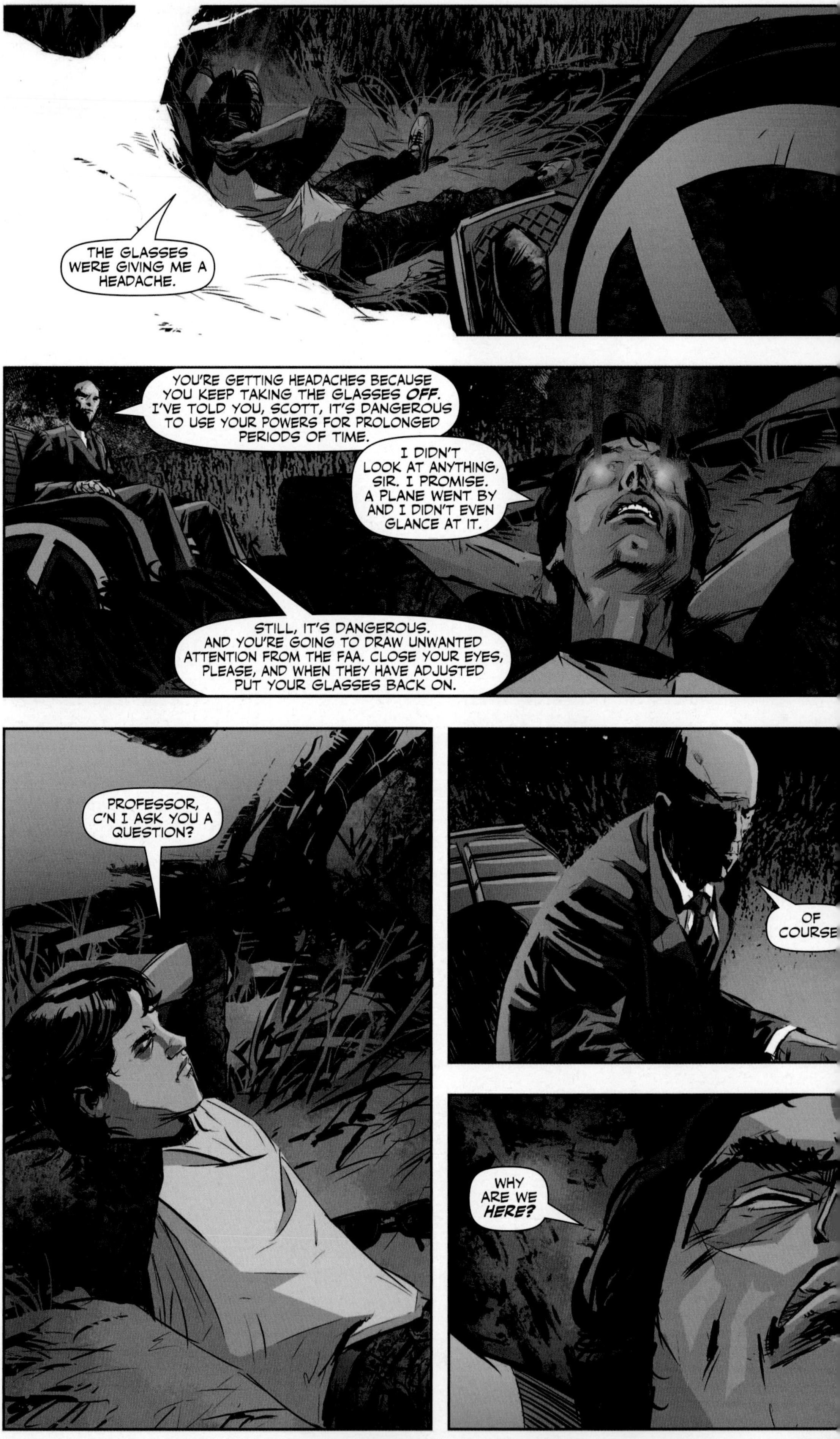
THE GLASSES WERE GIVING ME A HEADACHE.
YOU'RE GETTING HEADACHES BECAUSE YOU KEEP TAKING THE GLASSES *OFF*. I'VE TOLD YOU, SCOTT, IT'S DANGEROUS TO USE YOUR POWERS FOR PROLONGED PERIODS OF TIME.
I DIDN'T LOOK AT ANYTHING, SIR. I PROMISE. A PLANE WENT BY AND I DIDN'T EVEN GLANCE AT IT.
STILL, IT'S DANGEROUS. AND YOU'RE GOING TO DRAW UNWANTED ATTENTION FROM THE FAA. CLOSE YOUR EYES, PLEASE, AND WHEN THEY HAVE ADJUSTED PUT YOUR GLASSES BACK ON.
PROFESSOR, C'N I ASK YOU A QUESTION?
OF COURSE
WHY ARE WE ***HERE?***

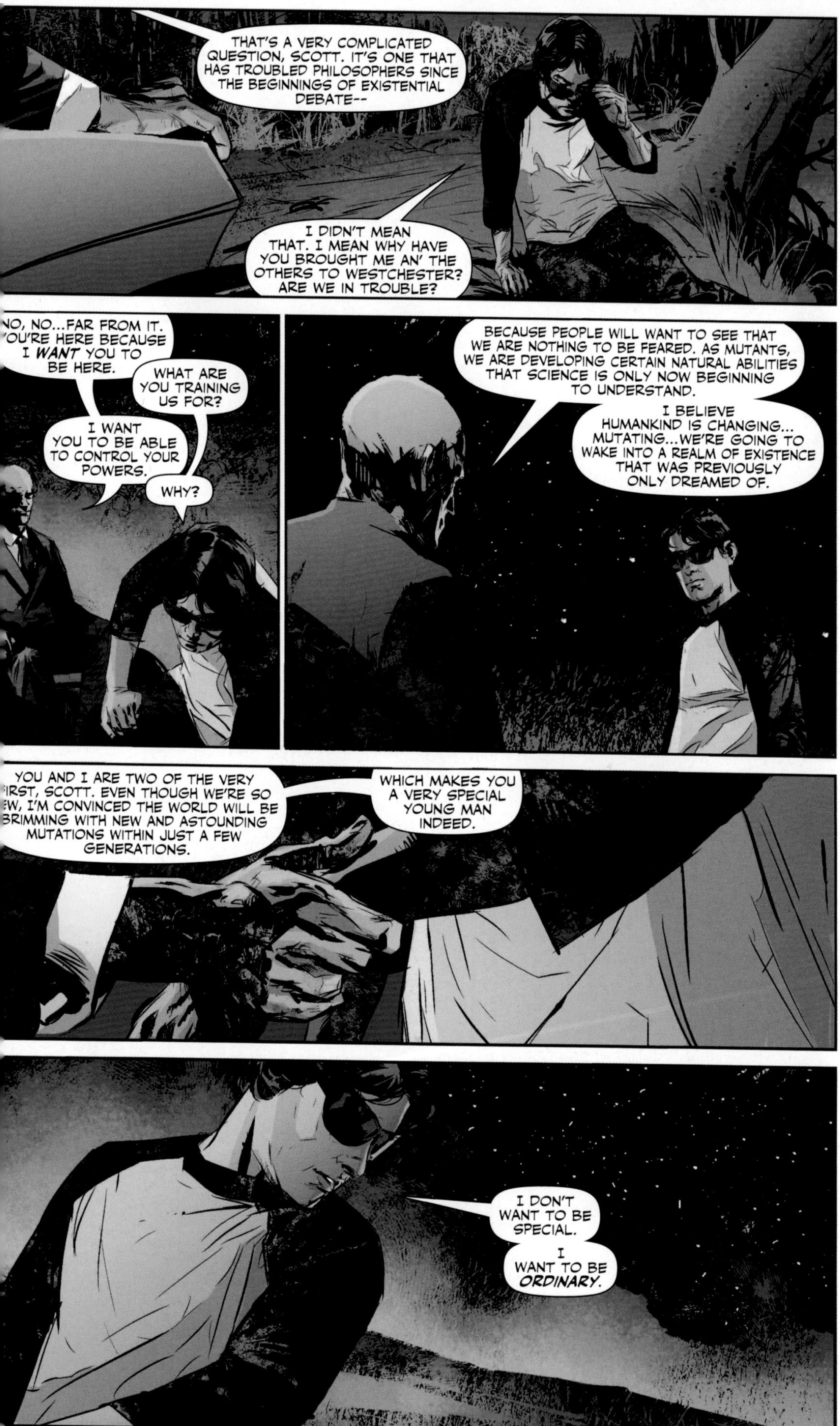
THAT'S A VERY COMPLICATED QUESTION, SCOTT. IT'S ONE THAT HAS TROUBLED PHILOSOPHERS SINCE THE BEGINNINGS OF EXISTENTIAL DEBATE--
I DIDN'T MEAN THAT. I MEAN WHY HAVE YOU BROUGHT ME AN' THE OTHERS TO WESTCHESTER? ARE WE IN TROUBLE?
NO, NO...FAR FROM IT. YOU'RE HERE BECAUSE I *WANT* YOU TO BE HERE.
WHAT ARE YOU TRAINING US FOR?
I WANT YOU TO BE ABLE TO CONTROL YOUR POWERS.
WHY?
BECAUSE PEOPLE WILL WANT TO SEE THAT WE ARE NOTHING TO BE FEARED. AS MUTANTS, WE ARE DEVELOPING CERTAIN NATURAL ABILITIES THAT SCIENCE IS ONLY NOW BEGINNING TO UNDERSTAND.
I BELIEVE HUMANKIND IS CHANGING... MUTATING...WE'RE GOING TO WAKE INTO A REALM OF EXISTENCE THAT WAS PREVIOUSLY ONLY DREAMED OF.
YOU AND I ARE TWO OF THE VERY FIRST, SCOTT. EVEN THOUGH WE'RE SO EW, I'M CONVINCED THE WORLD WILL BE BRIMMING WITH NEW AND ASTOUNDING MUTATIONS WITHIN JUST A FEW GENERATIONS.
WHICH MAKES YOU A VERY SPECIAL YOUNG MAN INDEED.
I DON'T WANT TO BE SPECIAL.
I WANT TO BE ***ORDINARY***.

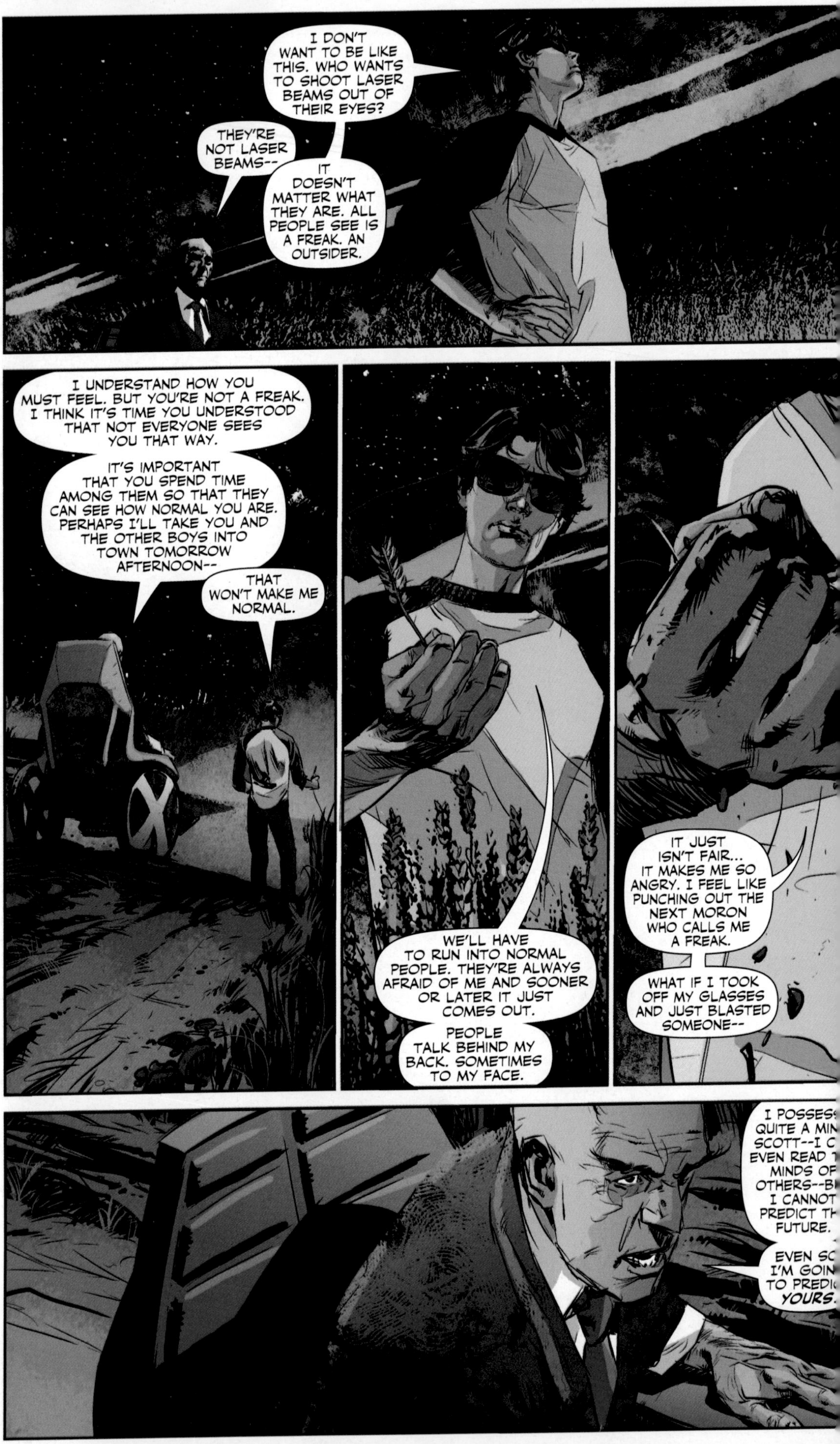

I DON'T WANT TO BE LIKE THIS. WHO WANTS TO SHOOT LASER BEAMS OUT OF THEIR EYES?
THEY'RE NOT LASER BEAMS--
IT DOESN'T MATTER WHAT THEY ARE. ALL PEOPLE SEE IS A FREAK. AN OUTSIDER.
I UNDERSTAND HOW YOU MUST FEEL. BUT YOU'RE NOT A FREAK. I THINK IT'S TIME YOU UNDERSTOOD THAT NOT EVERYONE SEES YOU THAT WAY.
IT'S IMPORTANT THAT YOU SPEND TIME AMONG THEM SO THAT THEY CAN SEE HOW NORMAL YOU ARE. PERHAPS I'LL TAKE YOU AND THE OTHER BOYS INTO TOWN TOMORROW AFTERNOON--
THAT WON'T MAKE ME NORMAL.
WE'LL HAVE TO RUN INTO NORMAL PEOPLE. THEY'RE ALWAYS AFRAID OF ME AND SOONER OR LATER IT JUST COMES OUT.
PEOPLE TALK BEHIND MY BACK. SOMETIMES TO MY FACE.
IT JUST ISN'T FAIR... IT MAKES ME SO ANGRY. I FEEL LIKE PUNCHING OUT THE NEXT MORON WHO CALLS ME A FREAK.
WHAT IF I TOOK OFF MY GLASSES AND JUST BLASTED SOMEONE--
I POSSES QUITE A MIN SCOTT--I C EVEN READ T MINDS OF OTHERS--B I CANNOT PREDICT TH FUTURE.
EVEN SO I'M GOIN TO PREDIC *YOURS*.

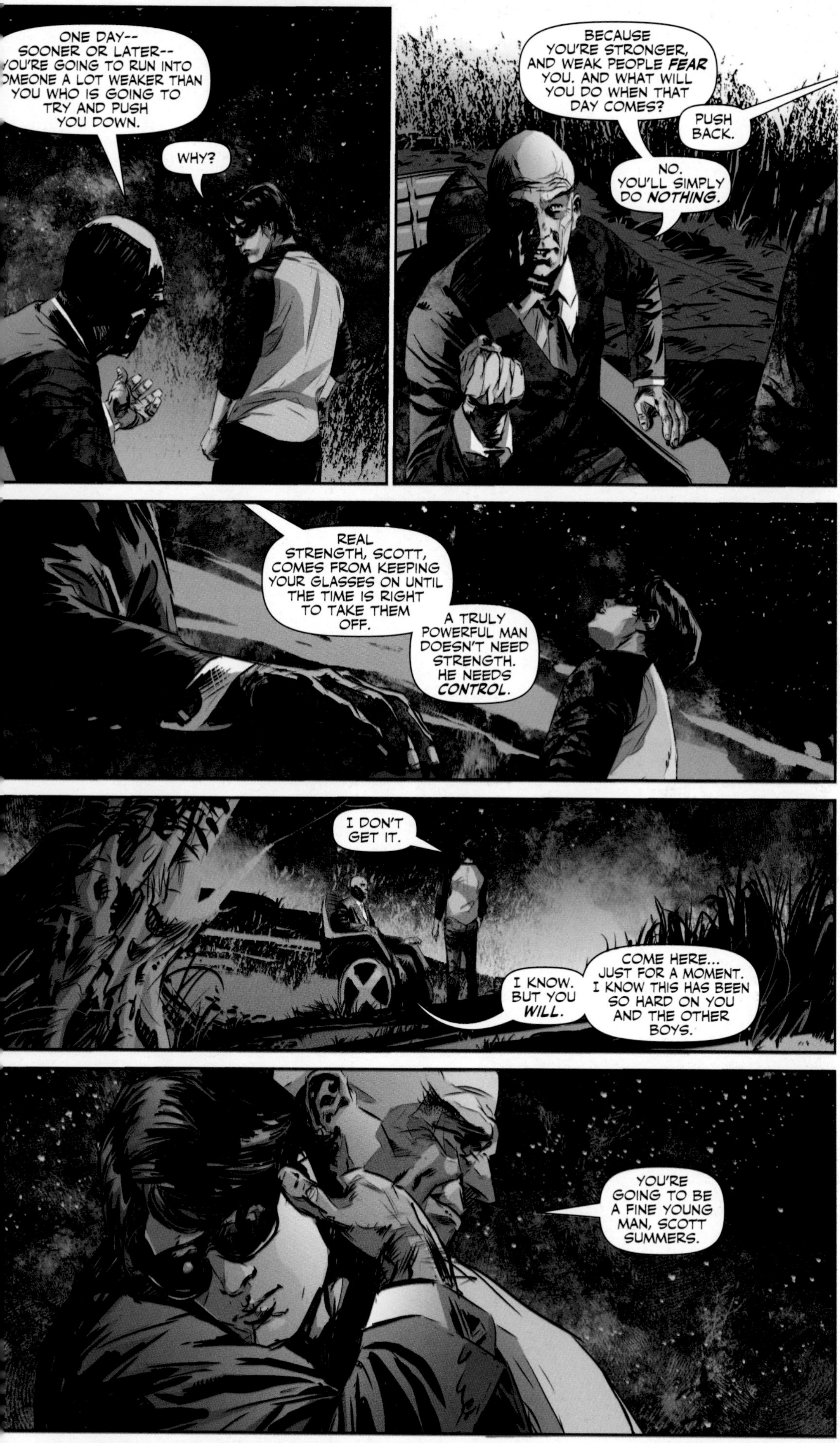
ONE DAY-- SOONER OR LATER-- YOU'RE GOING TO RUN INTO SOMEONE A LOT WEAKER THAN YOU WHO IS GOING TO TRY AND PUSH YOU DOWN.
WHY?
BECAUSE YOU'RE STRONGER, AND WEAK PEOPLE FEAR YOU. AND WHAT WILL YOU DO WHEN THAT DAY COMES?
PUSH BACK.
NO. YOU'LL SIMPLY DO NOTHING.
REAL STRENGTH, SCOTT, COMES FROM KEEPING YOUR GLASSES ON UNTIL THE TIME IS RIGHT TO TAKE THEM OFF.
A TRULY POWERFUL MAN DOESN'T NEED STRENGTH. HE NEEDS CONTROL.
I DON'T GET IT.
I KNOW. BUT YOU WILL.
COME HERE... JUST FOR A MOMENT. I KNOW THIS HAS BEEN SO HARD ON YOU AND THE OTHER BOYS.
YOU'RE GOING TO BE A FINE YOUNG MAN, SCOTT SUMMERS.

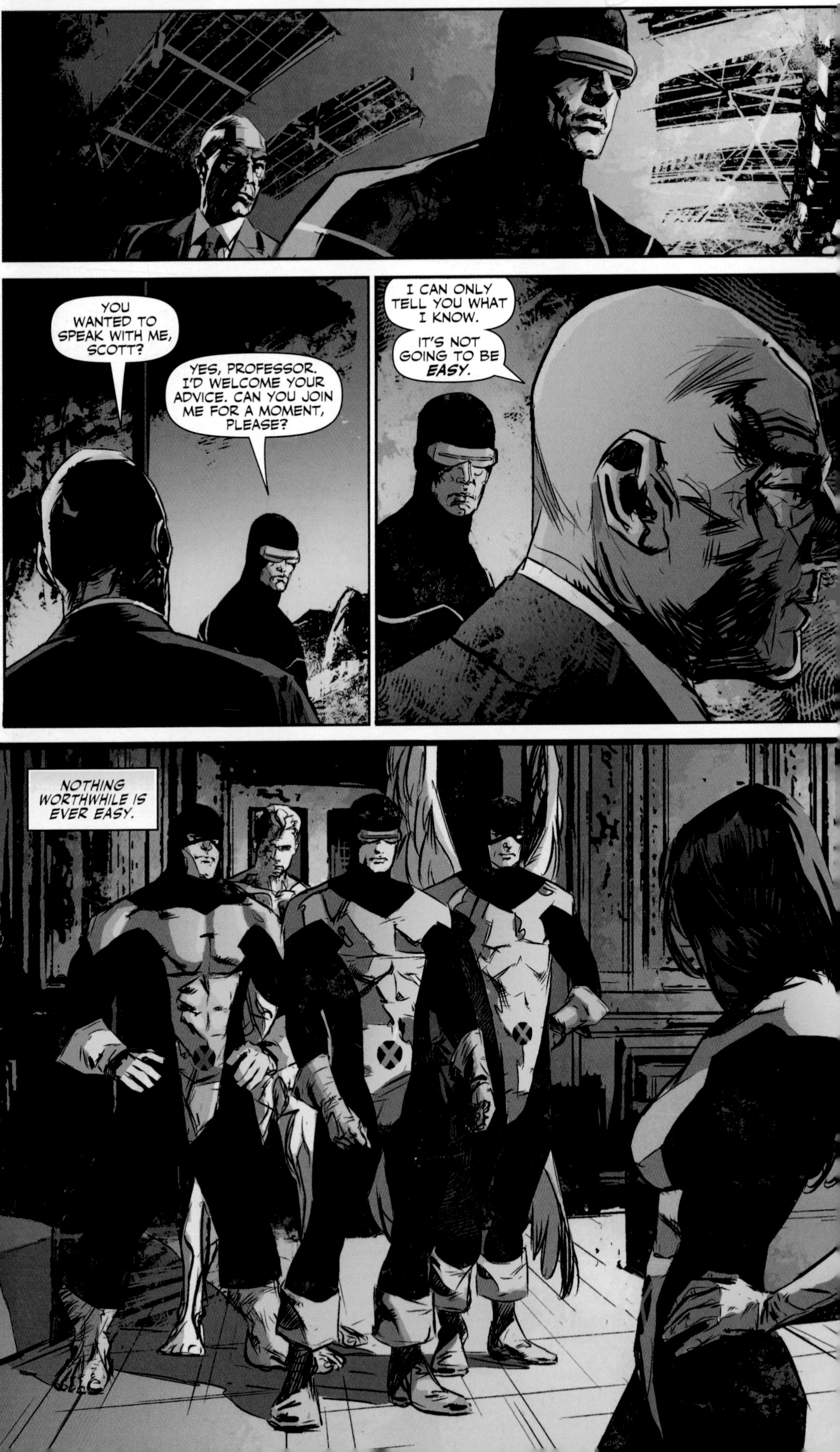

YOU WANTED TO SPEAK WITH ME, SCOTT?
YES, PROFESSOR. I'D WELCOME YOUR ADVICE. CAN YOU JOIN ME FOR A MOMENT, PLEASE?
I CAN ONLY TELL YOU WHAT I KNOW.
IT'S NOT GOING TO BE *EASY*.
NOTHING WORTHWHILE IS EVER EASY.

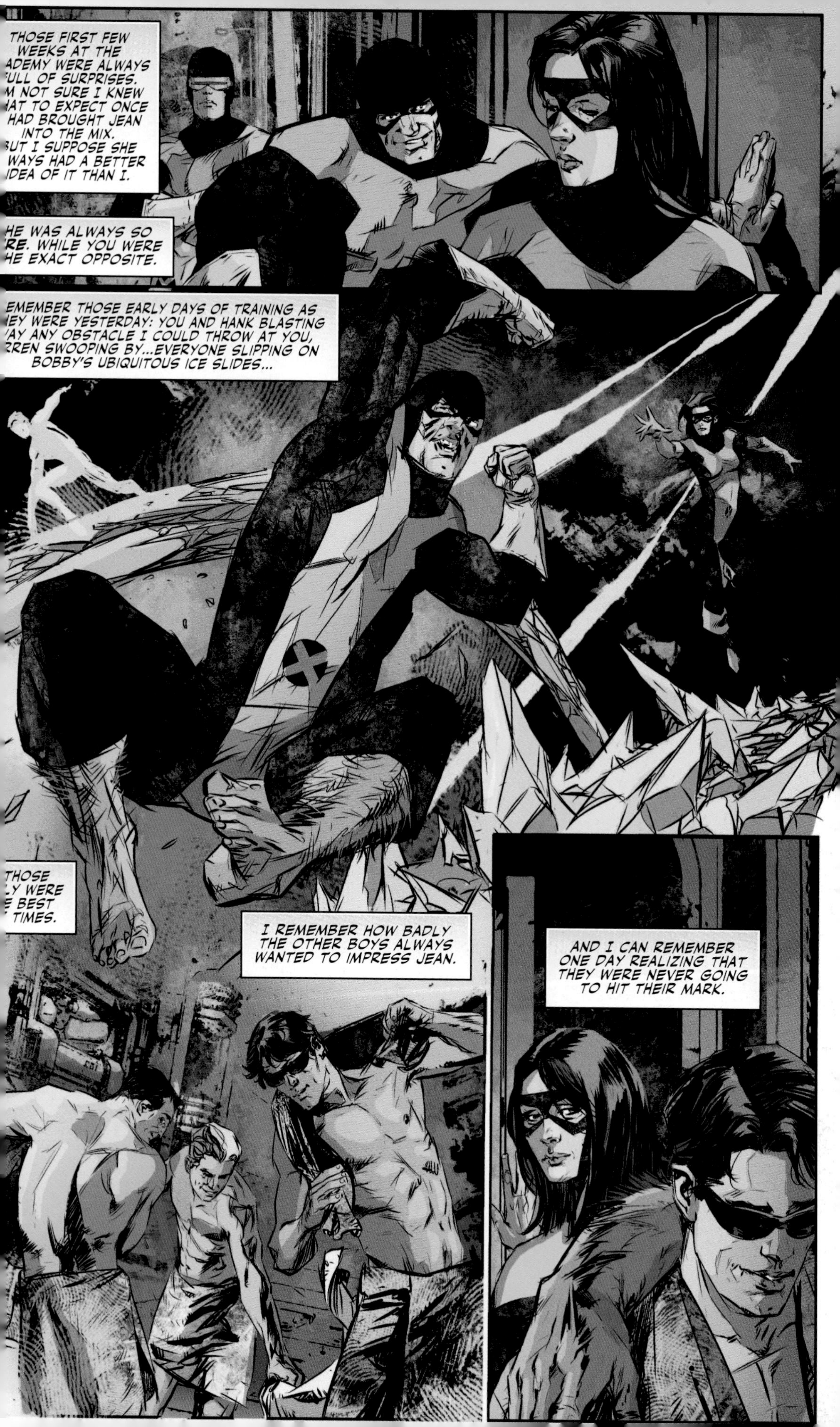
THOSE FIRST FEW WEEKS AT THE ADEMY WERE ALWAYS FULL OF SURPRISES. M NOT SURE I KNEW AT TO EXPECT ONCE HAD BROUGHT JEAN INTO THE MIX. BUT I SUPPOSE SHE WAYS HAD A BETTER IDEA OF IT THAN I.
HE WAS ALWAYS SO RE. WHILE YOU WERE HE EXACT OPPOSITE.
EMEMBER THOSE EARLY DAYS OF TRAINING AS EY WERE YESTERDAY: YOU AND HANK BLASTING AY ANY OBSTACLE I COULD THROW AT YOU, RREN SWOOPING BY...EVERYONE SLIPPING ON BOBBY'S UBIQUITOUS ICE SLIDES...
THOSE LY WERE E BEST TIMES.
I REMEMBER HOW BADLY THE OTHER BOYS ALWAYS WANTED TO IMPRESS JEAN.
AND I CAN REMEMBER ONE DAY REALIZING THAT THEY WERE NEVER GOING TO HIT THEIR MARK.

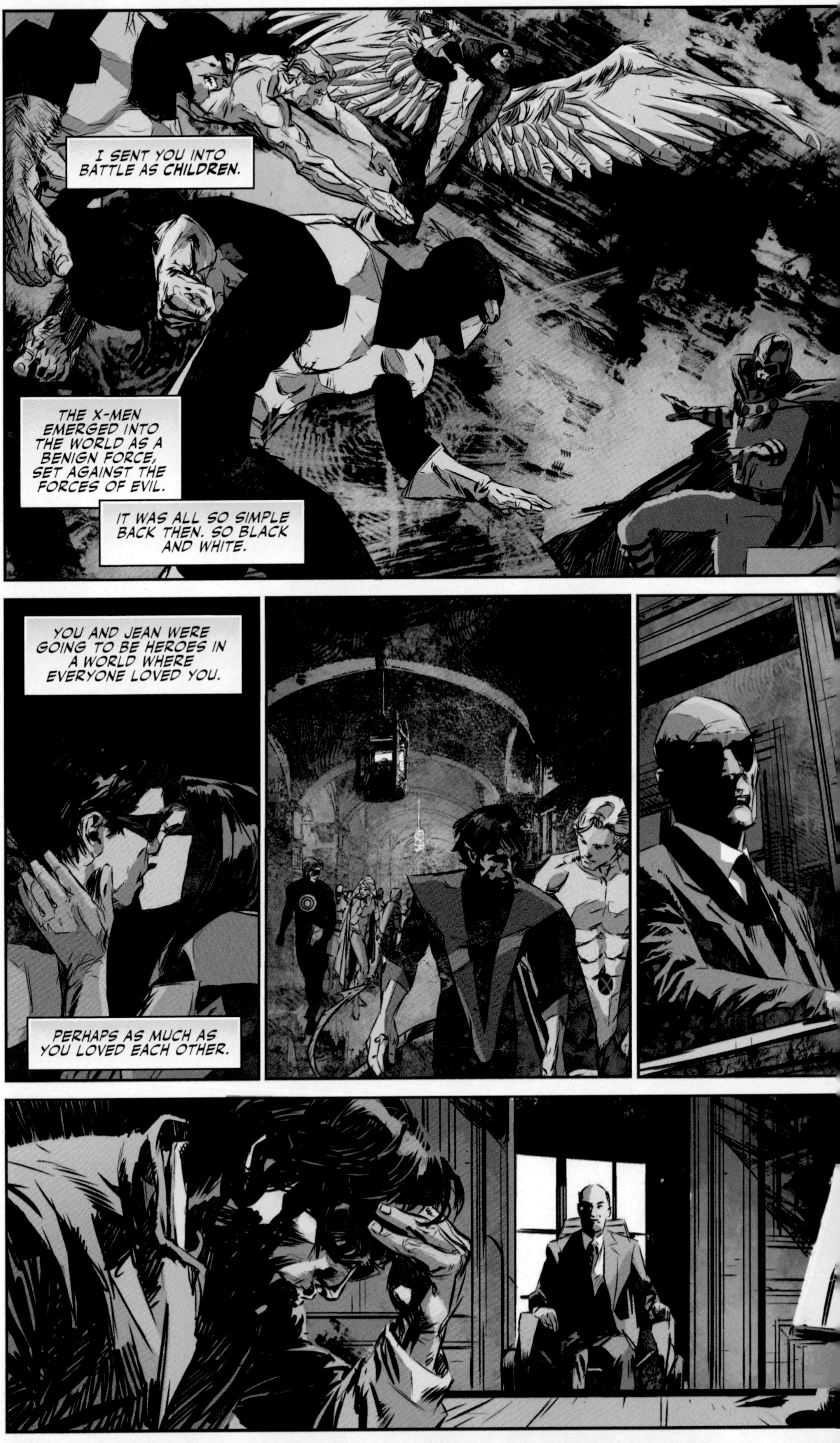
I SENT YOU INTO BATTLE AS CHILDREN.
THE X-MEN EMERGED INTO THE WORLD AS A BENIGN FORCE, SET AGAINST THE FORCES OF EVIL.
IT WAS ALL SO SIMPLE BACK THEN. SO BLACK AND WHITE.
YOU AND JEAN WERE GOING TO BE HEROES IN A WORLD WHERE EVERYONE LOVED YOU.
PERHAPS AS MUCH AS YOU LOVED EACH OTHER.

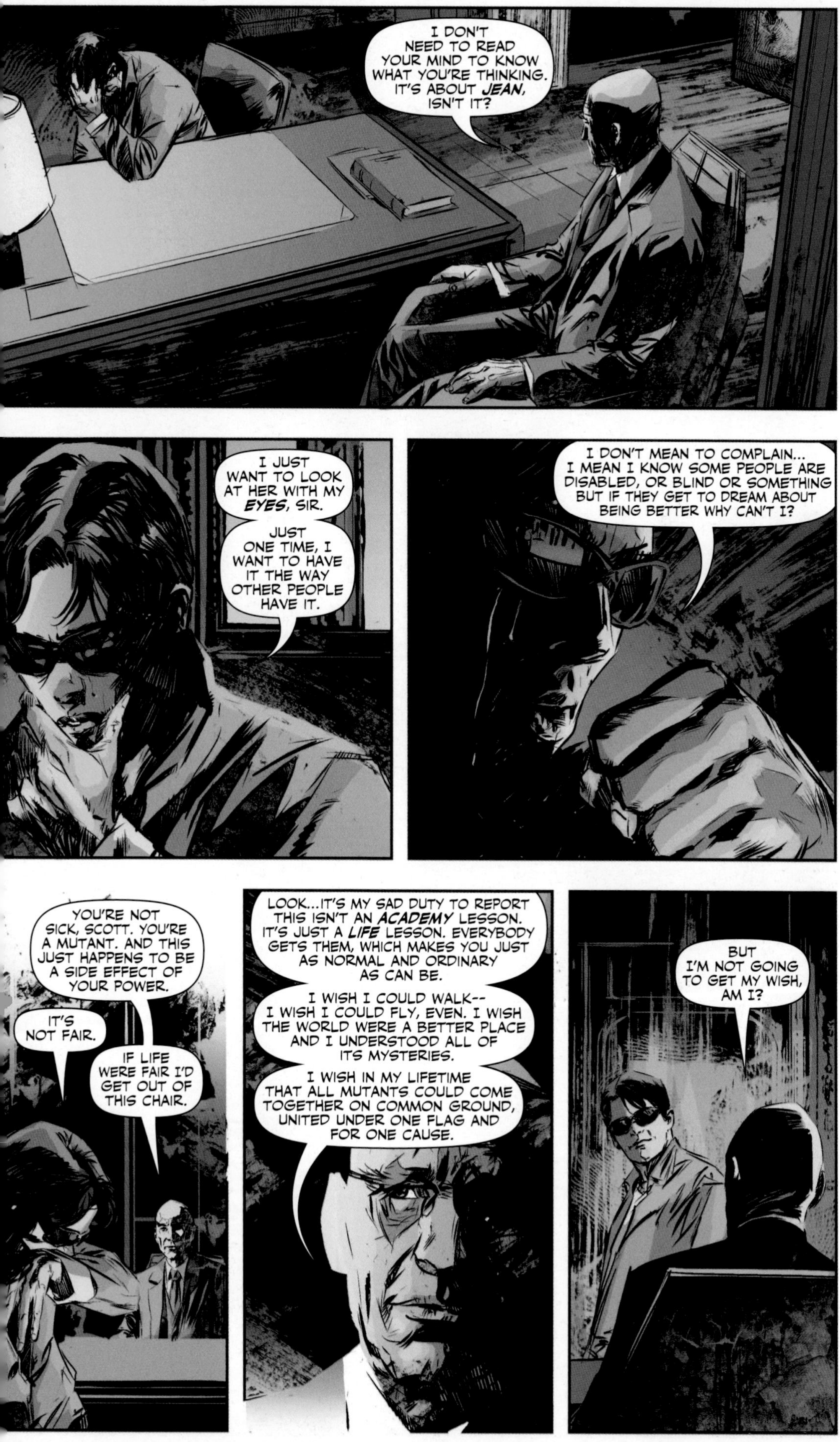
I DON'T NEED TO READ YOUR MIND TO KNOW WHAT YOU'RE THINKING. IT'S ABOUT *JEAN,* ISN'T IT?
I JUST WANT TO LOOK AT HER WITH MY *EYES*, SIR.
JUST ONE TIME, I WANT TO HAVE IT THE WAY OTHER PEOPLE HAVE IT.
I DON'T MEAN TO COMPLAIN... I MEAN I KNOW SOME PEOPLE ARE DISABLED, OR BLIND OR SOMETHING BUT IF THEY GET TO DREAM ABOUT BEING BETTER WHY CAN'T I?
YOU'RE NOT SICK, SCOTT. YOU'RE A MUTANT. AND THIS JUST HAPPENS TO BE A SIDE EFFECT OF YOUR POWER.
IT'S NOT FAIR.
IF LIFE WERE FAIR I'D GET OUT OF THIS CHAIR.
LOOK...IT'S MY SAD DUTY TO REPORT THIS ISN'T AN *ACADEMY* LESSON. IT'S JUST A *LIFE* LESSON. EVERYBODY GETS THEM, WHICH MAKES YOU JUST AS NORMAL AND ORDINARY AS CAN BE.
I WISH I COULD WALK-- I WISH I COULD FLY, EVEN. I WISH THE WORLD WERE A BETTER PLACE AND I UNDERSTOOD ALL OF ITS MYSTERIES.
I WISH IN MY LIFETIME THAT ALL MUTANTS COULD COME TOGETHER ON COMMON GROUND, UNITED UNDER ONE FLAG AND FOR ONE CAUSE.
BUT I'M NOT GOING TO GET MY WISH, AM I?

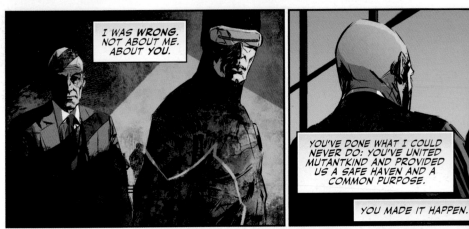

I WAS WRONG. NOT ABOUT ME. ABOUT YOU.

YOU'VE DONE WHAT I COULD NEVER DO: YOU'VE UNITED MUTANTKIND AND PROVIDED US A SAFE HAVEN AND A COMMON PURPOSE.

YOU MADE IT HAPPEN.

EXCEPT IT'S SUDDENLY NOT SO SAFE.

WE'VE ONLY JUST COME INTO BEING, YET IT MAY ALL BE GONE BY THIS TIME TOMORROW.

UNLESS YOU MAKE YOUR FIRST BIG DECISION AS OUR LEADER A GOOD ONE.

ALL OF THOSE SACRIFICES. WERE THEY WORTH IT?

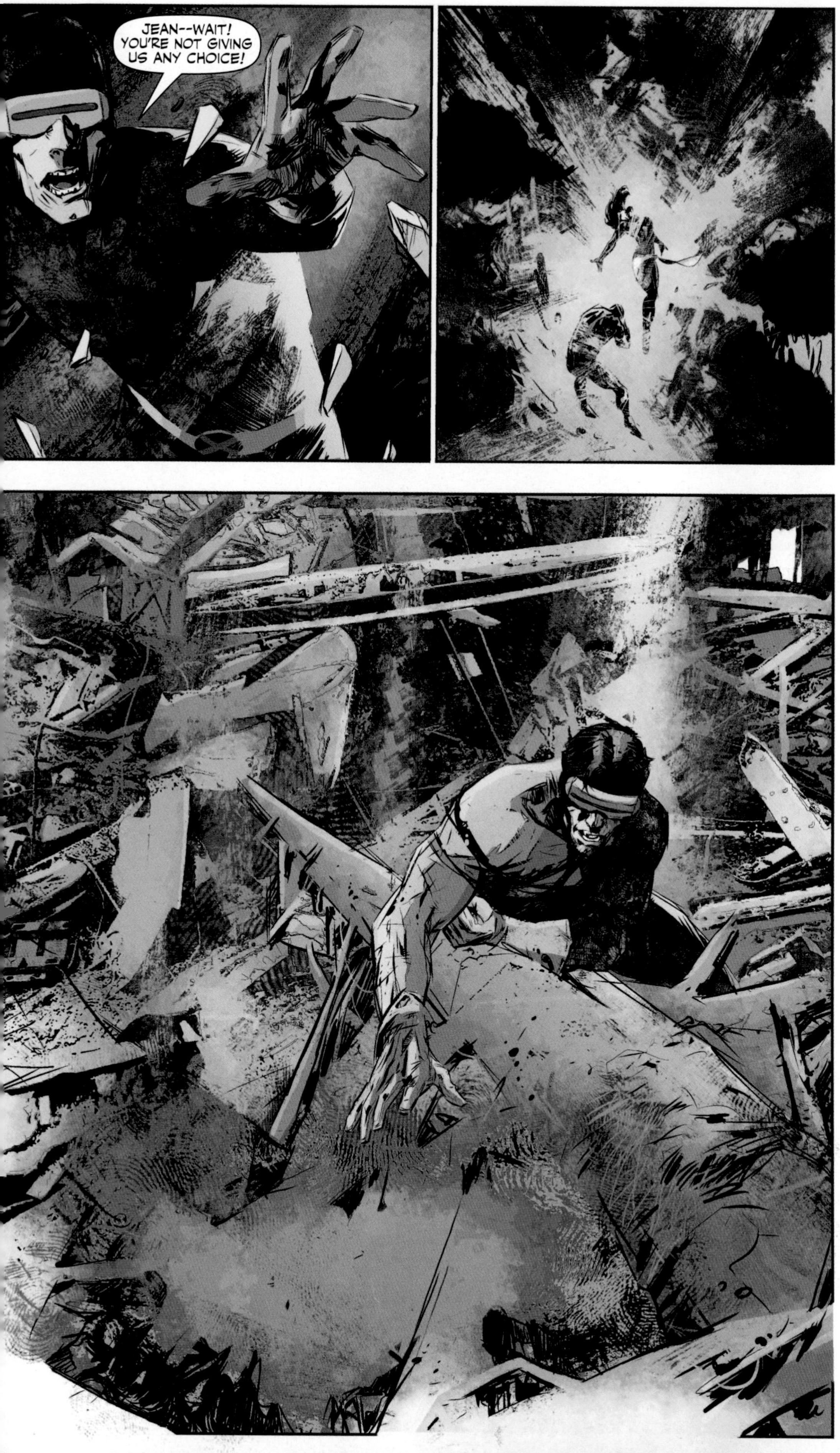
JEAN--WAIT! YOU'RE NOT GIVING US ANY CHOICE!

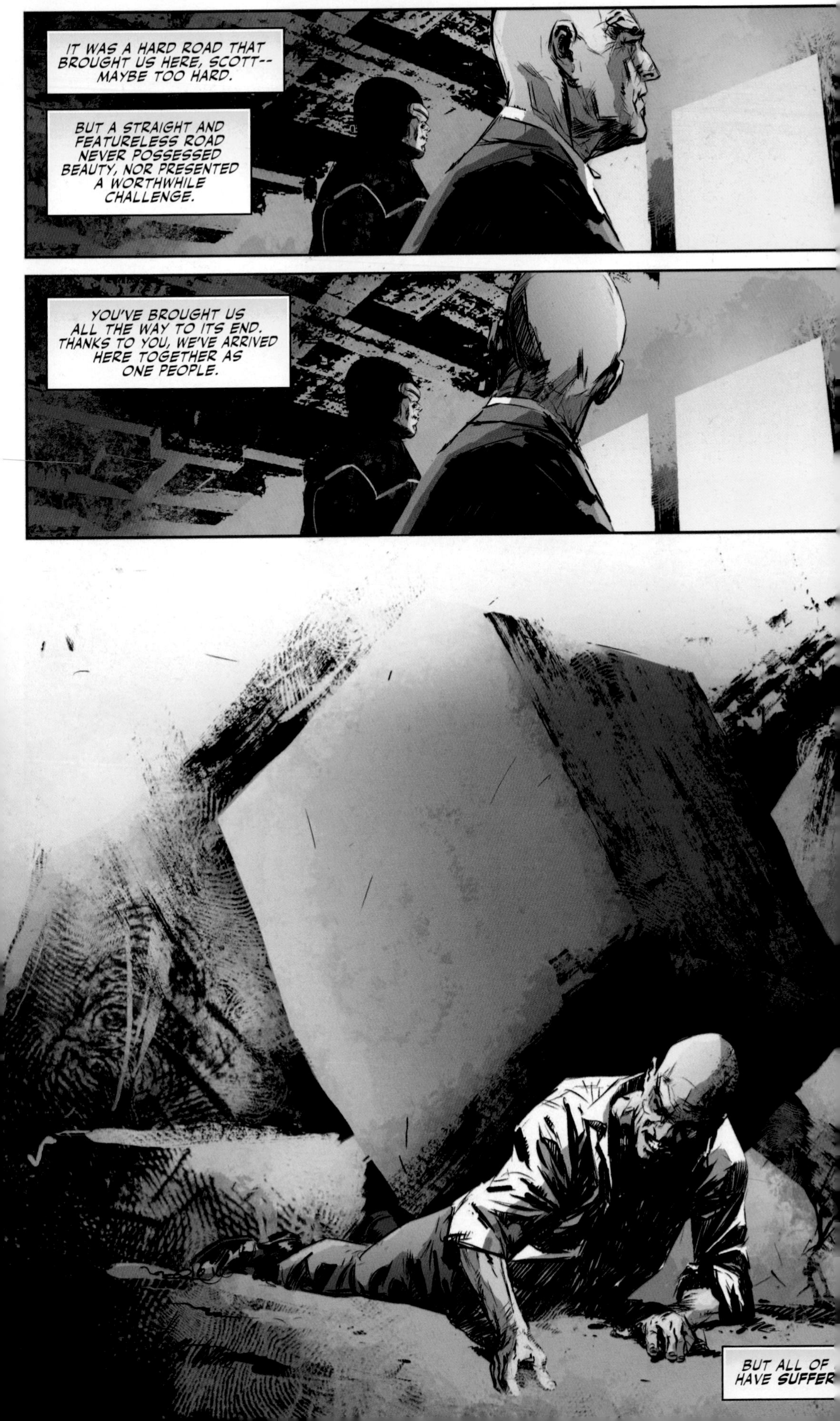
IT WAS A HARD ROAD THAT BROUGHT US HERE, SCOTT-- MAYBE TOO HARD.
BUT A STRAIGHT AND FEATURELESS ROAD NEVER POSSESSED BEAUTY, NOR PRESENTED A WORTHWHILE CHALLENGE.
YOU'VE BROUGHT US ALL THE WAY TO ITS END. THANKS TO YOU, WE'VE ARRIVED HERE TOGETHER AS ONE PEOPLE.
BUT ALL OF HAVE SUFFER

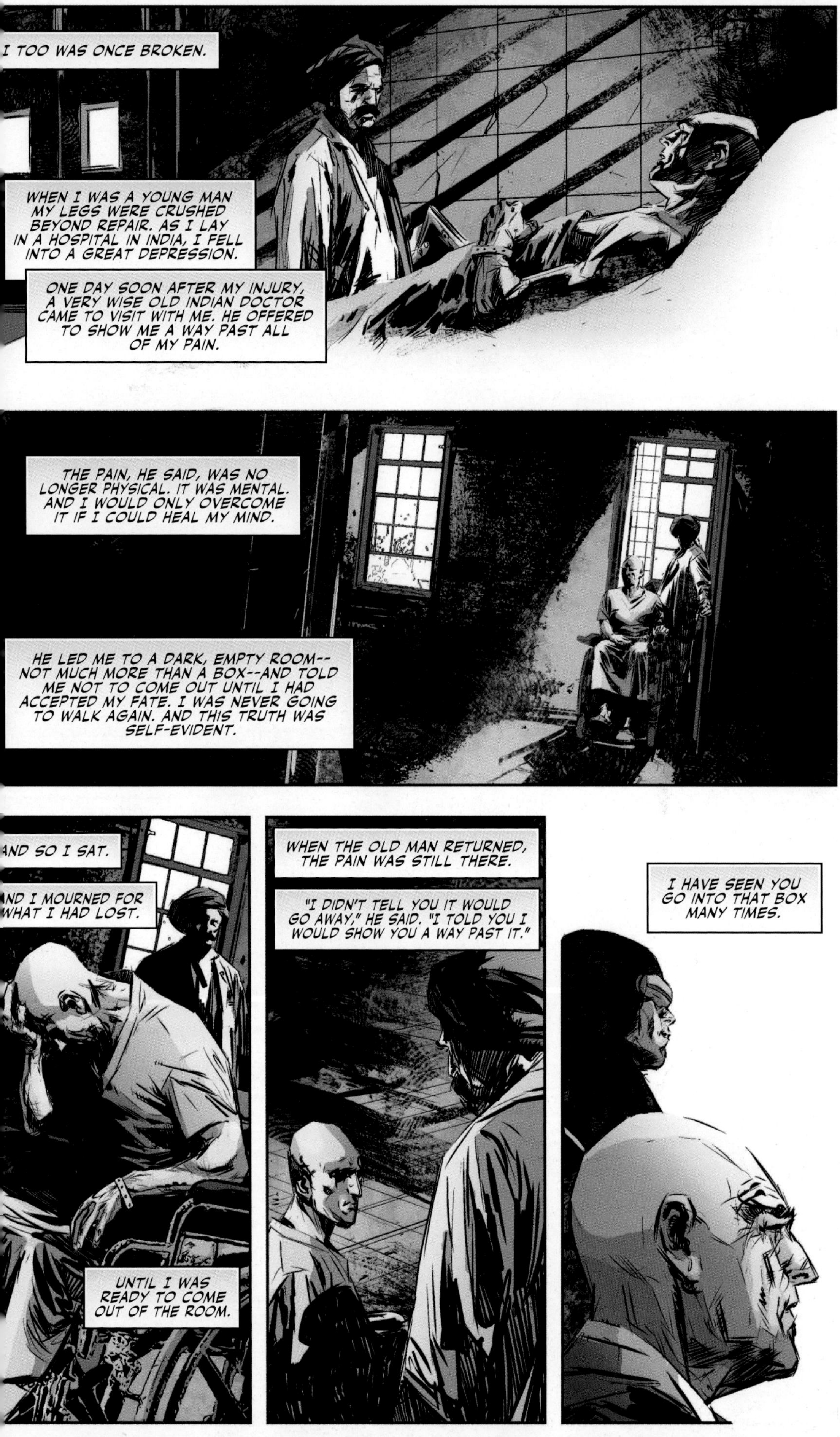
I TOO WAS ONCE BROKEN.
WHEN I WAS A YOUNG MAN MY LEGS WERE CRUSHED BEYOND REPAIR. AS I LAY IN A HOSPITAL IN INDIA, I FELL INTO A GREAT DEPRESSION.
ONE DAY SOON AFTER MY INJURY, A VERY WISE OLD INDIAN DOCTOR CAME TO VISIT WITH ME. HE OFFERED TO SHOW ME A WAY PAST ALL OF MY PAIN.
THE PAIN, HE SAID, WAS NO LONGER PHYSICAL. IT WAS MENTAL. AND I WOULD ONLY OVERCOME IT IF I COULD HEAL MY MIND.
HE LED ME TO A DARK, EMPTY ROOM--NOT MUCH MORE THAN A BOX--AND TOLD ME NOT TO COME OUT UNTIL I HAD ACCEPTED MY FATE. I WAS NEVER GOING TO WALK AGAIN. AND THIS TRUTH WAS SELF-EVIDENT.
AND SO I SAT.
AND I MOURNED FOR WHAT I HAD LOST.
UNTIL I WAS READY TO COME OUT OF THE ROOM.
WHEN THE OLD MAN RETURNED, THE PAIN WAS STILL THERE.
"I DIDN'T TELL YOU IT WOULD GO AWAY," HE SAID. "I TOLD YOU I WOULD SHOW YOU A WAY PAST IT."
I HAVE SEEN YOU GO INTO THAT BOX MANY TIMES.

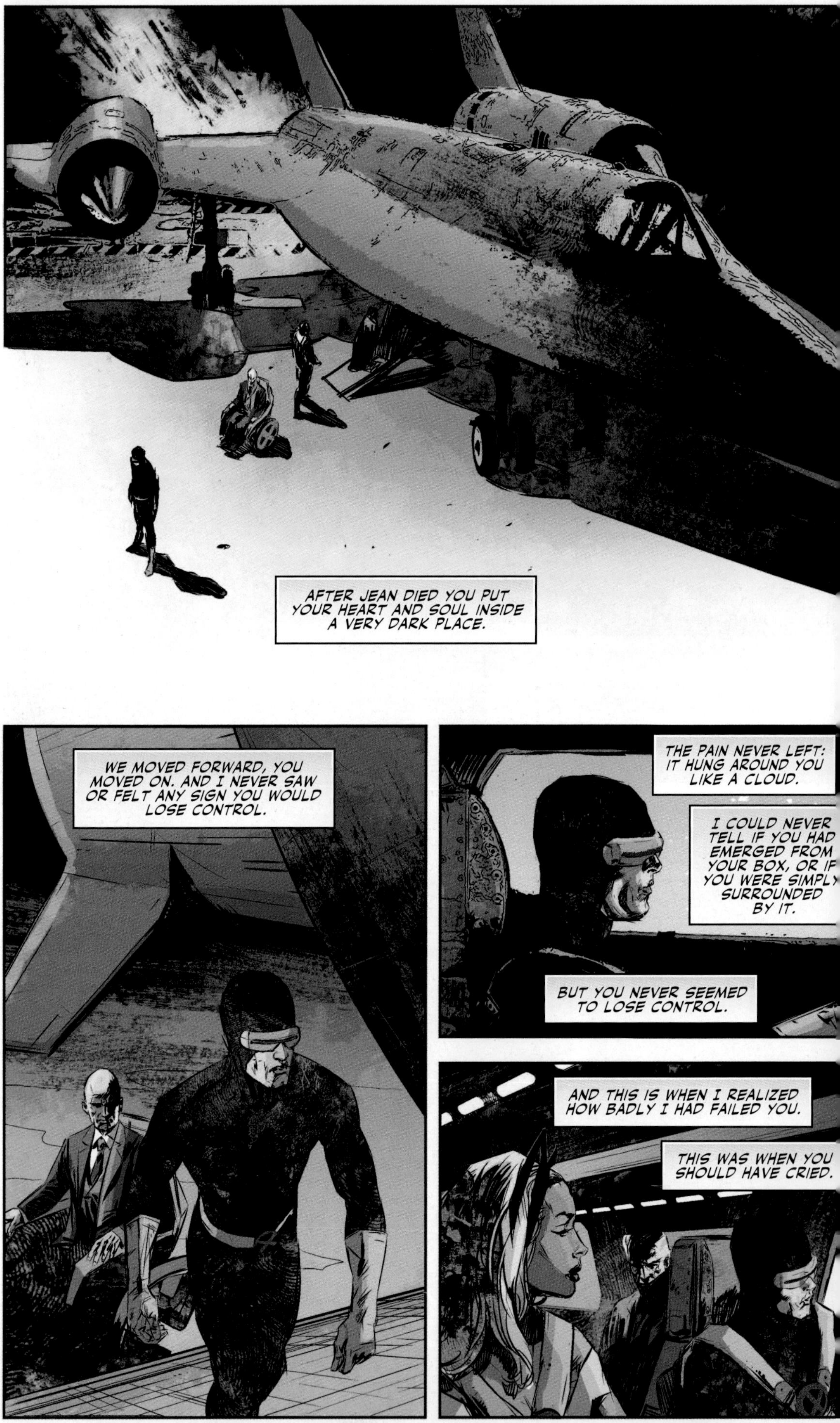
AFTER JEAN DIED YOU PUT YOUR HEART AND SOUL INSIDE A VERY DARK PLACE.
WE MOVED FORWARD, YOU MOVED ON. AND I NEVER SAW OR FELT ANY SIGN YOU WOULD LOSE CONTROL.
THE PAIN NEVER LEFT: IT HUNG AROUND YOU LIKE A CLOUD.
I COULD NEVER TELL IF YOU HAD EMERGED FROM YOUR BOX, OR IF YOU WERE SIMPLY SURROUNDED BY IT.
BUT YOU NEVER SEEMED TO LOSE CONTROL.
AND THIS IS WHEN I REALIZED HOW BADLY I HAD FAILED YOU.
THIS WAS WHEN YOU SHOULD HAVE CRIED.

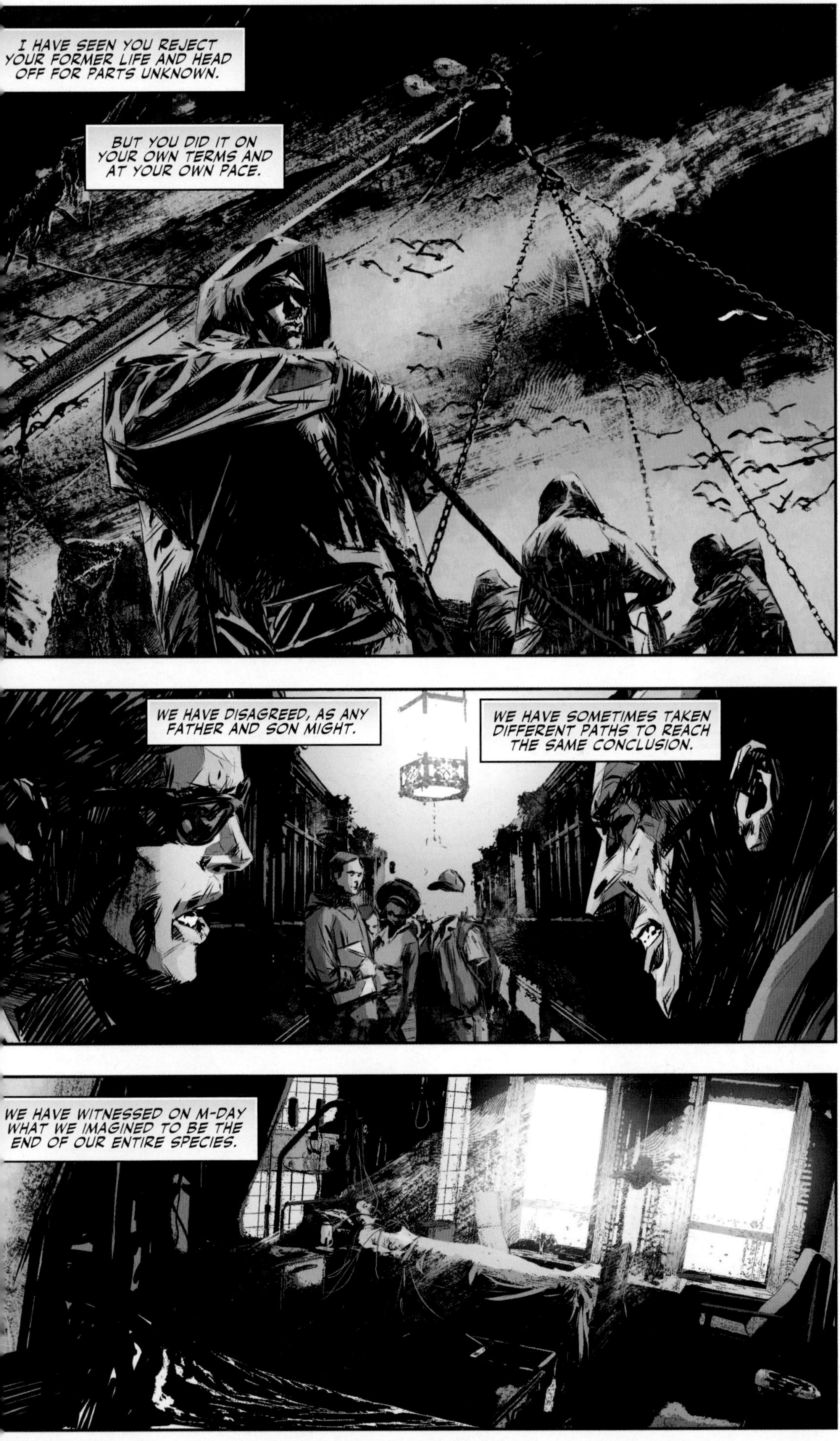
I HAVE SEEN YOU REJECT YOUR FORMER LIFE AND HEAD OFF FOR PARTS UNKNOWN.
BUT YOU DID IT ON YOUR OWN TERMS AND AT YOUR OWN PACE.
WE HAVE DISAGREED, AS ANY FATHER AND SON MIGHT.
WE HAVE SOMETIMES TAKEN DIFFERENT PATHS TO REACH THE SAME CONCLUSION.
WE HAVE WITNESSED ON M-DAY WHAT WE IMAGINED TO BE THE END OF OUR ENTIRE SPECIES.

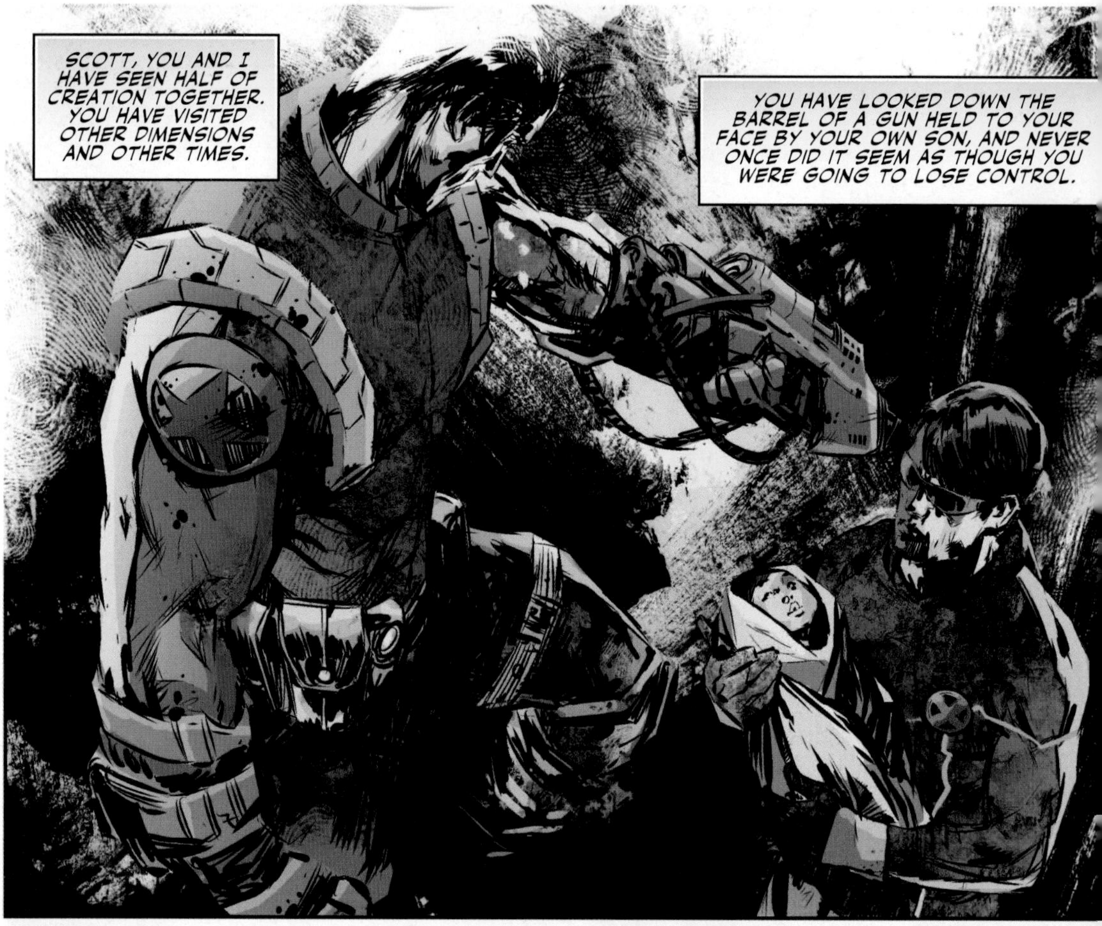
SCOTT, YOU AND I HAVE SEEN HALF OF CREATION TOGETHER. YOU HAVE VISITED OTHER DIMENSIONS AND OTHER TIMES.
YOU HAVE LOOKED DOWN THE BARREL OF A GUN HELD TO YOUR FACE BY YOUR OWN SON, AND NEVER ONCE DID IT SEEM AS THOUGH YOU WERE GOING TO LOSE CONTROL.

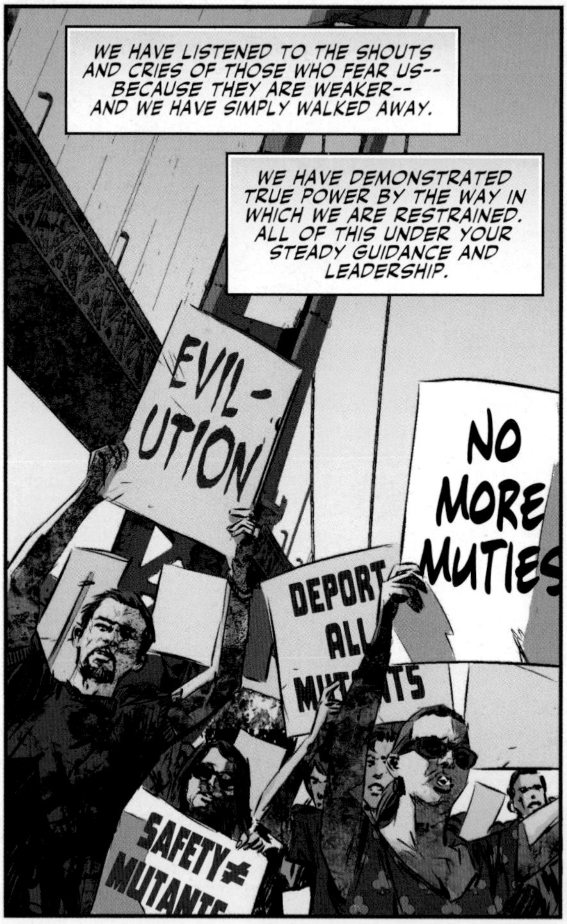
WE HAVE LISTENED TO THE SHOUTS AND CRIES OF THOSE WHO FEAR US-- BECAUSE THEY ARE WEAKER-- AND WE HAVE SIMPLY WALKED AWAY.
WE HAVE DEMONSTRATED TRUE POWER BY THE WAY IN WHICH WE ARE RESTRAINED. ALL OF THIS UNDER YOUR STEADY GUIDANCE AND LEADERSHIP.
EVIL-UTION
NO MORE MUTIES
DEPORT ALL MUTANTS

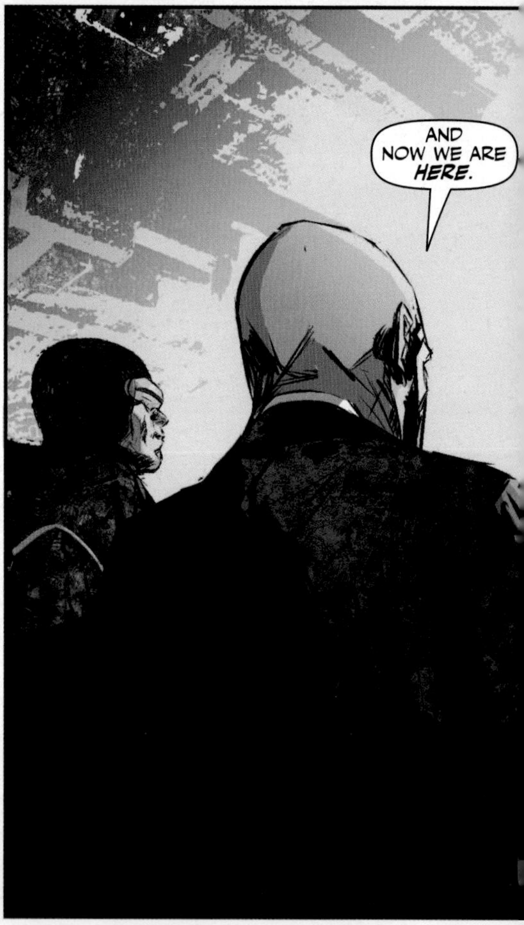
AND NOW WE ARE *HERE*.

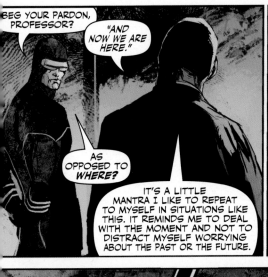

BEG YOUR PARDON, PROFESSOR?

"AND NOW WE ARE HERE."

AS OPPOSED TO *WHERE?*

IT'S A LITTLE MANTRA I LIKE TO REPEAT TO MYSELF IN SITUATIONS LIKE THIS. IT REMINDS ME TO DEAL WITH THE MOMENT AND NOT TO DISTRACT MYSELF WORRYING ABOUT THE PAST OR THE FUTURE.

THAT'S VERY PROFOUND. I CAN'T REMEMBER YOU EVER TELLING ME THAT BEFORE.

I'M FULL OF SURPRISES.

WELL, I *LIKE* IT. THOUGH I'D HAVE TO SAY I'M NOT SURE *EITHER* OF US HAS EVER BEEN IN A POSITION LIKE *THIS.*

TOUCHÉ.

DO YOU THINK WE SHOULD EVACUATE?

I'M NOT THINKING OF GIVING UP, IF THAT'S THE QUESTION.

THEN WE STAY AND FIGHT. IT HAS TO BE ALL OF US. EVERY SINGLE MUTANT IN UTOPIA.

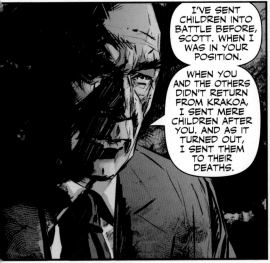

I'VE SENT CHILDREN INTO BATTLE BEFORE, SCOTT. WHEN I WAS IN YOUR POSITION.

WHEN YOU AND THE OTHERS DIDN'T RETURN FROM KRAKOA, I SENT MERE CHILDREN AFTER YOU. AND AS IT TURNED OUT, I SENT THEM TO THEIR DEATHS.

OF ALL THE DECISIONS I EVER MADE, IT REMAINS THE ONE I REGRET THE MOST.

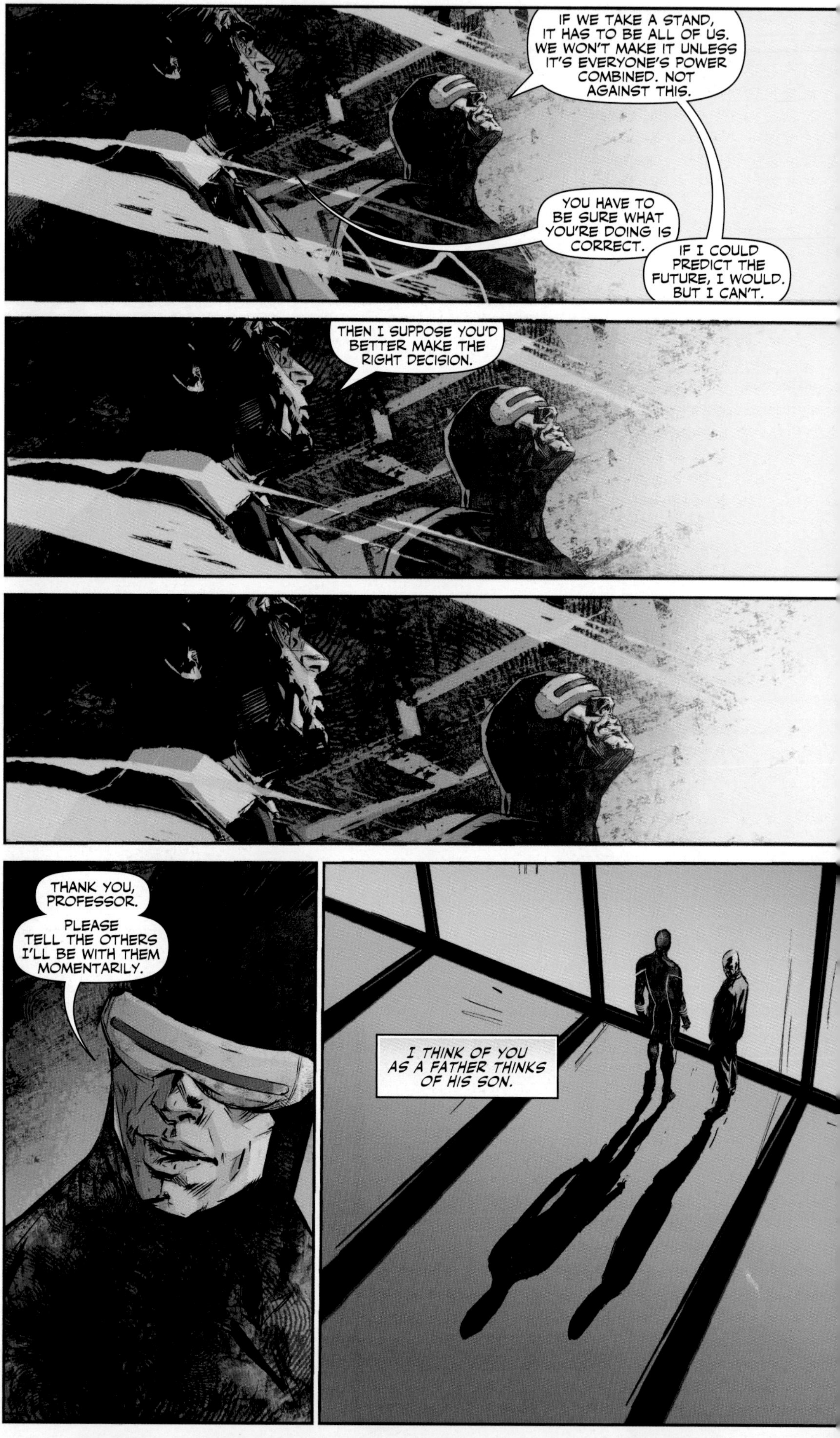
IF WE TAKE A STAND, IT HAS TO BE ALL OF US. WE WON'T MAKE IT UNLESS IT'S EVERYONE'S POWER COMBINED. NOT AGAINST THIS.
YOU HAVE TO BE SURE WHAT YOU'RE DOING IS CORRECT.
IF I COULD PREDICT THE FUTURE, I WOULD. BUT I CAN'T.
THEN I SUPPOSE YOU'D BETTER MAKE THE RIGHT DECISION.
THANK YOU, PROFESSOR.
PLEASE TELL THE OTHERS I'LL BE WITH THEM MOMENTARILY.
I THINK OF YOU AS A FATHER THINKS OF HIS SON.

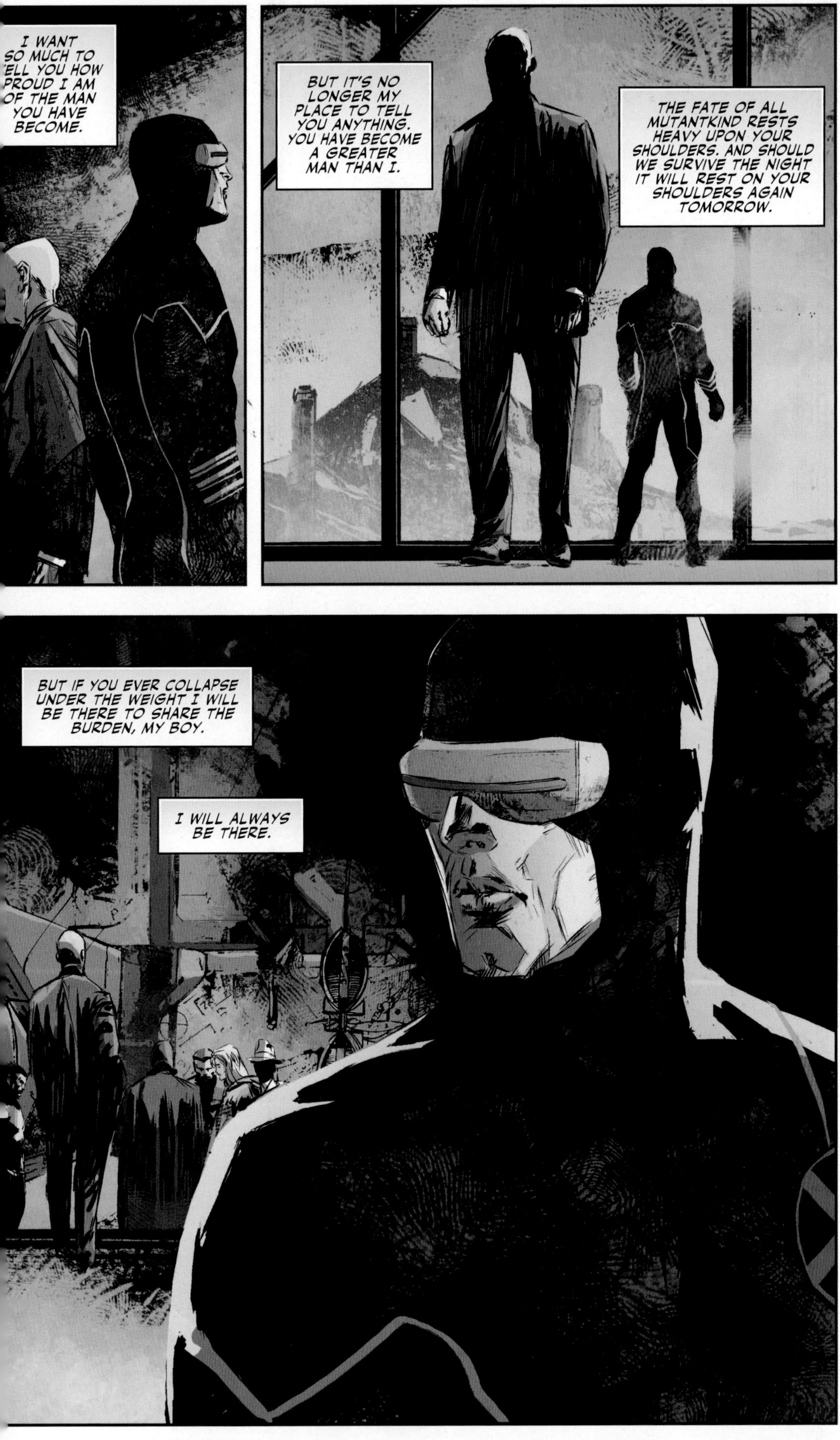
I WANT SO MUCH TO TELL YOU HOW PROUD I AM OF THE MAN YOU HAVE BECOME.
BUT IT'S NO LONGER MY PLACE TO TELL YOU ANYTHING. YOU HAVE BECOME A GREATER MAN THAN I.
THE FATE OF ALL MUTANTKIND RESTS HEAVY UPON YOUR SHOULDERS. AND SHOULD WE SURVIVE THE NIGHT IT WILL REST ON YOUR SHOULDERS AGAIN TOMORROW.
BUT IF YOU EVER COLLAPSE UNDER THE WEIGHT I WILL BE THERE TO SHARE THE BURDEN, MY BOY.
I WILL ALWAYS BE THERE.

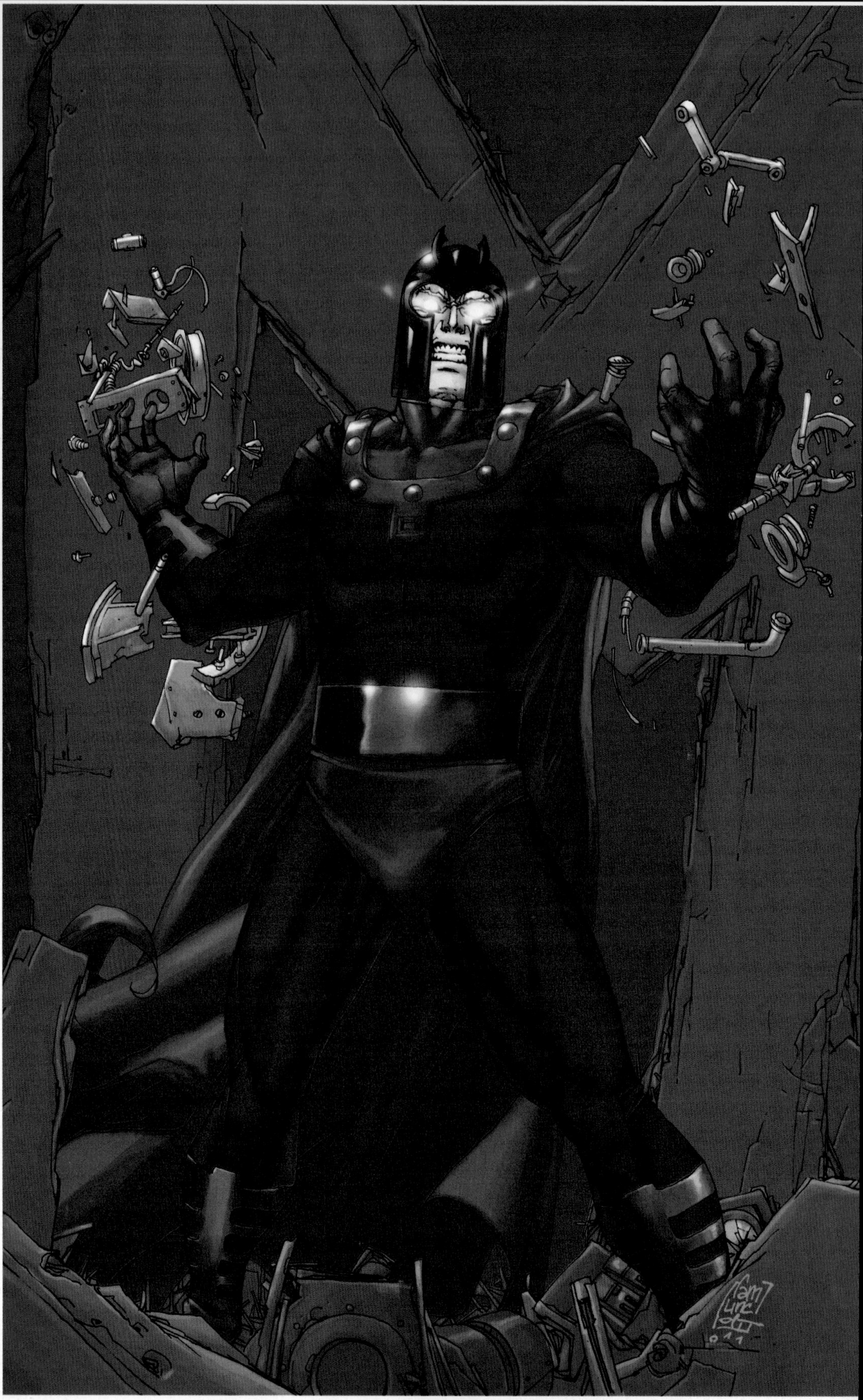

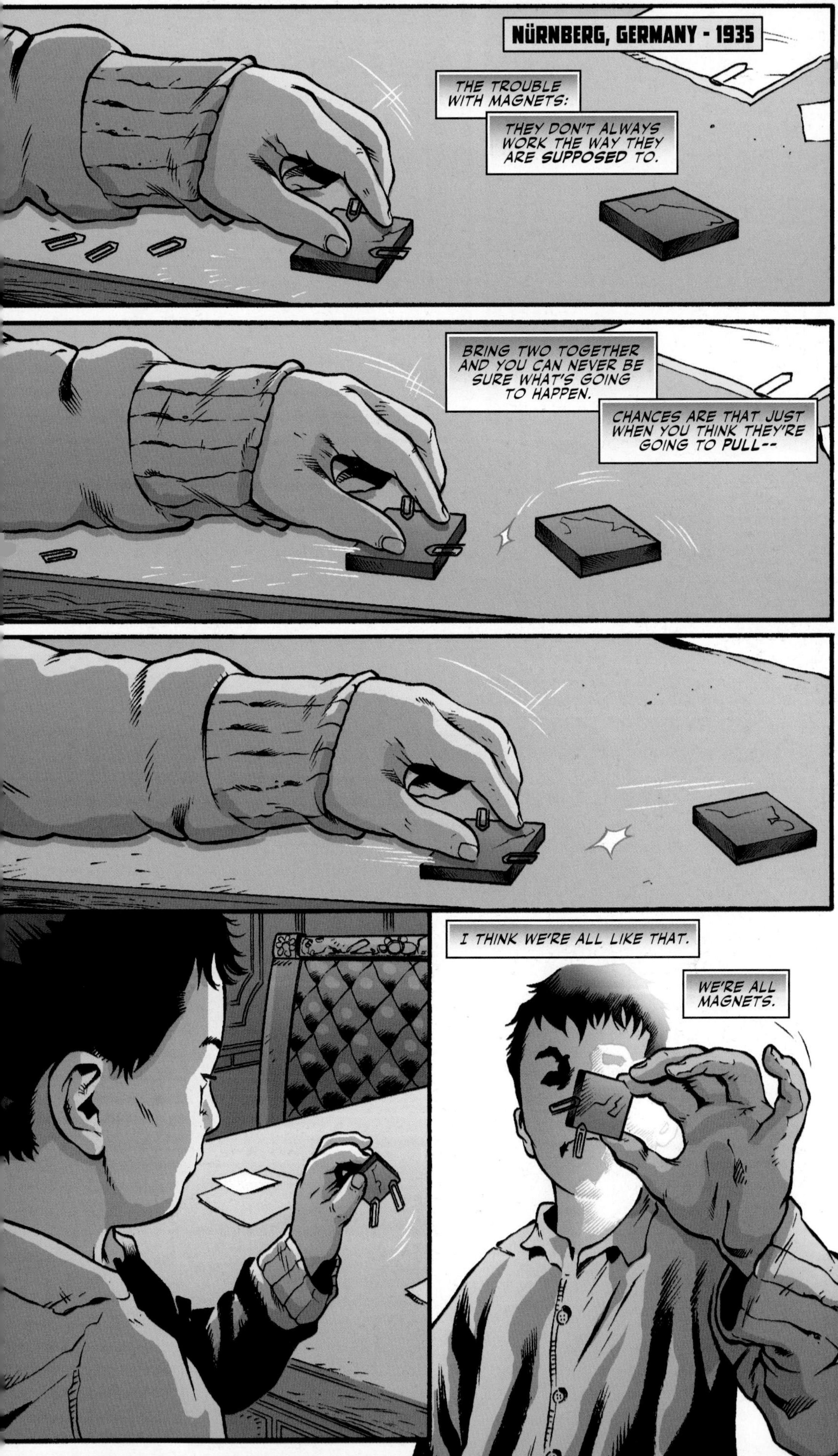
NÜRNBERG, GERMANY - 1935
THE TROUBLE WITH MAGNETS:
THEY DON'T ALWAYS WORK THE WAY THEY ARE SUPPOSED TO.
BRING TWO TOGETHER AND YOU CAN NEVER BE SURE WHAT'S GOING TO HAPPEN.
CHANCES ARE THAT JUST WHEN YOU THINK THEY'RE GOING TO PULL--
I THINK WE'RE ALL LIKE THAT.
WE'RE ALL MAGNETS.

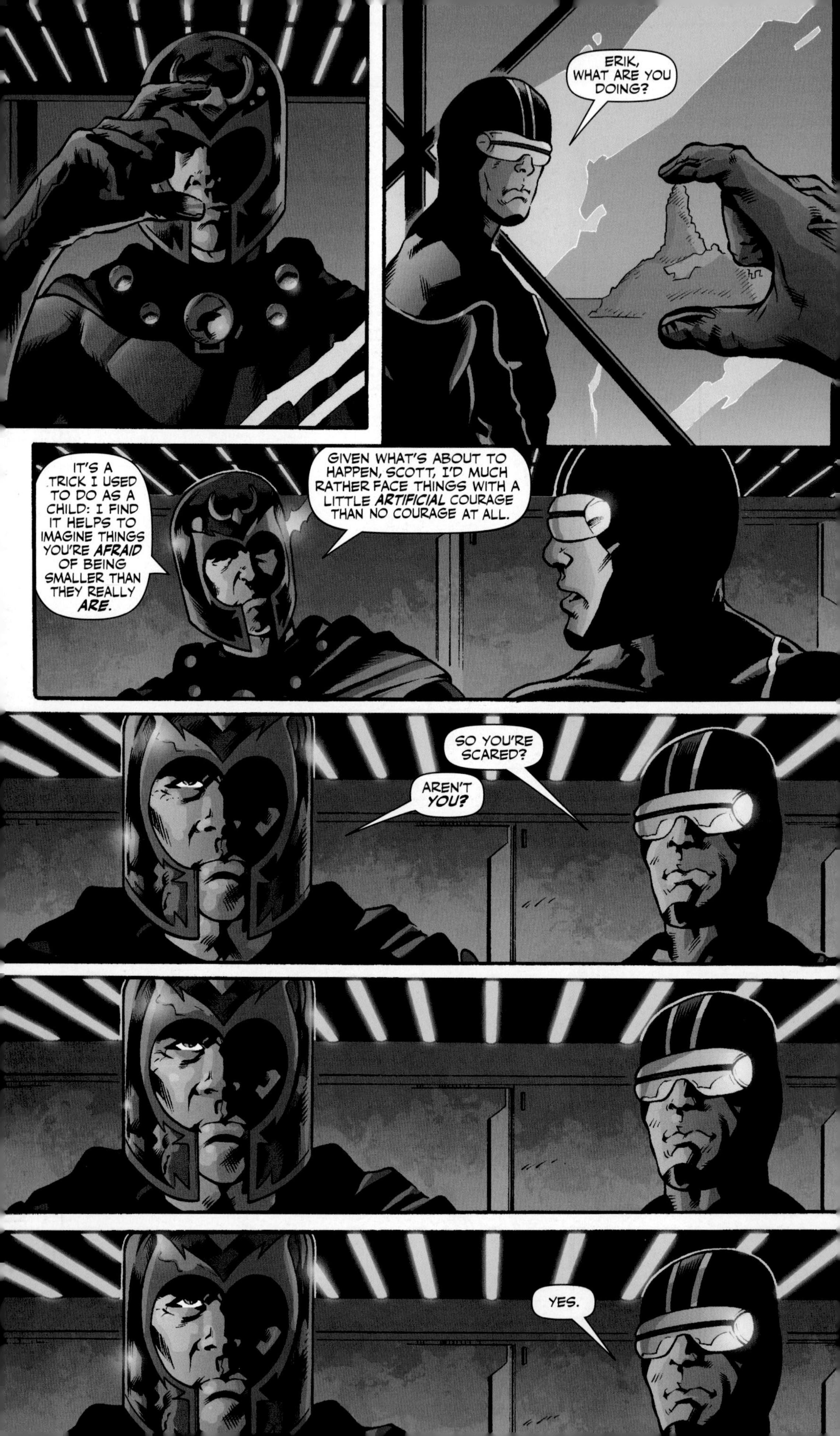
ERIK, WHAT ARE YOU DOING?
IT'S A TRICK I USED TO DO AS A CHILD: I FIND IT HELPS TO IMAGINE THINGS YOU'RE AFRAID OF BEING SMALLER THAN THEY REALLY ARE.
GIVEN WHAT'S ABOUT TO HAPPEN, SCOTT, I'D MUCH RATHER FACE THINGS WITH A LITTLE ARTIFICIAL COURAGE THAN NO COURAGE AT ALL.
SO YOU'RE SCARED?
AREN'T YOU?
YES.

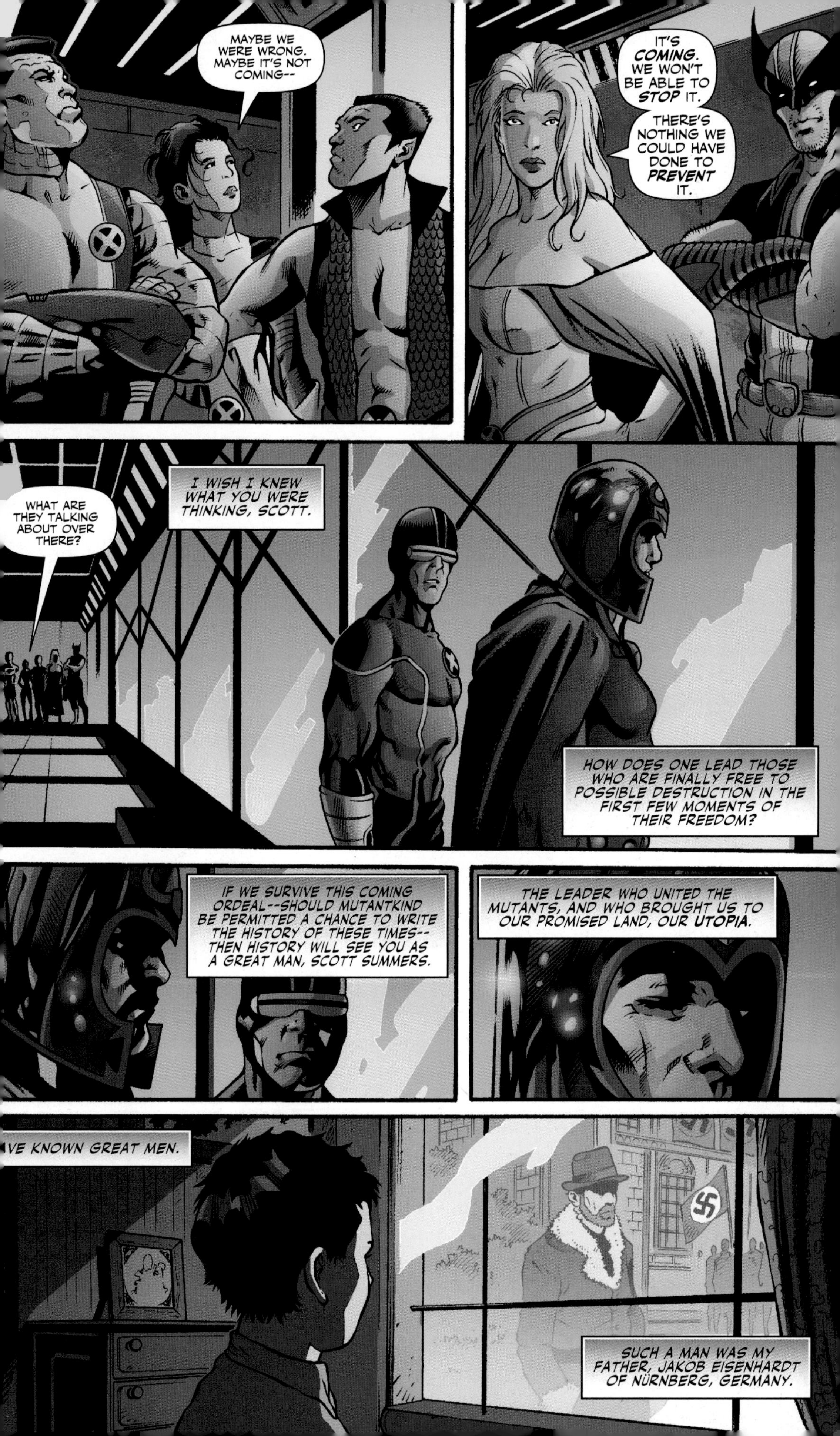

MAYBE WE WERE WRONG. MAYBE IT'S NOT COMING--
IT'S *COMING*. WE WON'T BE ABLE TO *STOP* IT.
THERE'S NOTHING WE COULD HAVE DONE TO *PREVENT* IT.
WHAT ARE THEY TALKING ABOUT OVER THERE?
I WISH I KNEW WHAT YOU WERE THINKING, SCOTT.
HOW DOES ONE LEAD THOSE WHO ARE FINALLY FREE TO POSSIBLE DESTRUCTION IN THE FIRST FEW MOMENTS OF THEIR FREEDOM?
IF WE SURVIVE THIS COMING ORDEAL--SHOULD MUTANTKIND BE PERMITTED A CHANCE TO WRITE THE HISTORY OF THESE TIMES--THEN HISTORY WILL SEE YOU AS A GREAT MAN, SCOTT SUMMERS.
THE LEADER WHO UNITED THE MUTANTS, AND WHO BROUGHT US TO OUR PROMISED LAND, OUR **UTOPIA**.
VE KNOWN GREAT MEN.
SUCH A MAN WAS MY FATHER, JAKOB EISENHARDT OF NÜRNBERG, GERMANY.

MY FATHER FOUGHT WITH THE GERMAN SIXTH ARMY AT YPRES IN OCTOBER OF 1914 IN A BATTLE KNOWN AS "DER KINDERMORD BEI YPERN," WHICH MEANT "THE MASSACRE OF THE INNOCENTS."

FORTY THOUSAND YOUNG MEN DIED IN THAT BATTLE. MY FATHER WAS BLINDED BY MUSTARD GAS AND SPENT FIVE DAYS IN A FIELD HOSPITAL.

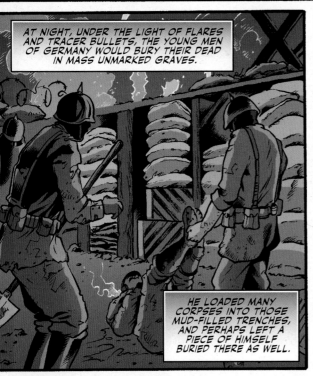

AT NIGHT, UNDER THE LIGHT OF FLARES AND TRACER BULLETS, THE YOUNG MEN OF GERMANY WOULD BURY THEIR DEAD IN MASS UNMARKED GRAVES.

HE LOADED MANY CORPSES INTO THOSE MUD-FILLED TRENCHES, AND PERHAPS LEFT A PIECE OF HIMSELF BURIED THERE AS WELL.

IN THE SUMMER OF 1916, MY FATHER-- SHOWING NO CONCERN FOR HIS OWN SAFETY-- PULLED A BAVARIAN MAJOR NAMED SCHARF TO THE SAFETY OF A NEARBY TRENCH UNDER HEAVY ENEMY FIRE.

FOR THIS, HE RECEIVED COMMENDATION FOR BRAV[ERY] AND THE UNDYING GRATIT[UDE] OF HIS SUPERIORS.

MONTHS LATER, THAT SAME OFFICER PINNED THE IRON CROSS TO MY FATHER'S LAPEL.

HE LOUDLY PROCLAIMED MY FATHER A "PROUD SON OF GERMANY."

AND A PROUD SON OF GERMANY MY FATHER REMAINED.

EVEN AS HIS COUNTRY GREW TO HATE HIM SIMPLY FOR THE ACCIDENT OF HIS BIRTH.

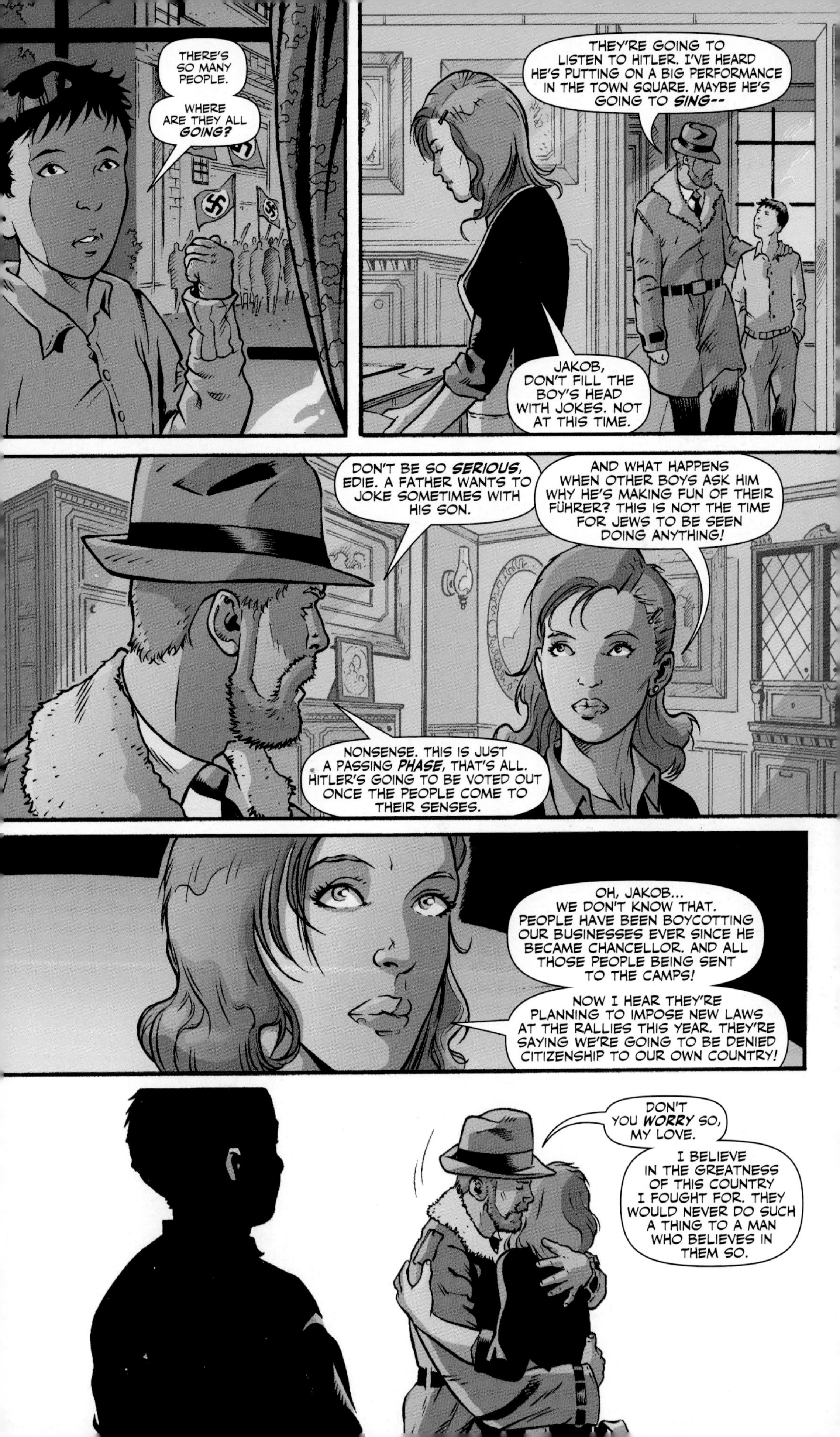
THERE'S SO MANY PEOPLE.
WHERE ARE THEY ALL GOING?
THEY'RE GOING TO LISTEN TO HITLER. I'VE HEARD HE'S PUTTING ON A BIG PERFORMANCE IN THE TOWN SQUARE. MAYBE HE'S GOING TO SING--
JAKOB, DON'T FILL THE BOY'S HEAD WITH JOKES. NOT AT THIS TIME.
DON'T BE SO SERIOUS, EDIE. A FATHER WANTS TO JOKE SOMETIMES WITH HIS SON.
AND WHAT HAPPENS WHEN OTHER BOYS ASK HIM WHY HE'S MAKING FUN OF THEIR FÜHRER? THIS IS NOT THE TIME FOR JEWS TO BE SEEN DOING ANYTHING!
NONSENSE. THIS IS JUST A PASSING PHASE, THAT'S ALL. HITLER'S GOING TO BE VOTED OUT ONCE THE PEOPLE COME TO THEIR SENSES.
OH, JAKOB... WE DON'T KNOW THAT. PEOPLE HAVE BEEN BOYCOTTING OUR BUSINESSES EVER SINCE HE BECAME CHANCELLOR. AND ALL THOSE PEOPLE BEING SENT TO THE CAMPS!
NOW I HEAR THEY'RE PLANNING TO IMPOSE NEW LAWS AT THE RALLIES THIS YEAR. THEY'RE SAYING WE'RE GOING TO BE DENIED CITIZENSHIP TO OUR OWN COUNTRY!
DON'T YOU WORRY SO, MY LOVE.
I BELIEVE IN THE GREATNESS OF THIS COUNTRY I FOUGHT FOR. THEY WOULD NEVER DO SUCH A THING TO A MAN WHO BELIEVES IN THEM SO.

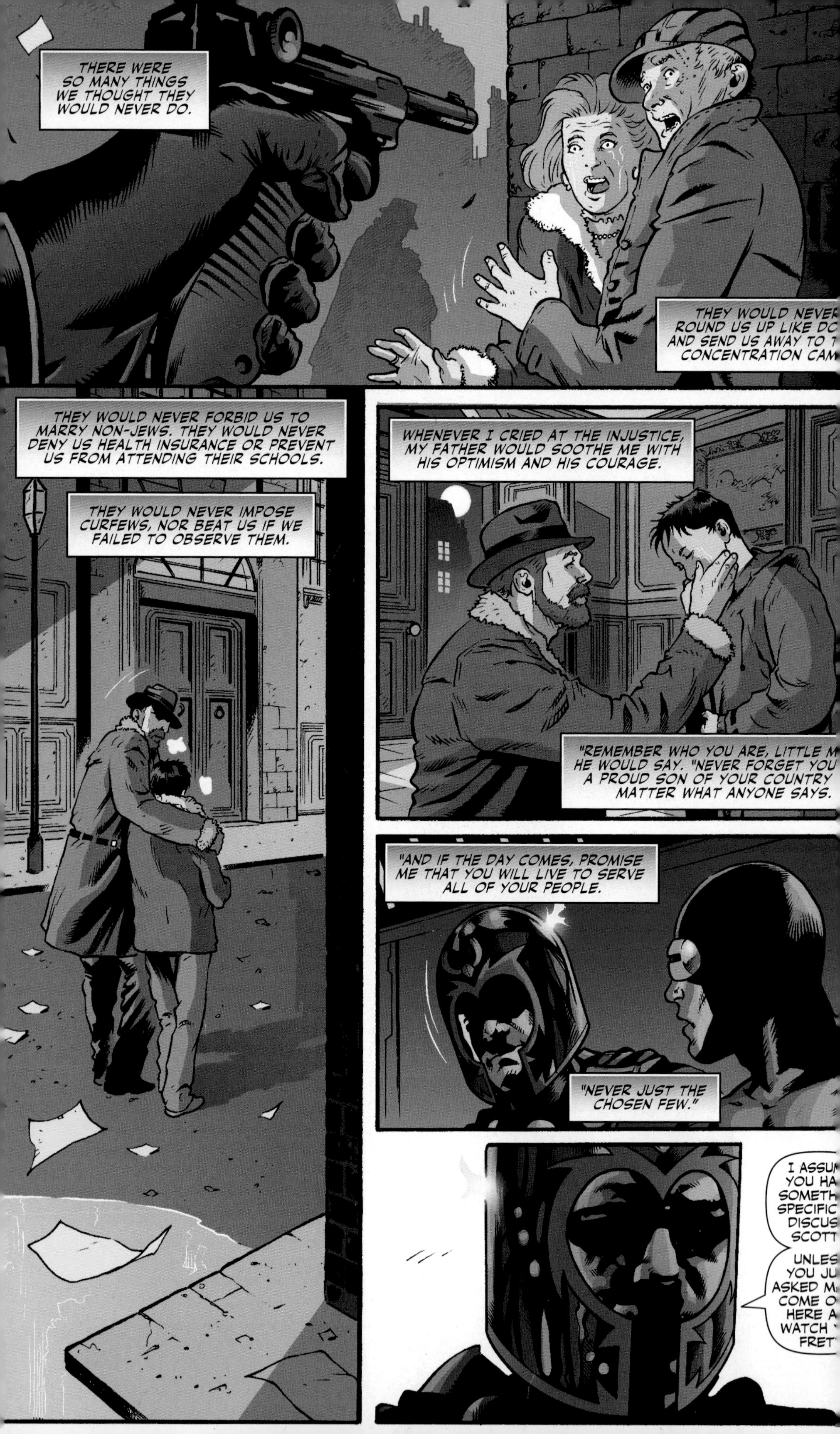

THERE WERE SO MANY THINGS WE THOUGHT THEY WOULD NEVER DO.
THEY WOULD NEVER ROUND US UP LIKE DO AND SEND US AWAY TO T CONCENTRATION CAM
THEY WOULD NEVER FORBID US TO MARRY NON-JEWS. THEY WOULD NEVER DENY US HEALTH INSURANCE OR PREVENT US FROM ATTENDING THEIR SCHOOLS.
THEY WOULD NEVER IMPOSE CURFEWS, NOR BEAT US IF WE FAILED TO OBSERVE THEM.
WHENEVER I CRIED AT THE INJUSTICE, MY FATHER WOULD SOOTHE ME WITH HIS OPTIMISM AND HIS COURAGE.
"REMEMBER WHO YOU ARE, LITTLE M HE WOULD SAY. "NEVER FORGET YOU A PROUD SON OF YOUR COUNTRY MATTER WHAT ANYONE SAYS.
"AND IF THE DAY COMES, PROMISE ME THAT YOU WILL LIVE TO SERVE ALL OF YOUR PEOPLE.
"NEVER JUST THE CHOSEN FEW."
I ASSU YOU HA SOMETH SPECIFIC DISCUS SCOTT
UNLES YOU JU ASKED M COME O HERE A WATCH FRET

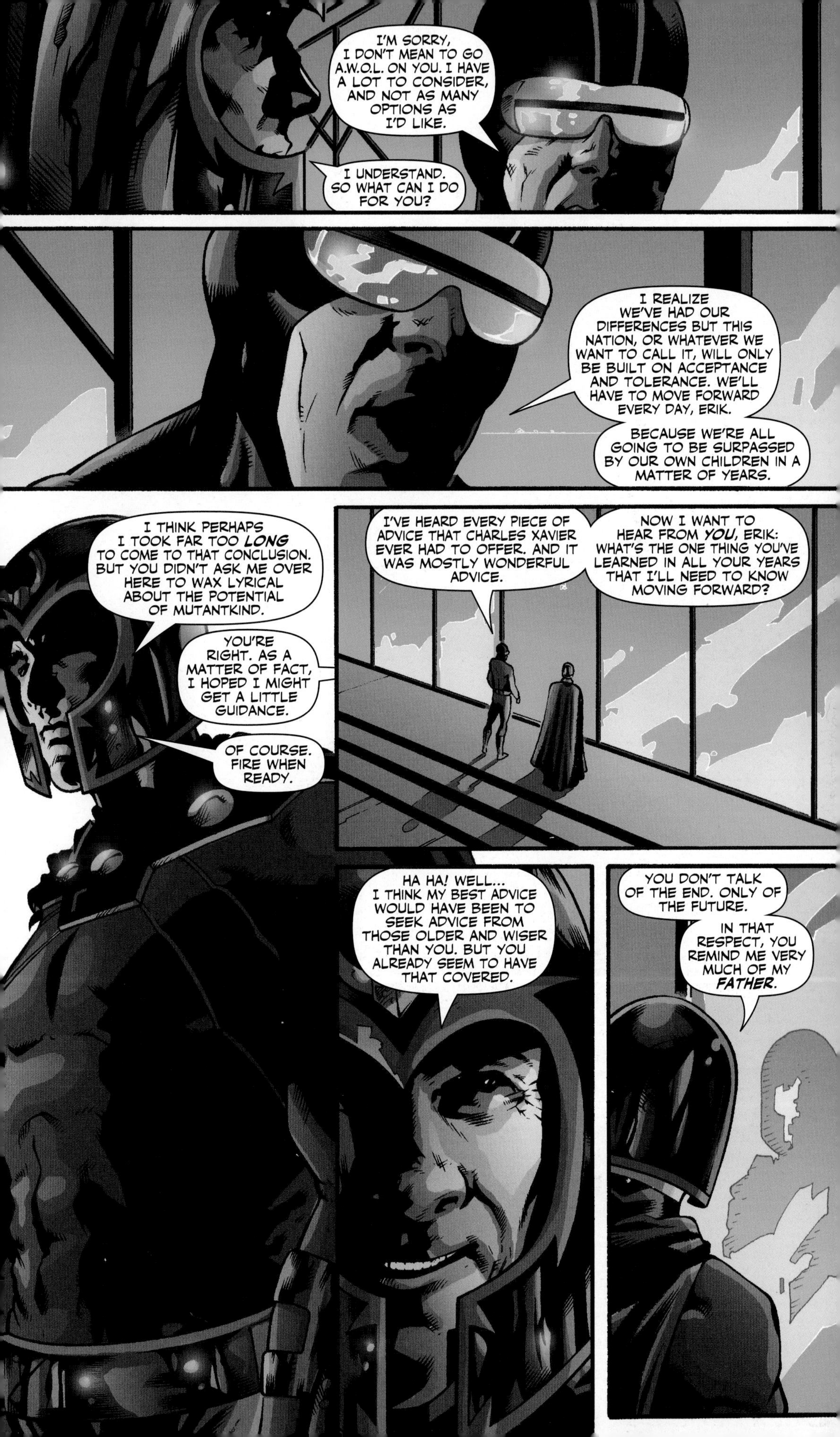
I'M SORRY, I DON'T MEAN TO GO A.W.O.L. ON YOU. I HAVE A LOT TO CONSIDER, AND NOT AS MANY OPTIONS AS I'D LIKE.
I UNDERSTAND. SO WHAT CAN I DO FOR YOU?
I REALIZE WE'VE HAD OUR DIFFERENCES BUT THIS NATION, OR WHATEVER WE WANT TO CALL IT, WILL ONLY BE BUILT ON ACCEPTANCE AND TOLERANCE. WE'LL HAVE TO MOVE FORWARD EVERY DAY, ERIK.
BECAUSE WE'RE ALL GOING TO BE SURPASSED BY OUR OWN CHILDREN IN A MATTER OF YEARS.
I THINK PERHAPS I TOOK FAR TOO *LONG* TO COME TO THAT CONCLUSION. BUT YOU DIDN'T ASK ME OVER HERE TO WAX LYRICAL ABOUT THE POTENTIAL OF MUTANTKIND.
YOU'RE RIGHT. AS A MATTER OF FACT, I HOPED I MIGHT GET A LITTLE GUIDANCE.
OF COURSE. FIRE WHEN READY.
I'VE HEARD EVERY PIECE OF ADVICE THAT CHARLES XAVIER EVER HAD TO OFFER. AND IT WAS MOSTLY WONDERFUL ADVICE.
NOW I WANT TO HEAR FROM *YOU*, ERIK: WHAT'S THE ONE THING YOU'VE LEARNED IN ALL YOUR YEARS THAT I'LL NEED TO KNOW MOVING FORWARD?
HA HA! WELL... I THINK MY BEST ADVICE WOULD HAVE BEEN TO SEEK ADVICE FROM THOSE OLDER AND WISER THAN YOU. BUT YOU ALREADY SEEM TO HAVE THAT COVERED.
YOU DON'T TALK OF THE END. ONLY OF THE FUTURE.
IN THAT RESPECT, YOU REMIND ME VERY MUCH OF MY ***FATHER***.

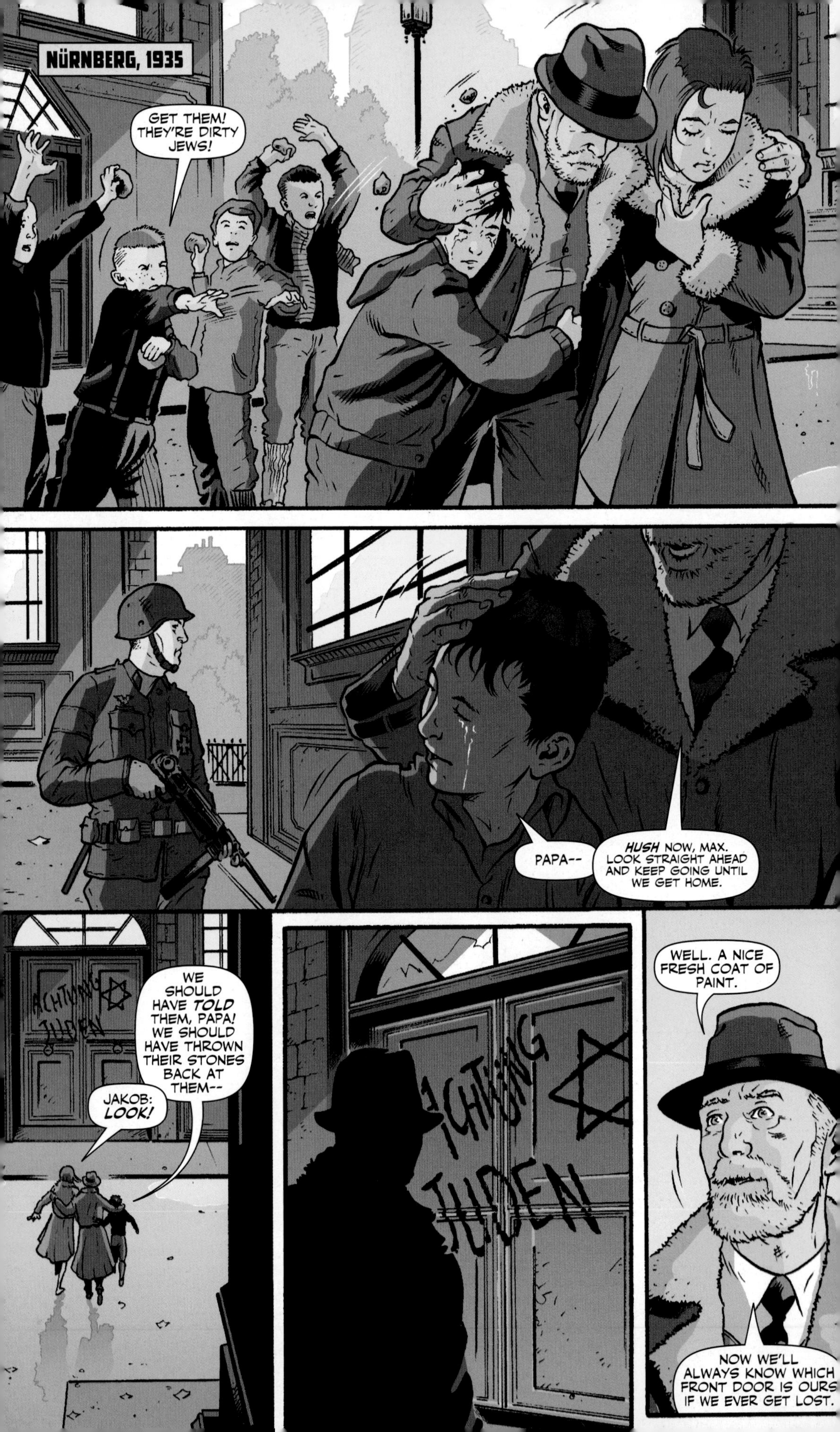
NÜRNBERG, 1935
GET THEM! THEY'RE DIRTY JEWS!
PAPA--
HUSH NOW, MAX. LOOK STRAIGHT AHEAD AND KEEP GOING UNTIL WE GET HOME.
ACHTUNG JUDEN
WE SHOULD HAVE TOLD THEM, PAPA! WE SHOULD HAVE THROWN THEIR STONES BACK AT THEM--
JAKOB: LOOK!
ACHTUNG JUDEN
WELL. A NICE FRESH COAT OF PAINT.
NOW WE'LL ALWAYS KNOW WHICH FRONT DOOR IS OURS IF WE EVER GET LOST.

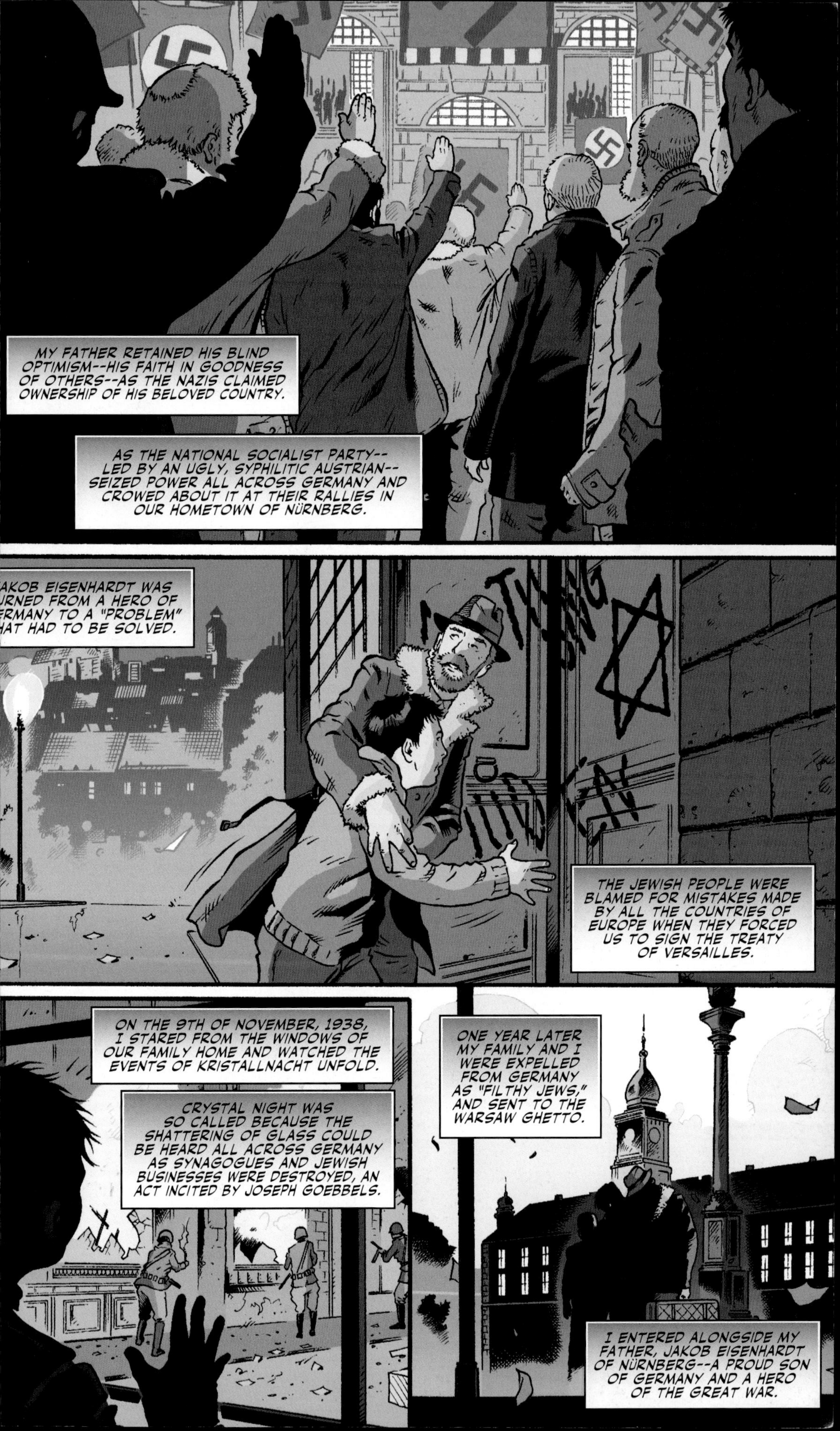
MY FATHER RETAINED HIS BLIND OPTIMISM--HIS FAITH IN GOODNESS OF OTHERS--AS THE NAZIS CLAIMED OWNERSHIP OF HIS BELOVED COUNTRY.
AS THE NATIONAL SOCIALIST PARTY--LED BY AN UGLY, SYPHILITIC AUSTRIAN--SEIZED POWER ALL ACROSS GERMANY AND CROWED ABOUT IT AT THEIR RALLIES IN OUR HOMETOWN OF NÜRNBERG.
AKOB EISENHARDT WAS URNED FROM A HERO OF ERMANY TO A "PROBLEM" HAT HAD TO BE SOLVED.
THE JEWISH PEOPLE WERE BLAMED FOR MISTAKES MADE BY ALL THE COUNTRIES OF EUROPE WHEN THEY FORCED US TO SIGN THE TREATY OF VERSAILLES.
ON THE 9TH OF NOVEMBER, 1938, I STARED FROM THE WINDOWS OF OUR FAMILY HOME AND WATCHED THE EVENTS OF KRISTALLNACHT UNFOLD.
CRYSTAL NIGHT WAS SO CALLED BECAUSE THE SHATTERING OF GLASS COULD BE HEARD ALL ACROSS GERMANY AS SYNAGOGUES AND JEWISH BUSINESSES WERE DESTROYED, AN ACT INCITED BY JOSEPH GOEBBELS.
ONE YEAR LATER MY FAMILY AND I WERE EXPELLED FROM GERMANY AS "FILTHY JEWS," AND SENT TO THE WARSAW GHETTO.
I ENTERED ALONGSIDE MY FATHER, JAKOB EISENHARDT OF NÜRNBERG--A PROUD SON OF GERMANY AND A HERO OF THE GREAT WAR.

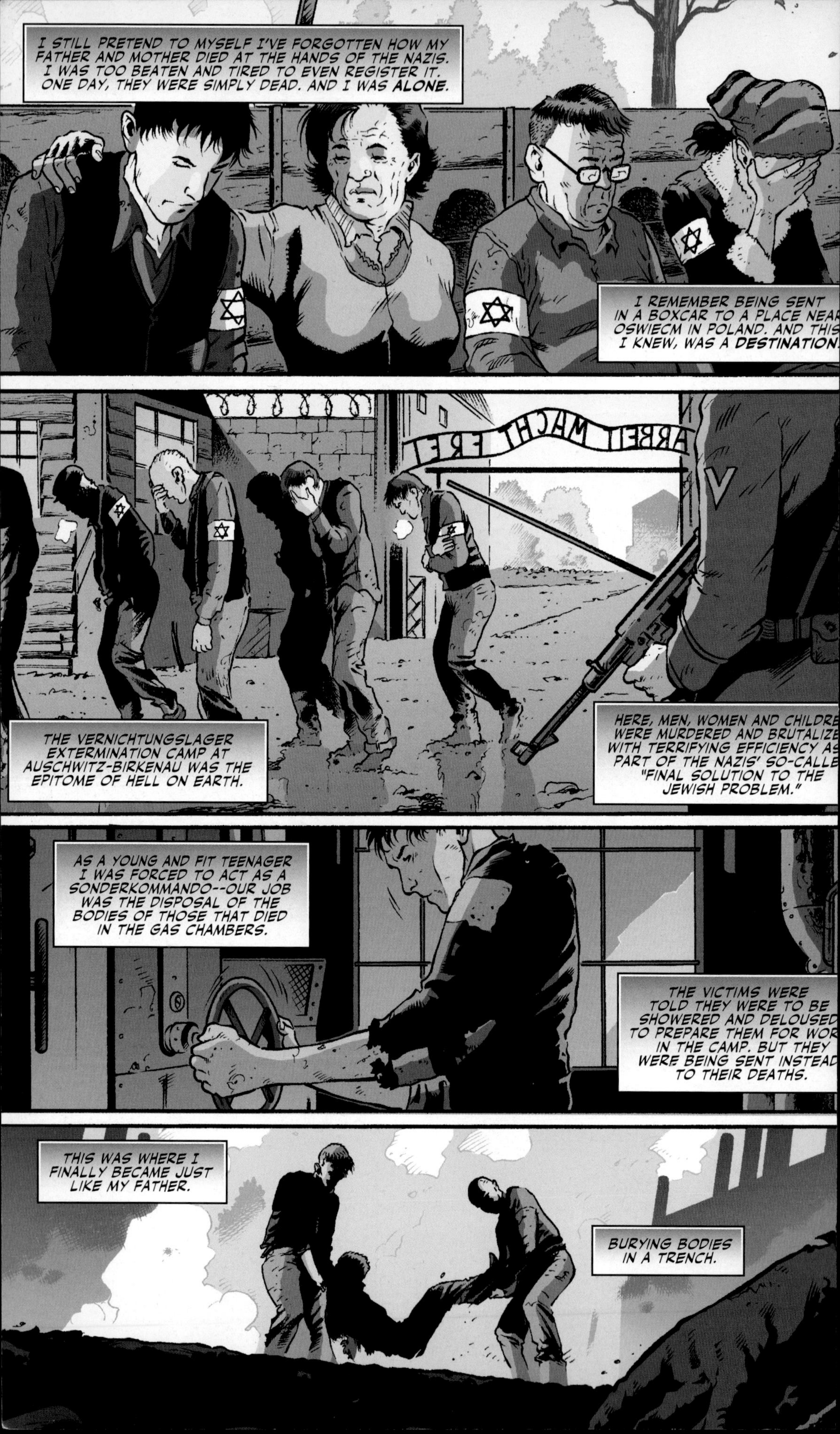
I STILL PRETEND TO MYSELF I'VE FORGOTTEN HOW MY FATHER AND MOTHER DIED AT THE HANDS OF THE NAZIS. I WAS TOO BEATEN AND TIRED TO EVEN REGISTER IT. ONE DAY, THEY WERE SIMPLY DEAD. AND I WAS **ALONE**.
I REMEMBER BEING SENT IN A BOXCAR TO A PLACE NEAR OSWIECM IN POLAND. AND THIS I KNEW, WAS A **DESTINATION**.
ARBEIT MACHT FREI
THE VERNICHTUNGSLAGER EXTERMINATION CAMP AT AUSCHWITZ-BIRKENAU WAS THE EPITOME OF HELL ON EARTH.
HERE, MEN, WOMEN AND CHILDRE WERE MURDERED AND BRUTALIZE WITH TERRIFYING EFFICIENCY AS PART OF THE NAZIS' SO-CALLE "FINAL SOLUTION TO THE JEWISH PROBLEM."
AS A YOUNG AND FIT TEENAGER I WAS FORCED TO ACT AS A SONDERKOMMANDO--OUR JOB WAS THE DISPOSAL OF THE BODIES OF THOSE THAT DIED IN THE GAS CHAMBERS.
THE VICTIMS WERE TOLD THEY WERE TO BE SHOWERED AND DELOUSED TO PREPARE THEM FOR WOR IN THE CAMP. BUT THEY WERE BEING SENT INSTEAD TO THEIR DEATHS.
THIS WAS WHERE I FINALLY BECAME JUST LIKE MY FATHER.
BURYING BODIES IN A TRENCH.

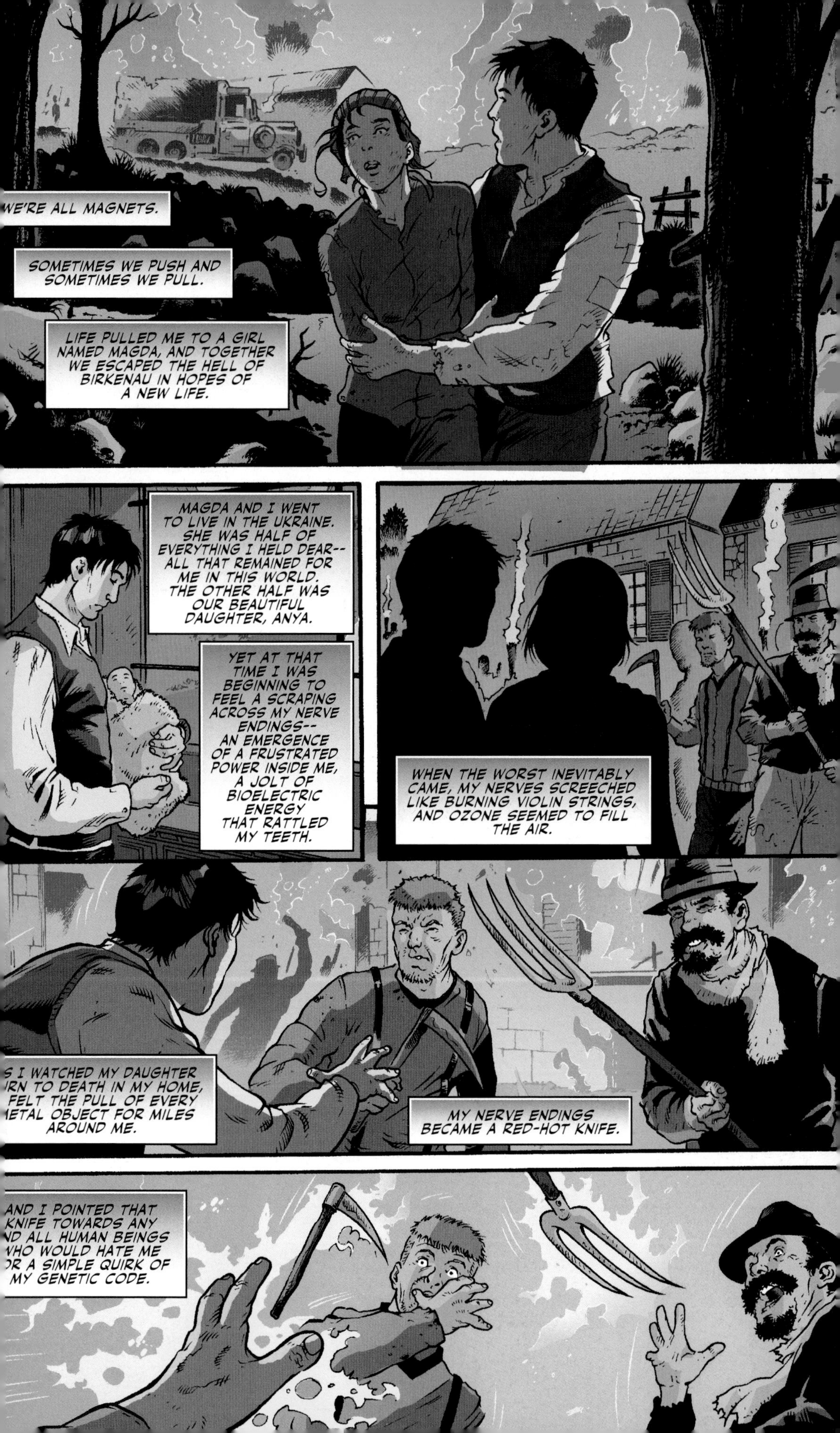
WE'RE ALL MAGNETS.
SOMETIMES WE PUSH AND SOMETIMES WE PULL.
LIFE PULLED ME TO A GIRL NAMED MAGDA, AND TOGETHER WE ESCAPED THE HELL OF BIRKENAU IN HOPES OF A NEW LIFE.
MAGDA AND I WENT TO LIVE IN THE UKRAINE. SHE WAS HALF OF EVERYTHING I HELD DEAR-- ALL THAT REMAINED FOR ME IN THIS WORLD. THE OTHER HALF WAS OUR BEAUTIFUL DAUGHTER, ANYA.
YET AT THAT TIME I WAS BEGINNING TO FEEL A SCRAPING ACROSS MY NERVE ENDINGS-- AN EMERGENCE OF A FRUSTRATED POWER INSIDE ME, A JOLT OF BIOELECTRIC ENERGY THAT RATTLED MY TEETH.
WHEN THE WORST INEVITABLY CAME, MY NERVES SCREECHED LIKE BURNING VIOLIN STRINGS, AND OZONE SEEMED TO FILL THE AIR.
S I WATCHED MY DAUGHTER IRN TO DEATH IN MY HOME, FELT THE PULL OF EVERY IETAL OBJECT FOR MILES AROUND ME.
MY NERVE ENDINGS BECAME A RED-HOT KNIFE.
AND I POINTED THAT KNIFE TOWARDS ANY ND ALL HUMAN BEINGS WHO WOULD HATE ME OR A SIMPLE QUIRK OF MY GENETIC CODE.

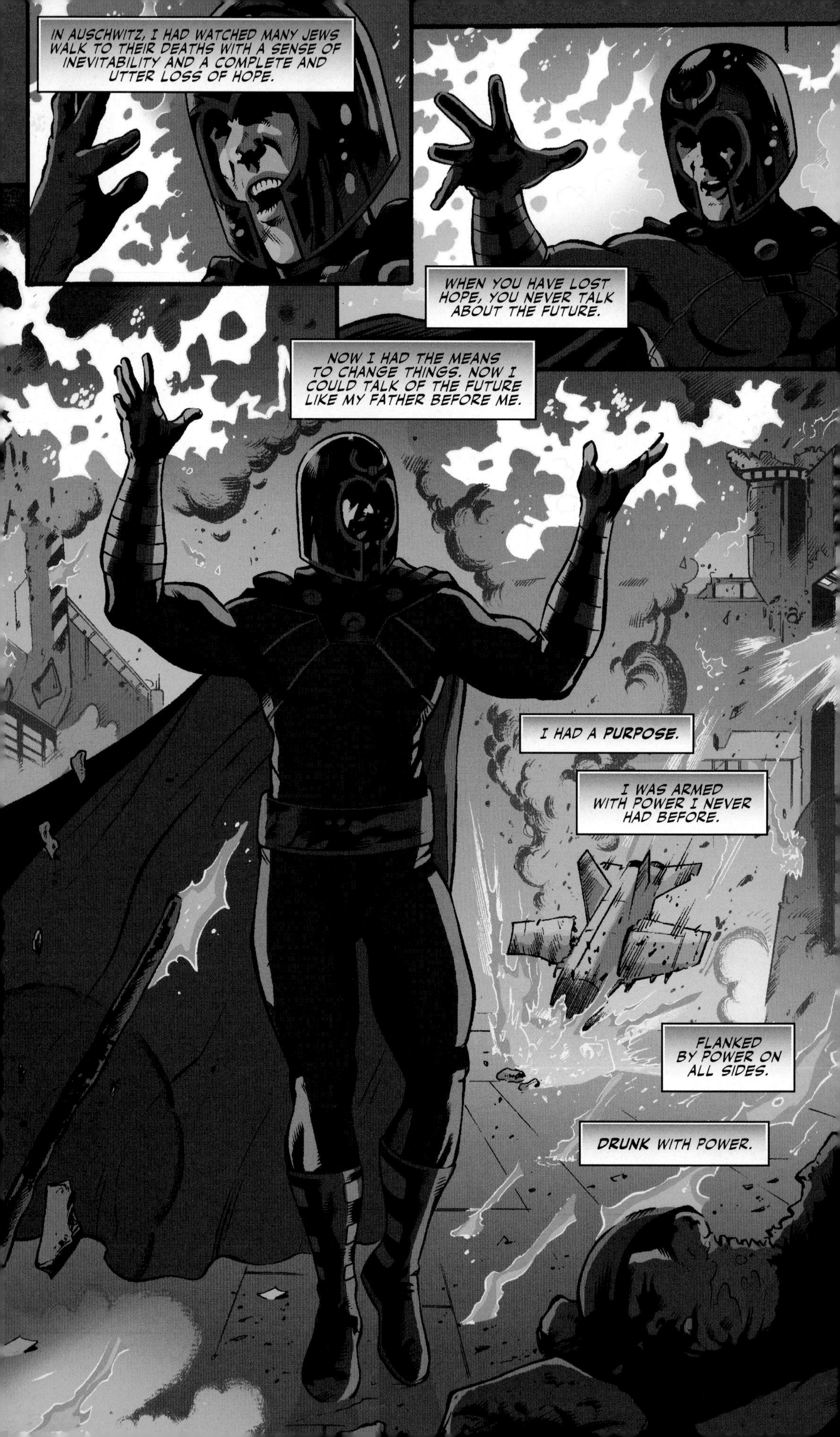
IN AUSCHWITZ, I HAD WATCHED MANY JEWS WALK TO THEIR DEATHS WITH A SENSE OF INEVITABILITY AND A COMPLETE AND UTTER LOSS OF HOPE.
WHEN YOU HAVE LOST HOPE, YOU NEVER TALK ABOUT THE FUTURE.
NOW I HAD THE MEANS TO CHANGE THINGS. NOW I COULD TALK OF THE FUTURE LIKE MY FATHER BEFORE ME.
I HAD A PURPOSE.
I WAS ARMED WITH POWER I NEVER HAD BEFORE.
FLANKED BY POWER ON ALL SIDES.
DRUNK WITH POWER.

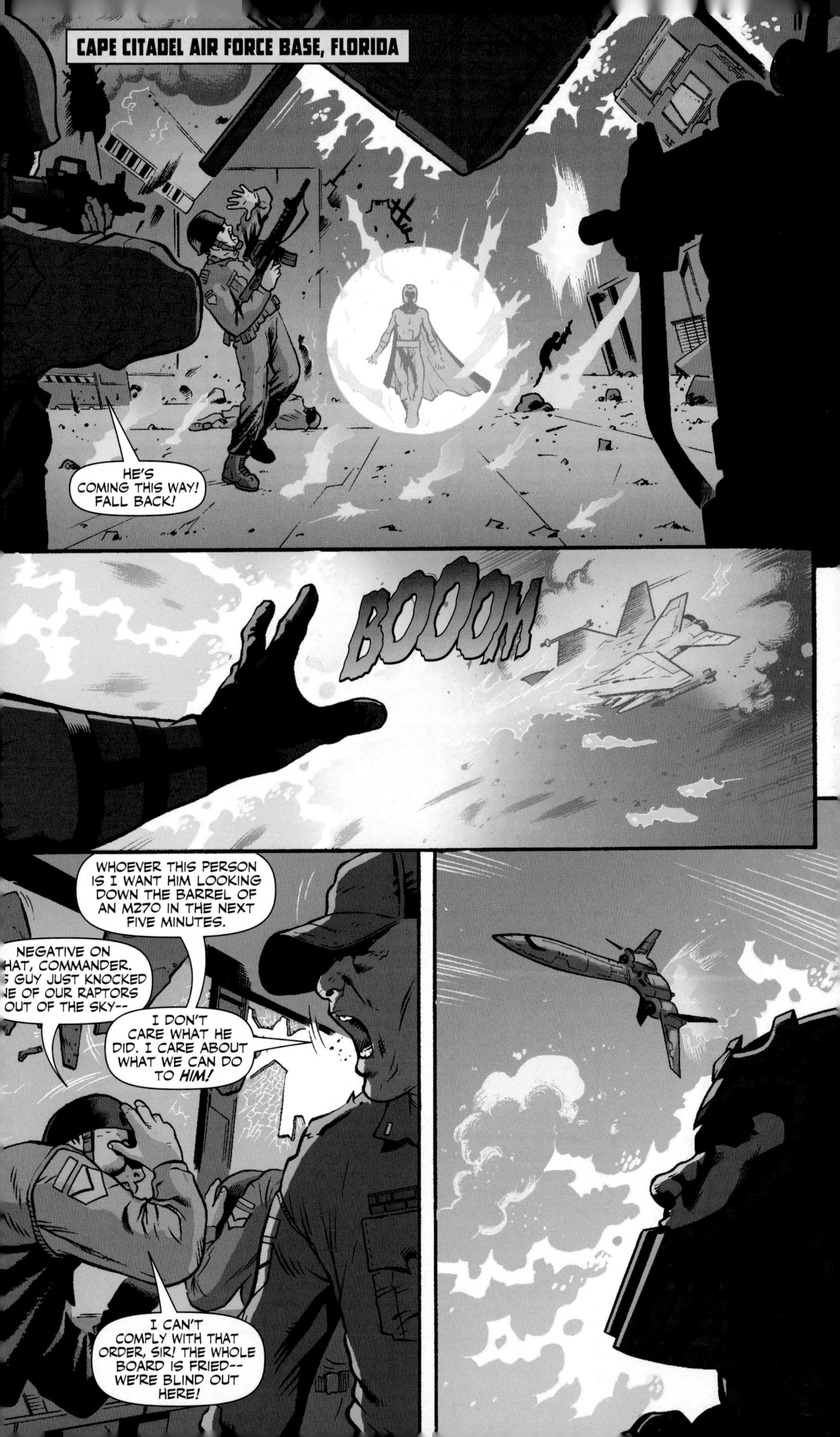
CAPE CITADEL AIR FORCE BASE, FLORIDA
HE'S COMING THIS WAY! FALL BACK!
BOOOM
WHOEVER THIS PERSON IS I WANT HIM LOOKING DOWN THE BARREL OF AN M270 IN THE NEXT FIVE MINUTES.
NEGATIVE ON HAT, COMMANDER. GUY JUST KNOCKED NE OF OUR RAPTORS OUT OF THE SKY--
I DON'T CARE WHAT HE DID. I CARE ABOUT WHAT WE CAN DO TO *HIM!*
I CAN'T COMPLY WITH THAT ORDER, SIR! THE WHOLE BOARD IS FRIED-- WE'RE BLIND OUT HERE!

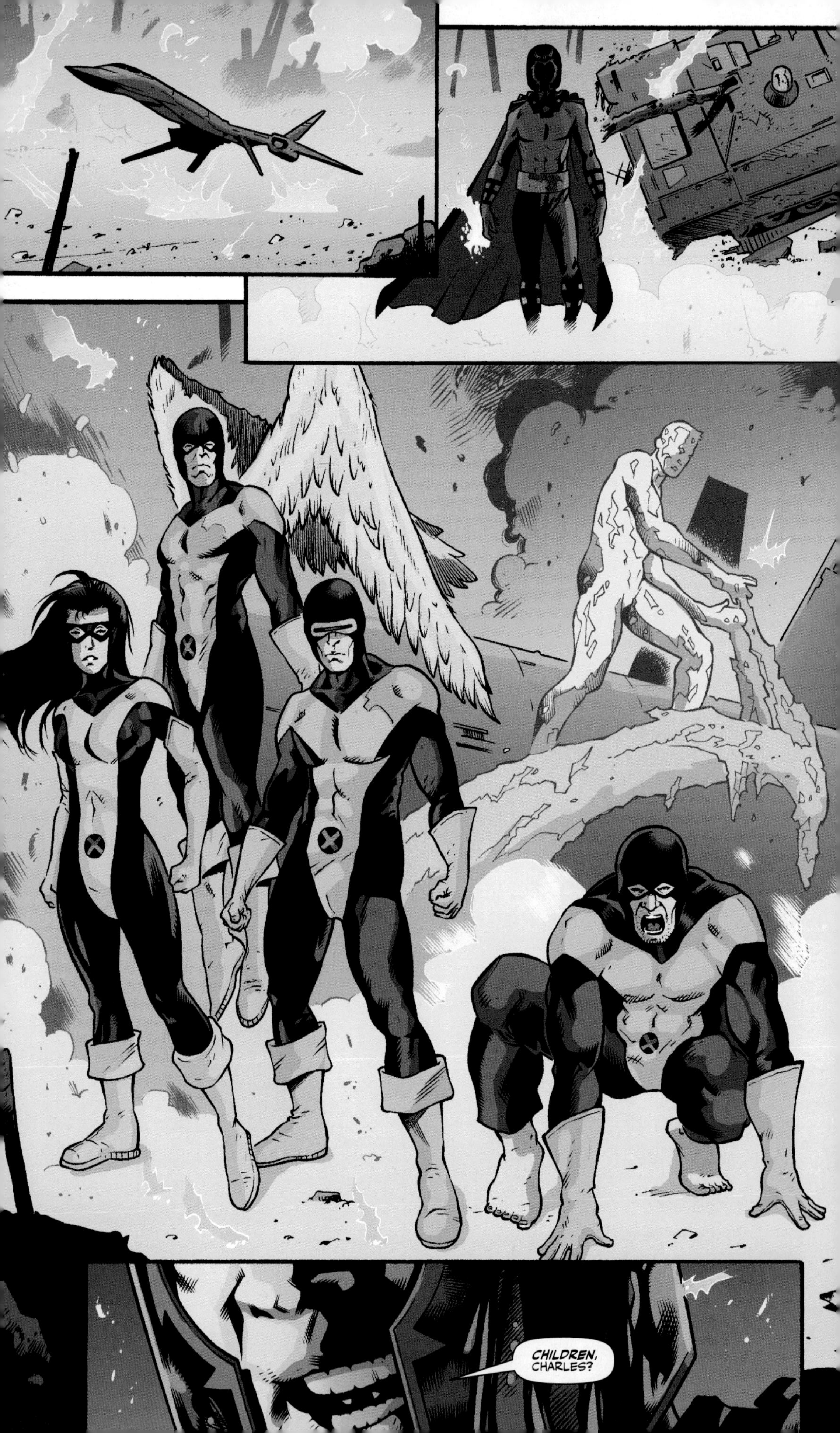
CHILDREN, CHARLES?

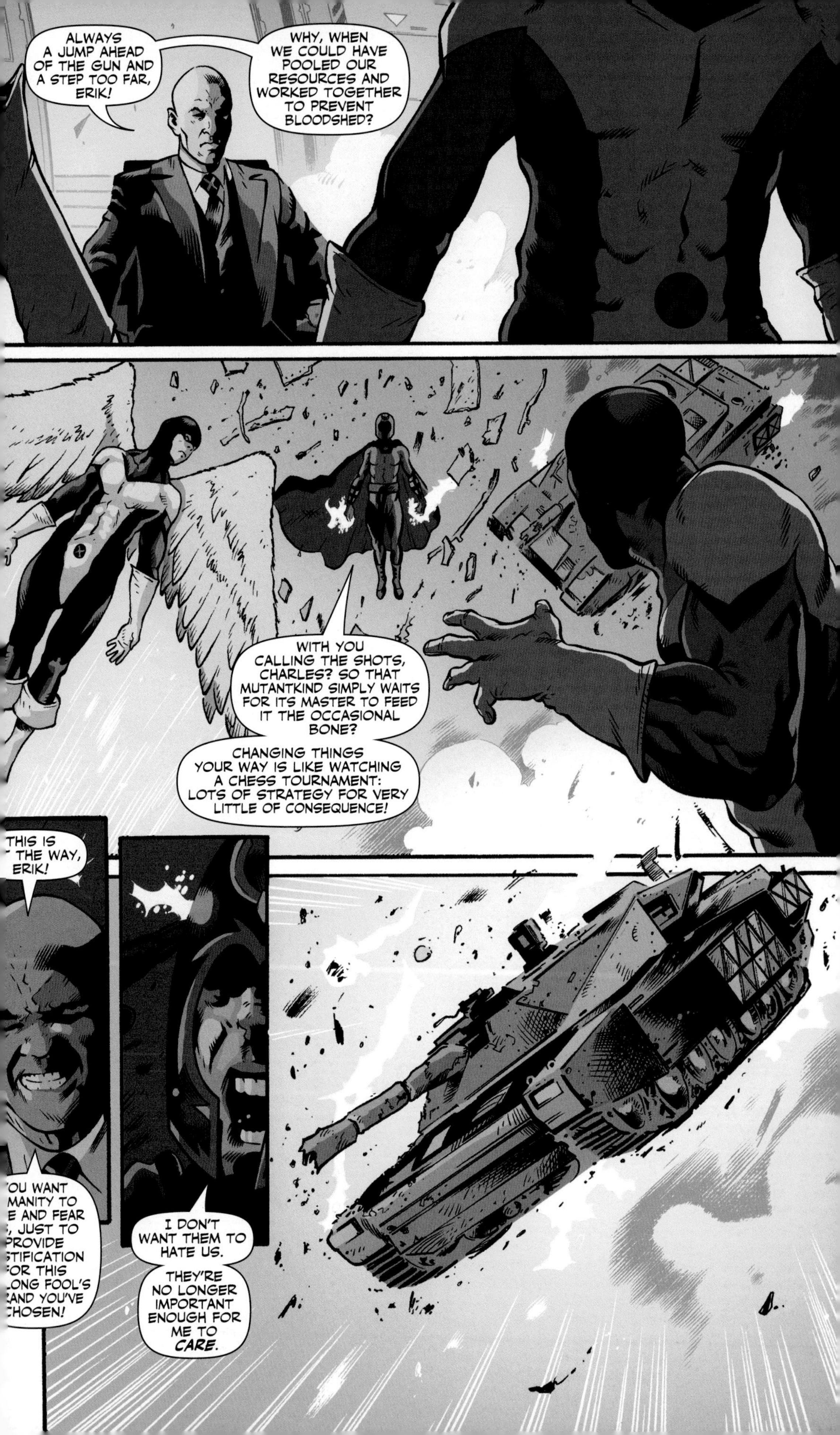
ALWAYS A JUMP AHEAD OF THE GUN AND A STEP TOO FAR, ERIK!
WHY, WHEN WE COULD HAVE POOLED OUR RESOURCES AND WORKED TOGETHER TO PREVENT BLOODSHED?
WITH YOU CALLING THE SHOTS, CHARLES? SO THAT MUTANTKIND SIMPLY WAITS FOR ITS MASTER TO FEED IT THE OCCASIONAL BONE?
CHANGING THINGS YOUR WAY IS LIKE WATCHING A CHESS TOURNAMENT: LOTS OF STRATEGY FOR VERY LITTLE OF CONSEQUENCE!
THIS IS THE WAY, ERIK!
OU WANT MANITY TO E AND FEAR , JUST TO PROVIDE STIFICATION FOR THIS LONG FOOL'S AND YOU'VE CHOSEN!
I DON'T WANT THEM TO HATE US.
THEY'RE NO LONGER IMPORTANT ENOUGH FOR ME TO *CARE*.

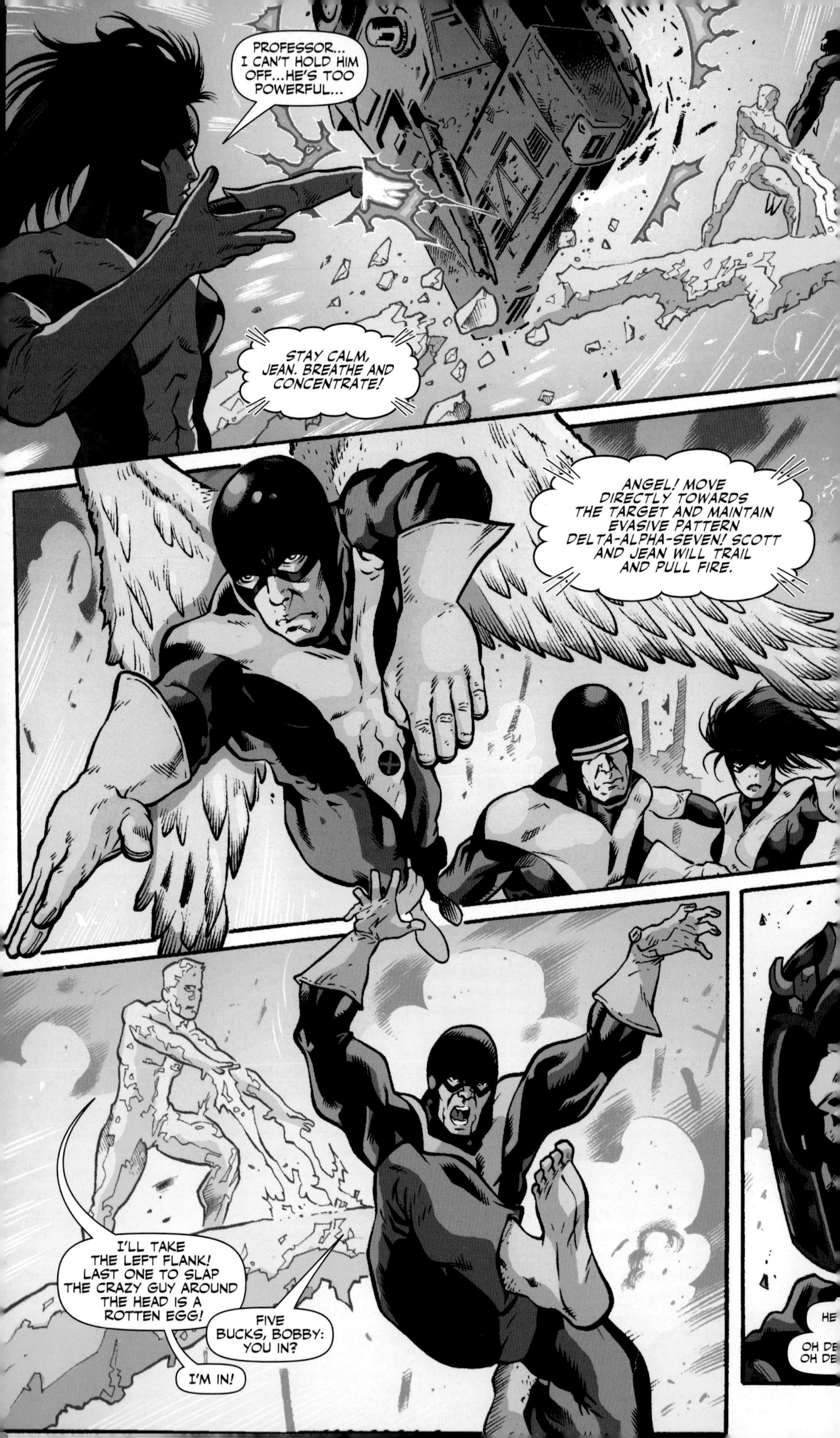
PROFESSOR... I CAN'T HOLD HIM OFF...HE'S TOO POWERFUL...
STAY CALM, JEAN. BREATHE AND CONCENTRATE!
ANGEL! MOVE DIRECTLY TOWARDS THE TARGET AND MAINTAIN EVASIVE PATTERN DELTA-ALPHA-SEVEN! SCOTT AND JEAN WILL TRAIL AND PULL FIRE.
I'LL TAKE THE LEFT FLANK! LAST ONE TO SLAP THE CRAZY GUY AROUND THE HEAD IS A ROTTEN EGG!
FIVE BUCKS, BOBBY: YOU IN?
I'M IN!

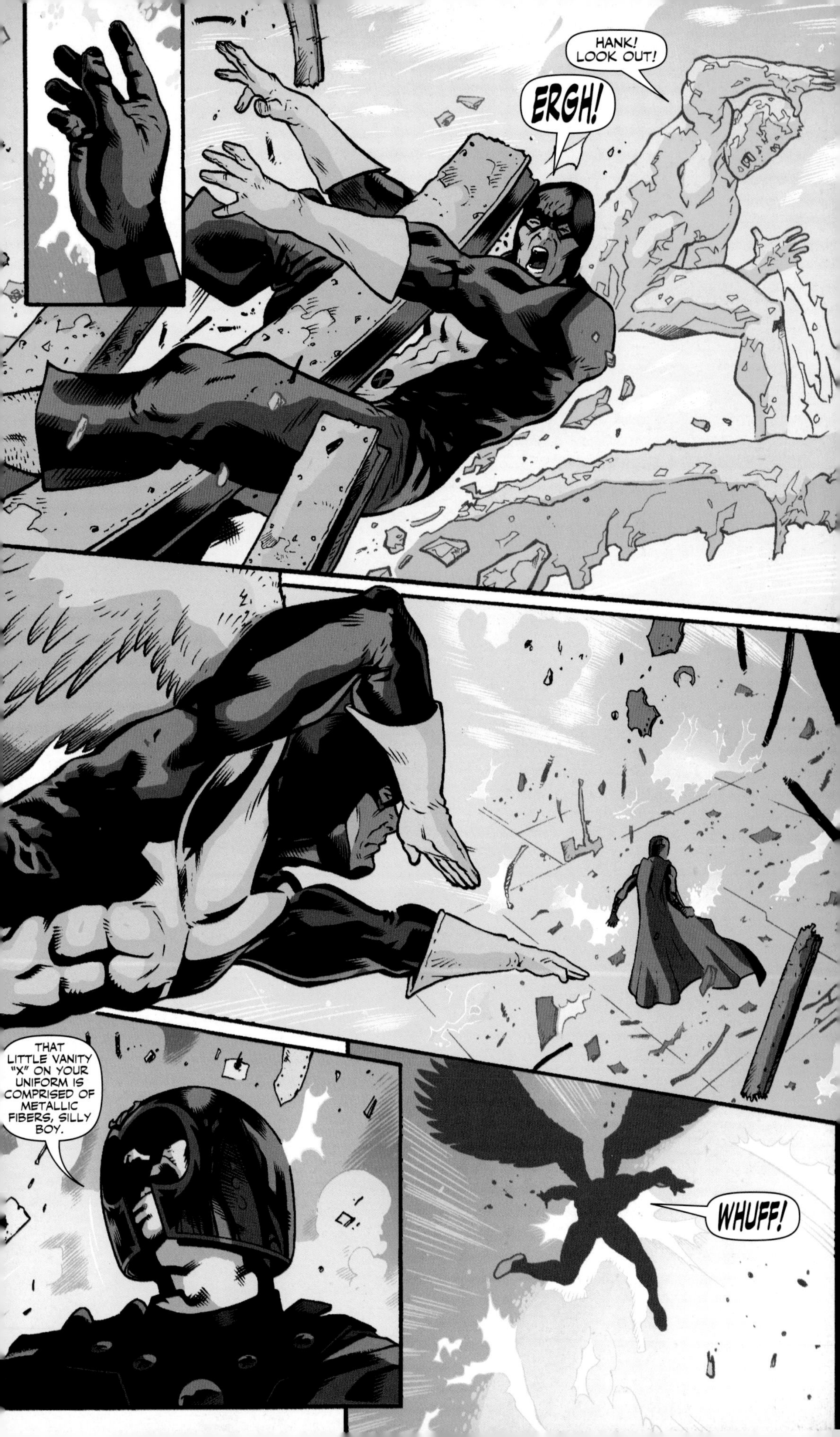
HANK! LOOK OUT!
ERGH!
THAT LITTLE VANITY "X" ON YOUR UNIFORM IS COMPRISED OF METALLIC FIBERS, SILLY BOY.
WHUFF!

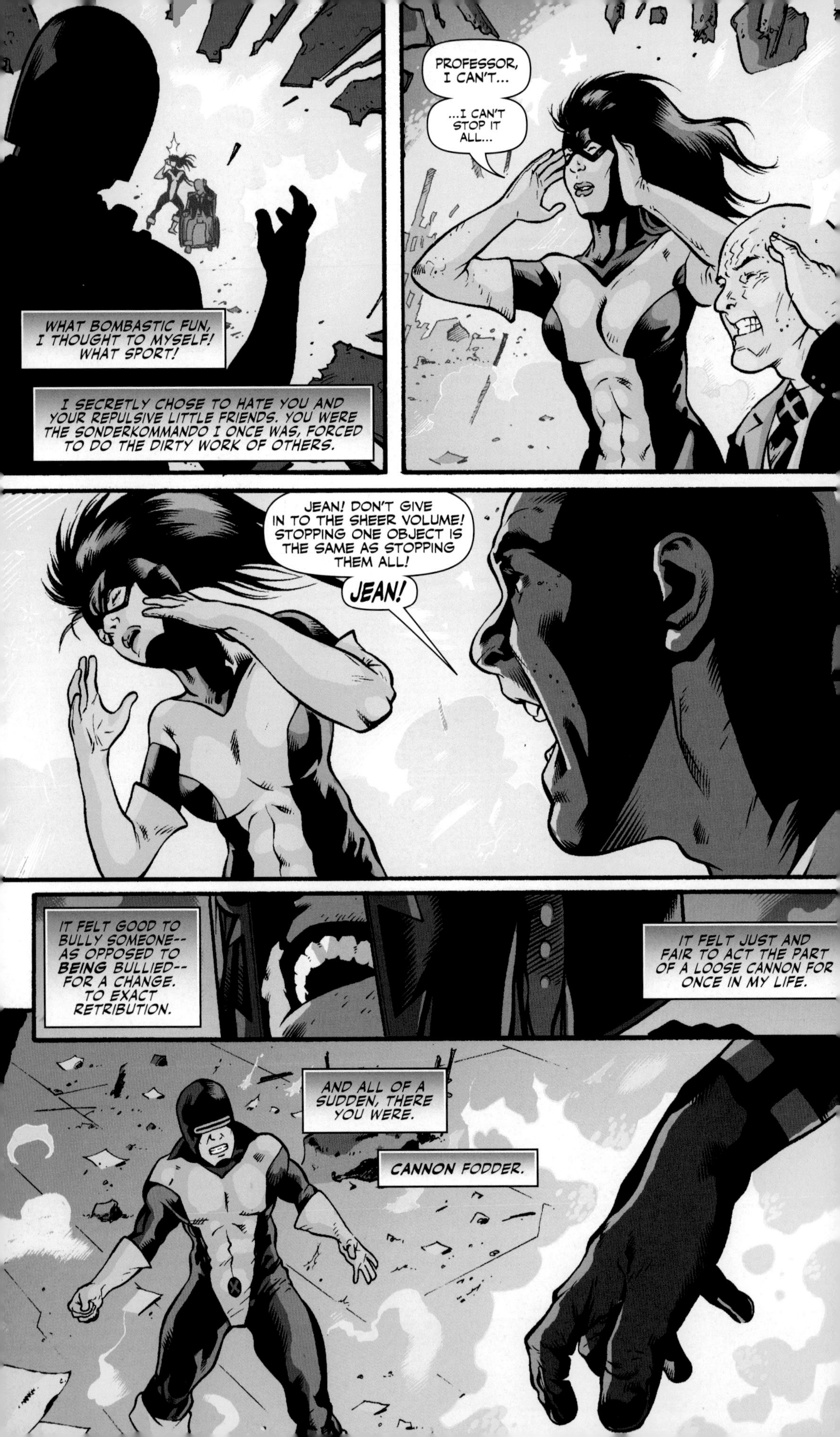

WHAT BOMBASTIC FUN, I THOUGHT TO MYSELF! WHAT SPORT!
I SECRETLY CHOSE TO HATE YOU AND YOUR REPULSIVE LITTLE FRIENDS. YOU WERE THE SONDERKOMMANDO I ONCE WAS, FORCED TO DO THE DIRTY WORK OF OTHERS.
PROFESSOR, I CAN'T...
...I CAN'T STOP IT ALL...
JEAN! DON'T GIVE IN TO THE SHEER VOLUME! STOPPING ONE OBJECT IS THE SAME AS STOPPING THEM ALL!
JEAN!
IT FELT GOOD TO BULLY SOMEONE-- AS OPPOSED TO BEING BULLIED-- FOR A CHANGE. TO EXACT RETRIBUTION.
IT FELT JUST AND FAIR TO ACT THE PART OF A LOOSE CANNON FOR ONCE IN MY LIFE.
AND ALL OF A SUDDEN, THERE YOU WERE.
CANNON FODDER.

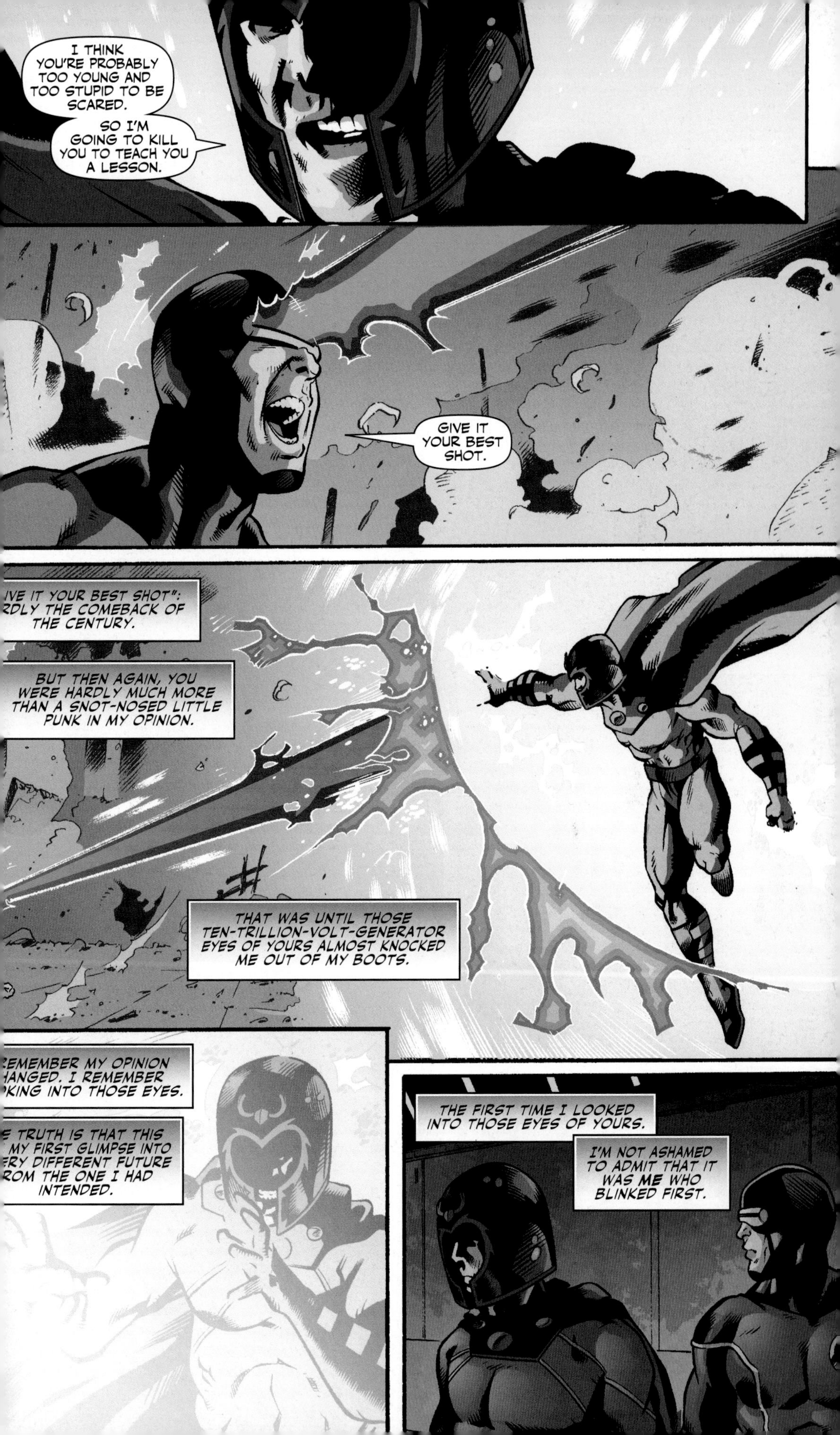

I THINK YOU'RE PROBABLY TOO YOUNG AND TOO STUPID TO BE SCARED.
SO I'M GOING TO KILL YOU TO TEACH YOU A LESSON.
GIVE IT YOUR BEST SHOT.
IVE IT YOUR BEST SHOT": RDLY THE COMEBACK OF THE CENTURY.
BUT THEN AGAIN, YOU WERE HARDLY MUCH MORE THAN A SNOT-NOSED LITTLE PUNK IN MY OPINION.
THAT WAS UNTIL THOSE TEN-TRILLION-VOLT-GENERATOR EYES OF YOURS ALMOST KNOCKED ME OUT OF MY BOOTS.
REMEMBER MY OPINION HANGED. I REMEMBER OKING INTO THOSE EYES.
E TRUTH IS THAT THIS MY FIRST GLIMPSE INTO ERY DIFFERENT FUTURE ROM THE ONE I HAD INTENDED.
THE FIRST TIME I LOOKED INTO THOSE EYES OF YOURS.
I'M NOT ASHAMED TO ADMIT THAT IT WAS ME WHO BLINKED FIRST.

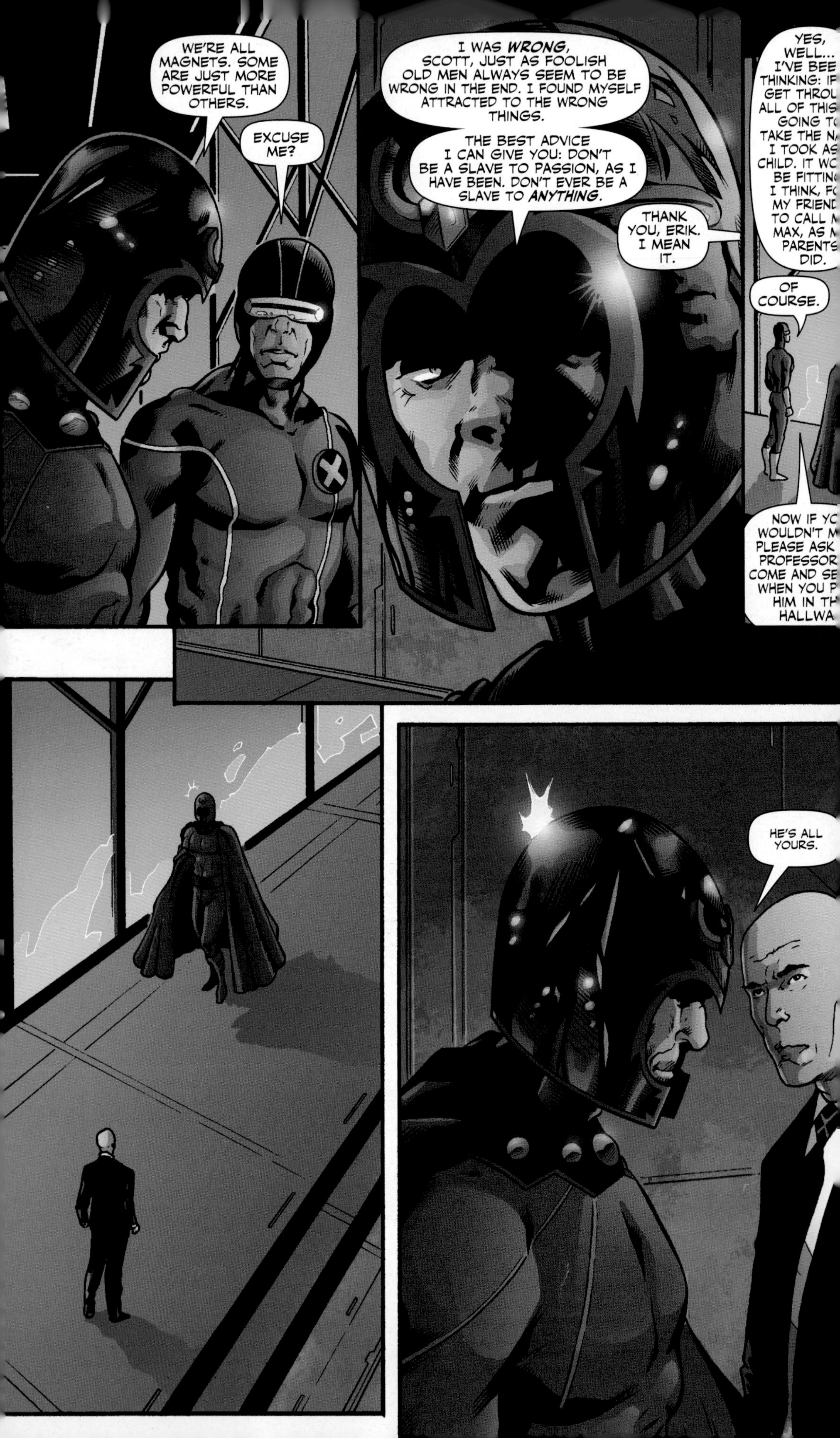
WE'RE ALL MAGNETS. SOME ARE JUST MORE POWERFUL THAN OTHERS.
EXCUSE ME?
I WAS *WRONG*, SCOTT, JUST AS FOOLISH OLD MEN ALWAYS SEEM TO BE WRONG IN THE END. I FOUND MYSELF ATTRACTED TO THE WRONG THINGS.
THE BEST ADVICE I CAN GIVE YOU: DON'T BE A SLAVE TO PASSION, AS I HAVE BEEN. DON'T EVER BE A SLAVE TO *ANYTHING*.
THANK YOU, ERIK. I MEAN IT.
YES, WELL... I'VE BEE THINKING: IF GET THROU ALL OF THIS GOING TO TAKE THE NA I TOOK AS CHILD. IT WO BE FITTIN I THINK, FO MY FRIEND TO CALL M MAX, AS M PARENTS DID.
OF COURSE.
NOW IF YO WOULDN'T M PLEASE ASK PROFESSOR COME AND SE WHEN YOU P HIM IN TH HALLWA
HE'S ALL YOURS.

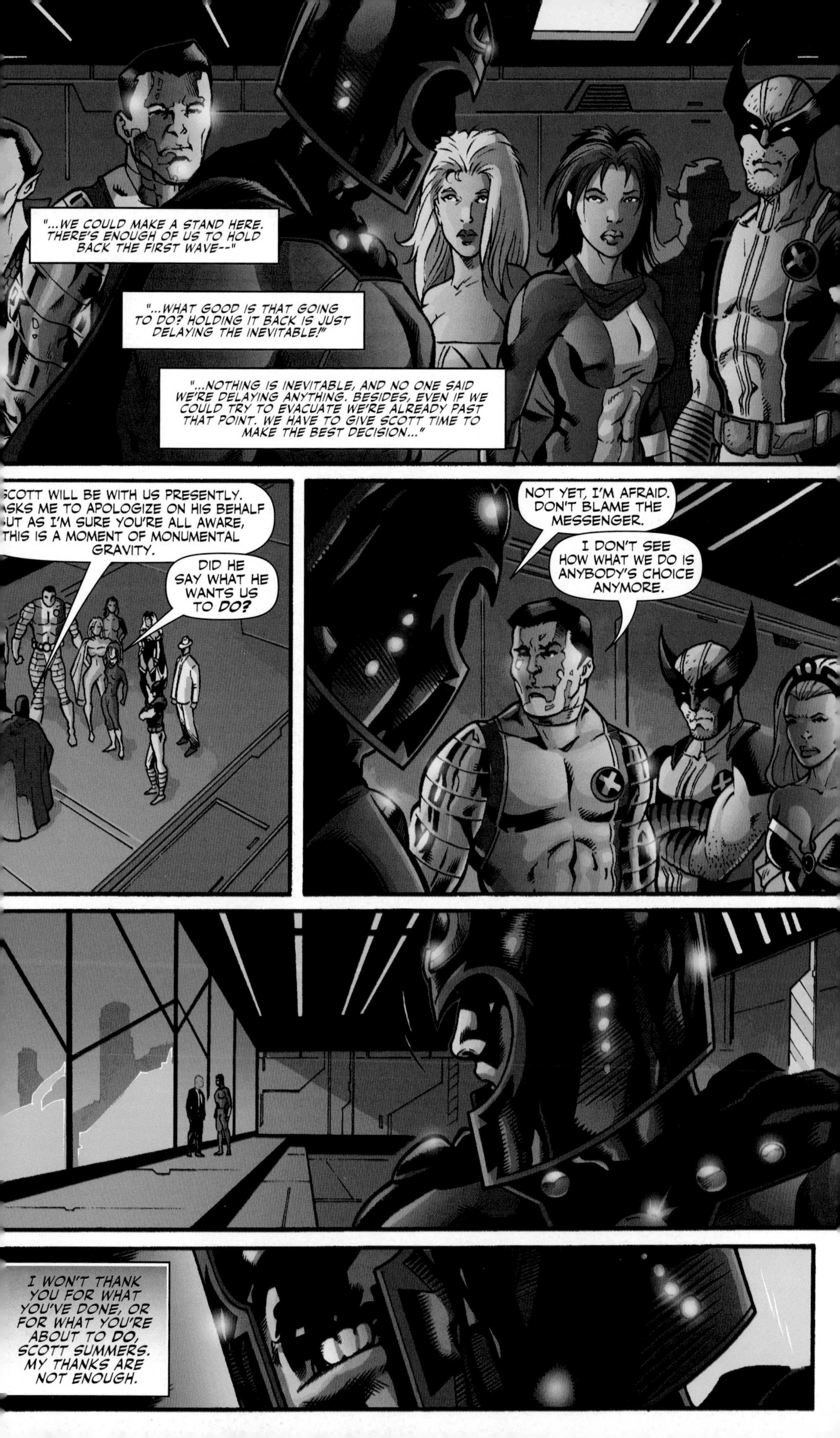
"...WE COULD MAKE A STAND HERE. THERE'S ENOUGH OF US TO HOLD BACK THE FIRST WAVE--"
"...WHAT GOOD IS THAT GOING TO DO? HOLDING IT BACK IS JUST DELAYING THE INEVITABLE!"
"...NOTHING IS INEVITABLE, AND NO ONE SAID WE'RE DELAYING ANYTHING. BESIDES, EVEN IF WE COULD TRY TO EVACUATE WE'RE ALREADY PAST THAT POINT. WE HAVE TO GIVE SCOTT TIME TO MAKE THE BEST DECISION..."
SCOTT WILL BE WITH US PRESENTLY. ASKS ME TO APOLOGIZE ON HIS BEHALF BUT AS I'M SURE YOU'RE ALL AWARE, THIS IS A MOMENT OF MONUMENTAL GRAVITY.
DID HE SAY WHAT HE WANTS US TO DO?
NOT YET, I'M AFRAID. DON'T BLAME THE MESSENGER.
I DON'T SEE HOW WHAT WE DO IS ANYBODY'S CHOICE ANYMORE.
I WON'T THANK YOU FOR WHAT YOU'VE DONE, OR FOR WHAT YOU'RE ABOUT TO DO, SCOTT SUMMERS. MY THANKS ARE NOT ENOUGH.

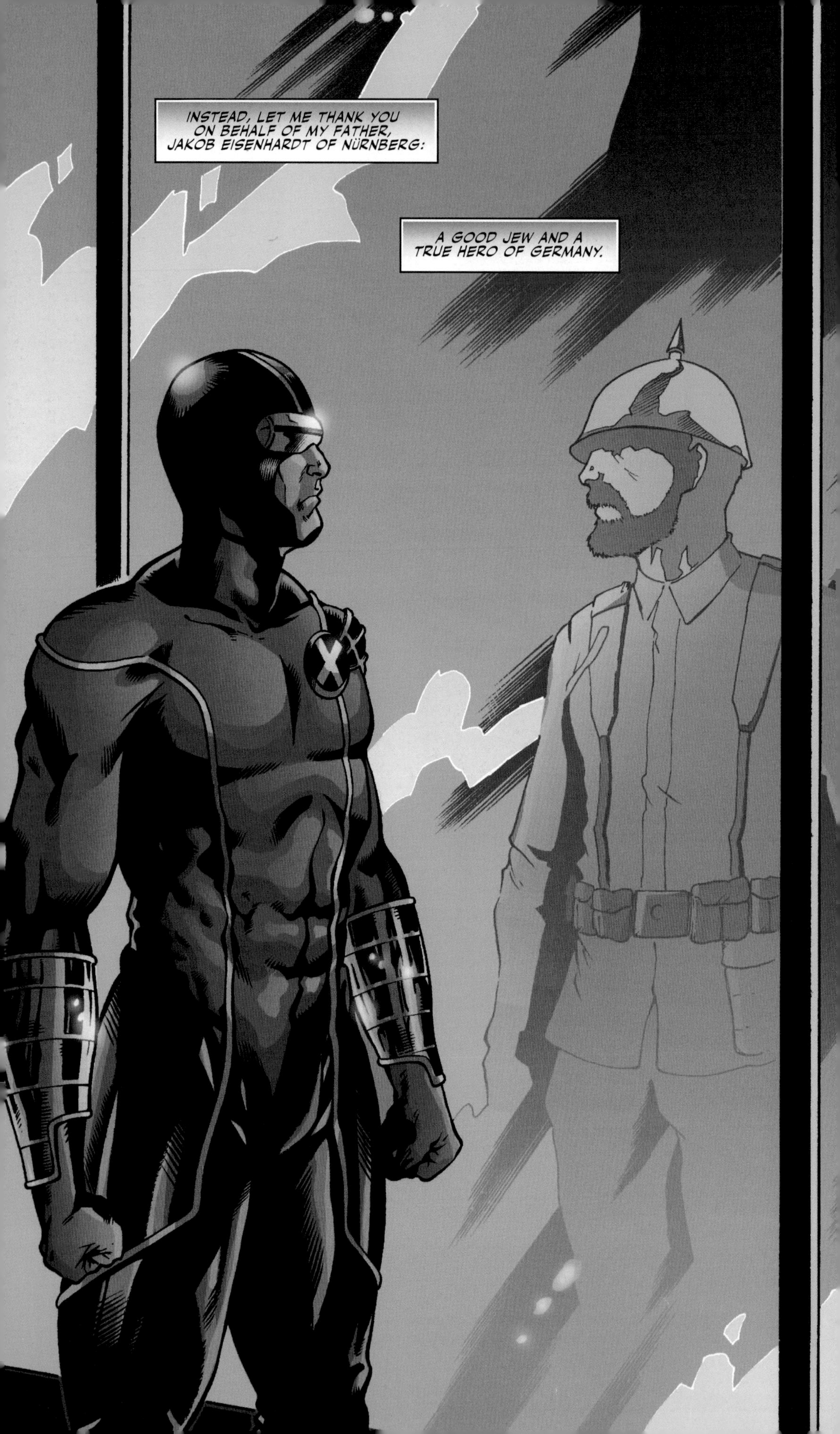
INSTEAD, LET ME THANK YOU ON BEHALF OF MY FATHER, JAKOB EISENHARDT OF NÜRNBERG:
A GOOD JEW AND A TRUE HERO OF GERMANY.

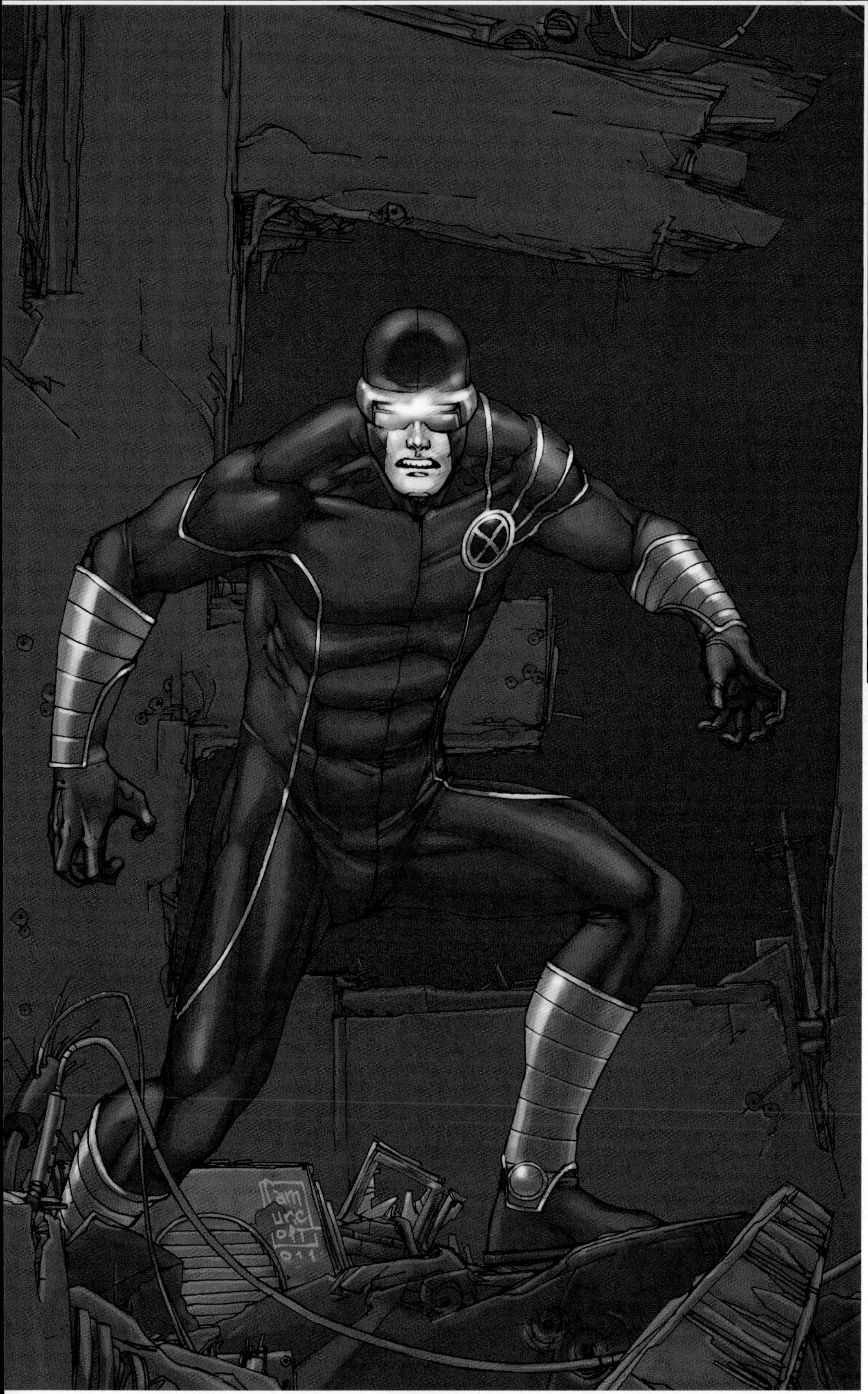

3

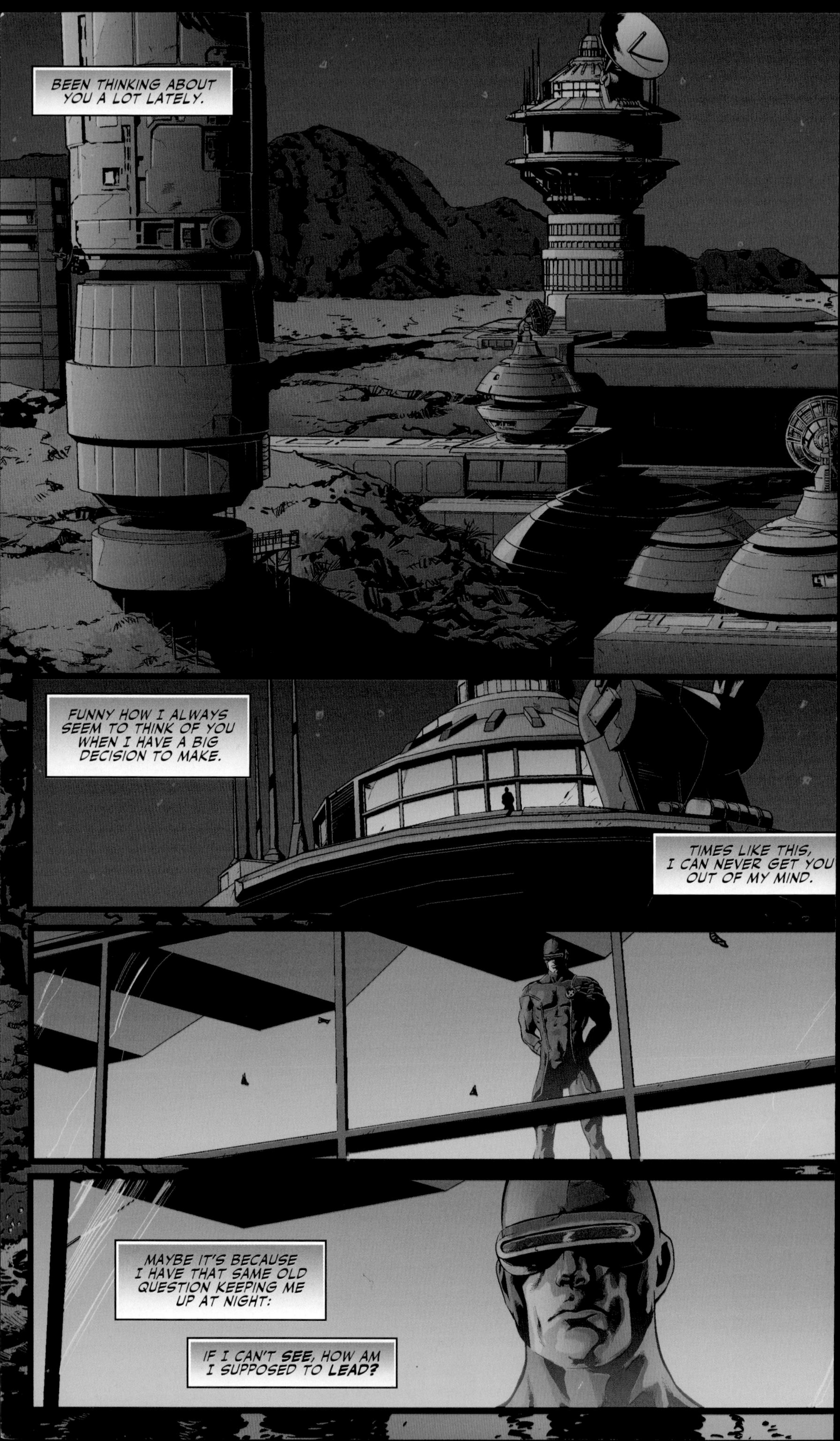
BEEN THINKING ABOUT YOU A LOT LATELY.
FUNNY HOW I ALWAYS SEEM TO THINK OF YOU WHEN I HAVE A BIG DECISION TO MAKE.
TIMES LIKE THIS, I CAN NEVER GET YOU OUT OF MY MIND.
MAYBE IT'S BECAUSE I HAVE THAT SAME OLD QUESTION KEEPING ME UP AT NIGHT:
IF I CAN'T **SEE**, HOW AM I SUPPOSED TO **LEAD?**

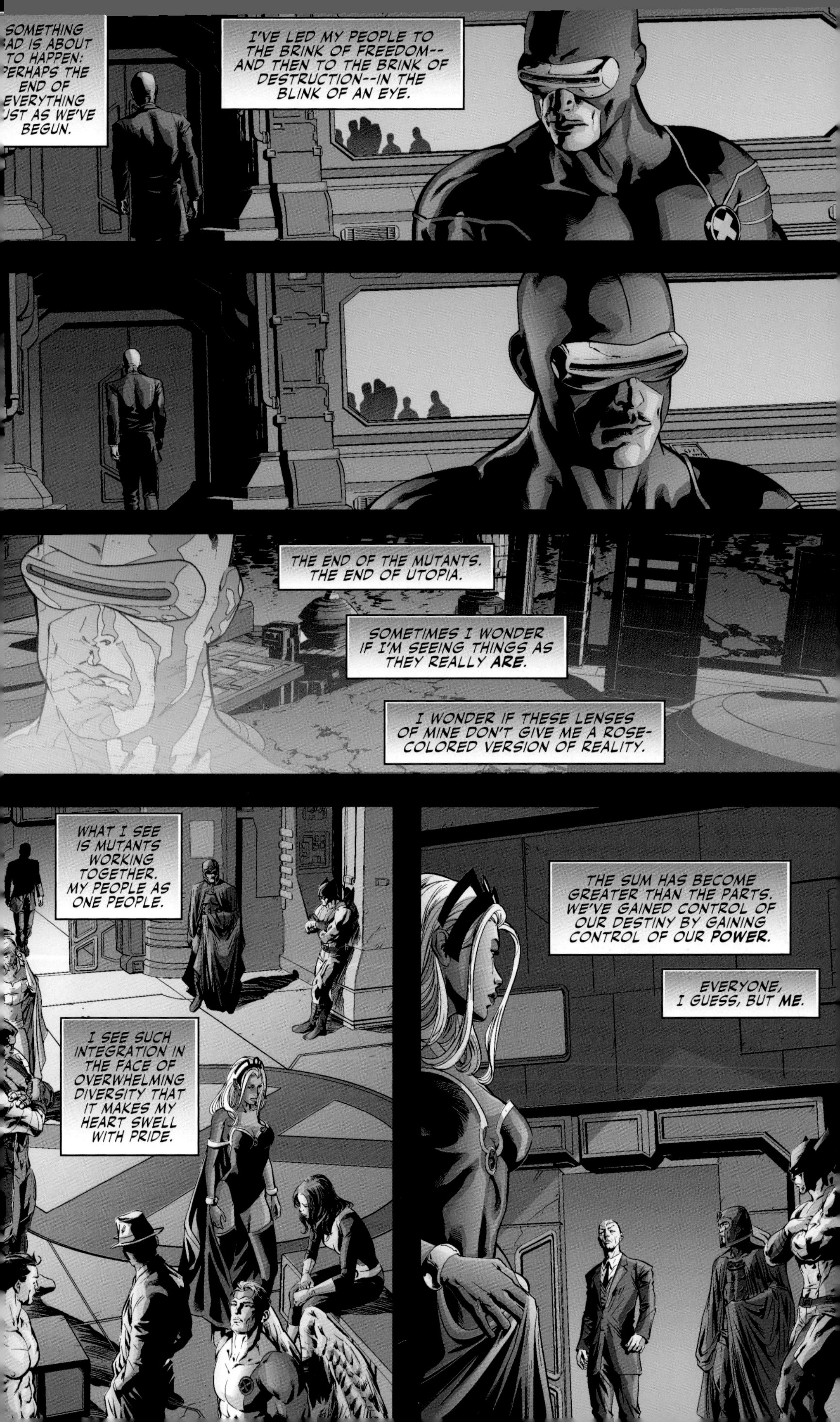

SOMETHING BAD IS ABOUT TO HAPPEN: PERHAPS THE END OF EVERYTHING JUST AS WE'VE BEGUN.
I'VE LED MY PEOPLE TO THE BRINK OF FREEDOM--AND THEN TO THE BRINK OF DESTRUCTION--IN THE BLINK OF AN EYE.
THE END OF THE MUTANTS. THE END OF UTOPIA.
SOMETIMES I WONDER IF I'M SEEING THINGS AS THEY REALLY ARE.
I WONDER IF THESE LENSES OF MINE DON'T GIVE ME A ROSE-COLORED VERSION OF REALITY.
WHAT I SEE IS MUTANTS WORKING TOGETHER. MY PEOPLE AS ONE PEOPLE.
I SEE SUCH INTEGRATION IN THE FACE OF OVERWHELMING DIVERSITY THAT IT MAKES MY HEART SWELL WITH PRIDE.
THE SUM HAS BECOME GREATER THAN THE PARTS. WE'VE GAINED CONTROL OF OUR DESTINY BY GAINING CONTROL OF OUR POWER.
EVERYONE, I GUESS, BUT ME.

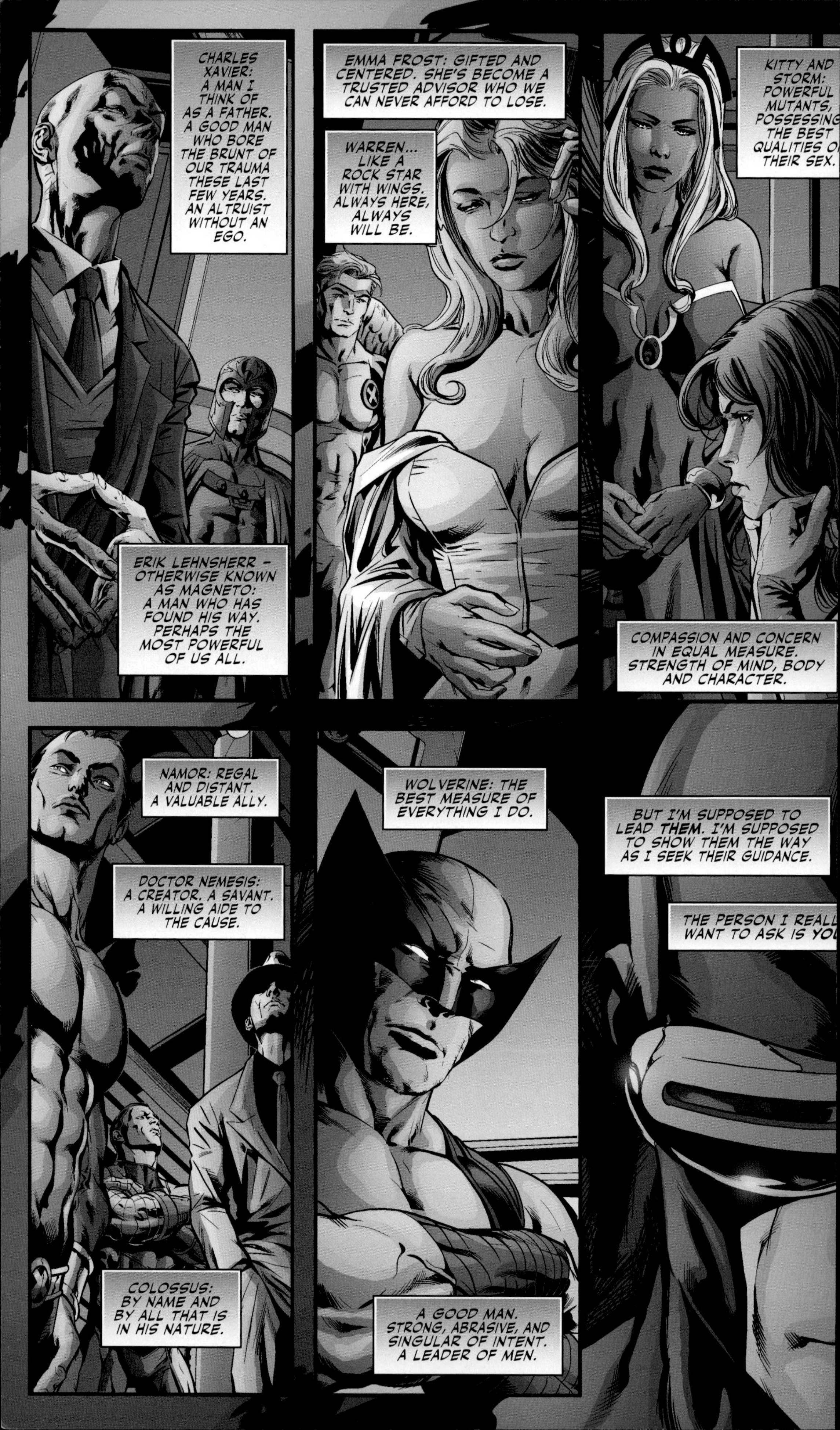
CHARLES XAVIER: A MAN I THINK OF AS A FATHER. A GOOD MAN WHO BORE THE BRUNT OF OUR TRAUMA THESE LAST FEW YEARS. AN ALTRUIST WITHOUT AN EGO.
ERIK LEHNSHERR – OTHERWISE KNOWN AS MAGNETO: A MAN WHO HAS FOUND HIS WAY. PERHAPS THE MOST POWERFUL OF US ALL.
EMMA FROST: GIFTED AND CENTERED. SHE'S BECOME A TRUSTED ADVISOR WHO WE CAN NEVER AFFORD TO LOSE.
WARREN... LIKE A ROCK STAR WITH WINGS. ALWAYS HERE, ALWAYS WILL BE.
KITTY AND STORM: POWERFUL MUTANTS, POSSESSING THE BEST QUALITIES OF THEIR SEX.
COMPASSION AND CONCERN IN EQUAL MEASURE. STRENGTH OF MIND, BODY AND CHARACTER.
NAMOR: REGAL AND DISTANT. A VALUABLE ALLY.
DOCTOR NEMESIS: A CREATOR. A SAVANT. A WILLING AIDE TO THE CAUSE.
COLOSSUS: BY NAME AND BY ALL THAT IS IN HIS NATURE.
WOLVERINE: THE BEST MEASURE OF EVERYTHING I DO.
A GOOD MAN. STRONG, ABRASIVE, AND SINGULAR OF INTENT. A LEADER OF MEN.
BUT I'M SUPPOSED TO LEAD THEM. I'M SUPPOSED TO SHOW THEM THE WAY AS I SEEK THEIR GUIDANCE.
THE PERSON I REALL WANT TO ASK IS YO

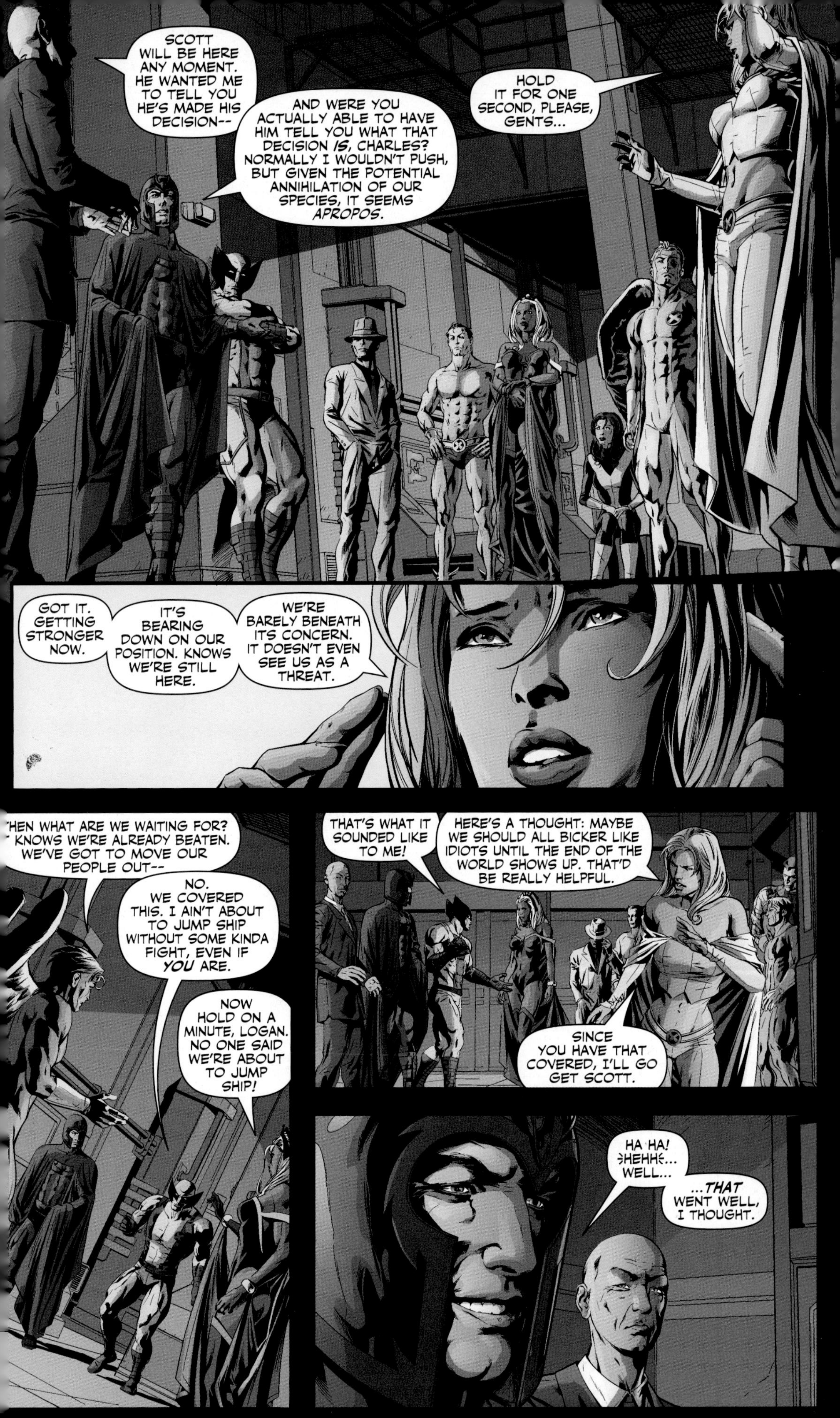
SCOTT WILL BE HERE ANY MOMENT. HE WANTED ME TO TELL YOU HE'S MADE HIS DECISION--
AND WERE YOU ACTUALLY ABLE TO HAVE HIM TELL YOU WHAT THAT DECISION *IS*, CHARLES? NORMALLY I WOULDN'T PUSH, BUT GIVEN THE POTENTIAL ANNIHILATION OF OUR SPECIES, IT SEEMS *APROPOS*.
HOLD IT FOR ONE SECOND, PLEASE, GENTS...
GOT IT. GETTING STRONGER NOW.
IT'S BEARING DOWN ON OUR POSITION. KNOWS WE'RE STILL HERE.
WE'RE BARELY BENEATH ITS CONCERN. IT DOESN'T EVEN SEE US AS A THREAT.
THEN WHAT ARE WE WAITING FOR? IT KNOWS WE'RE ALREADY BEATEN. WE'VE GOT TO MOVE OUR PEOPLE OUT--
NO. WE COVERED THIS. I AIN'T ABOUT TO JUMP SHIP WITHOUT SOME KINDA FIGHT, EVEN IF *YOU* ARE.
NOW HOLD ON A MINUTE, LOGAN. NO ONE SAID WE'RE ABOUT TO JUMP SHIP!
THAT'S WHAT IT SOUNDED LIKE TO ME!
HERE'S A THOUGHT: MAYBE WE SHOULD ALL BICKER LIKE IDIOTS UNTIL THE END OF THE WORLD SHOWS UP. THAT'D BE REALLY HELPFUL.
SINCE YOU HAVE THAT COVERED, I'LL GO GET SCOTT.
HA HA! HEHH... WELL...
...*THAT* WENT WELL, I THOUGHT.

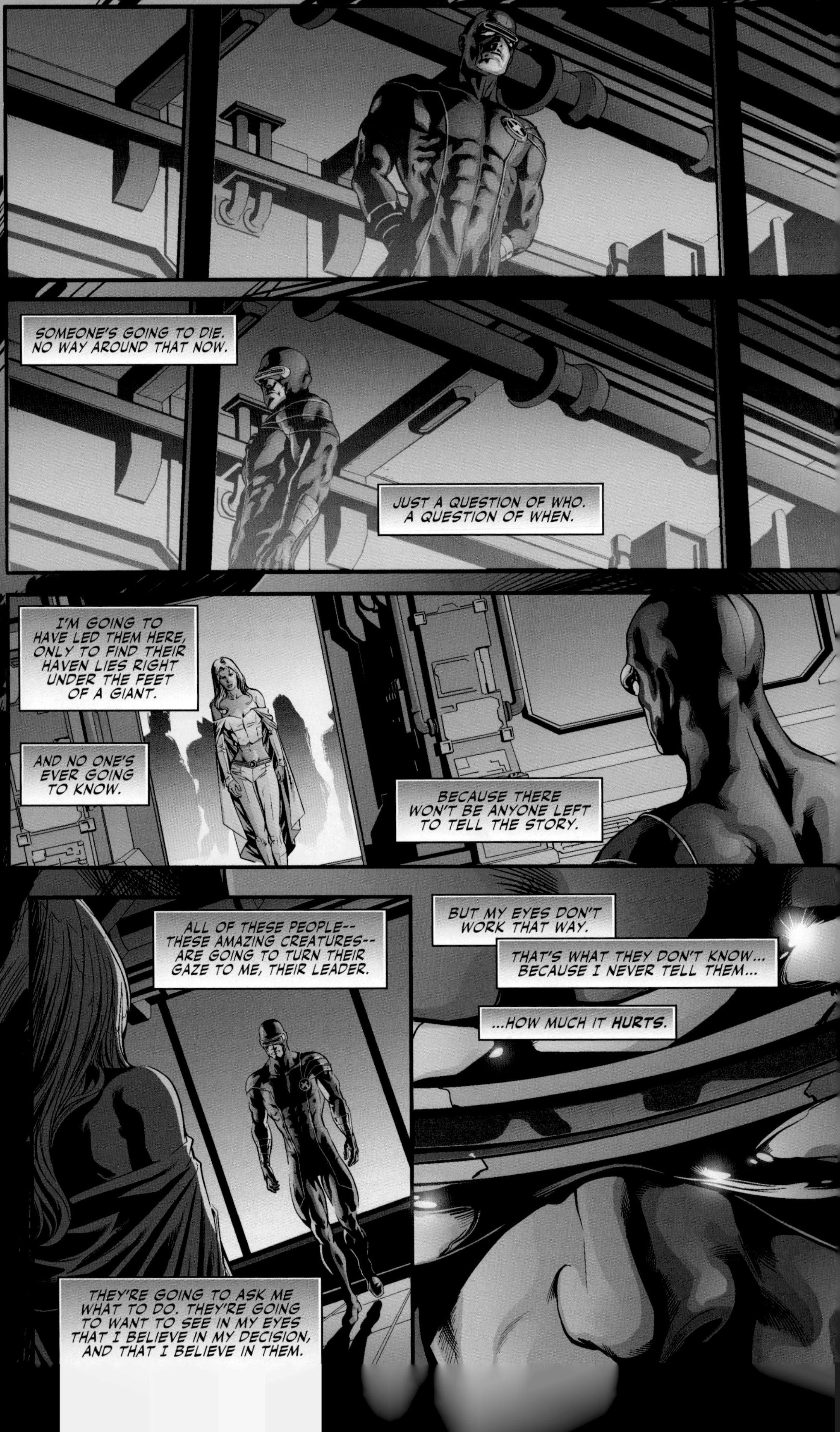
SOMEONE'S GOING TO DIE. NO WAY AROUND THAT NOW.
JUST A QUESTION OF WHO. A QUESTION OF WHEN.
I'M GOING TO HAVE LED THEM HERE, ONLY TO FIND THEIR HAVEN LIES RIGHT UNDER THE FEET OF A GIANT.
AND NO ONE'S EVER GOING TO KNOW.
BECAUSE THERE WON'T BE ANYONE LEFT TO TELL THE STORY.
ALL OF THESE PEOPLE-- THESE AMAZING CREATURES-- ARE GOING TO TURN THEIR GAZE TO ME, THEIR LEADER.
THEY'RE GOING TO ASK ME WHAT TO DO. THEY'RE GOING TO WANT TO SEE IN MY EYES THAT I BELIEVE IN MY DECISION, AND THAT I BELIEVE IN THEM.
BUT MY EYES DON'T WORK THAT WAY.
THAT'S WHAT THEY DON'T KNOW... BECAUSE I NEVER TELL THEM...
...HOW MUCH IT HURTS.

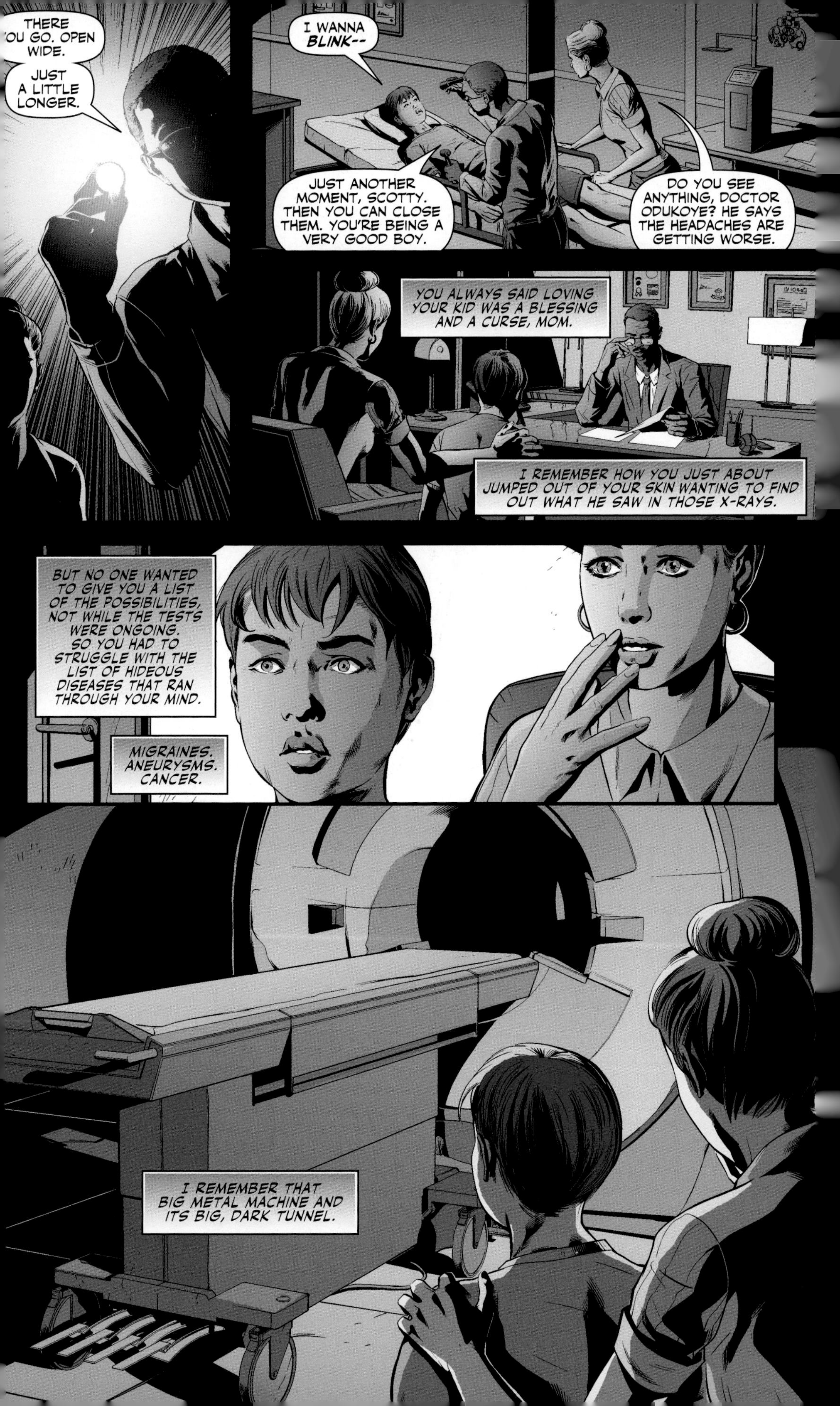

THERE YOU GO. OPEN WIDE.
JUST A LITTLE LONGER.
I WANNA BLINK--
JUST ANOTHER MOMENT, SCOTTY. THEN YOU CAN CLOSE THEM. YOU'RE BEING A VERY GOOD BOY.
DO YOU SEE ANYTHING, DOCTOR ODUKOYE? HE SAYS THE HEADACHES ARE GETTING WORSE.
YOU ALWAYS SAID LOVING YOUR KID WAS A BLESSING AND A CURSE, MOM.
I REMEMBER HOW YOU JUST ABOUT JUMPED OUT OF YOUR SKIN WANTING TO FIND OUT WHAT HE SAW IN THOSE X-RAYS.
BUT NO ONE WANTED TO GIVE YOU A LIST OF THE POSSIBILITIES, NOT WHILE THE TESTS WERE ONGOING. SO YOU HAD TO STRUGGLE WITH THE LIST OF HIDEOUS DISEASES THAT RAN THROUGH YOUR MIND.
MIGRAINES. ANEURYSMS. CANCER.
I REMEMBER THAT BIG METAL MACHINE AND ITS BIG, DARK TUNNEL.

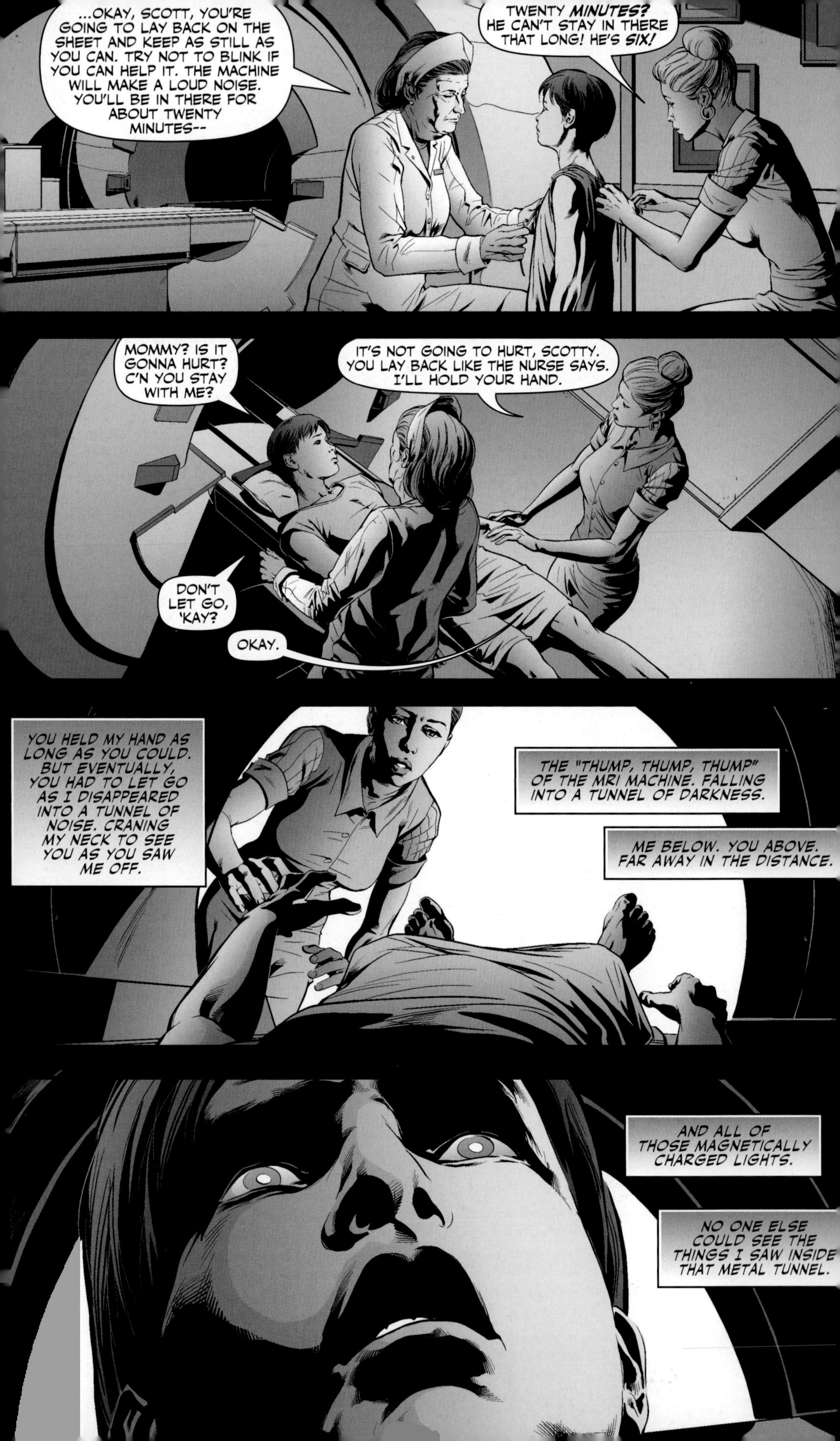

...OKAY, SCOTT, YOU'RE GOING TO LAY BACK ON THE SHEET AND KEEP AS STILL AS YOU CAN. TRY NOT TO BLINK IF YOU CAN HELP IT. THE MACHINE WILL MAKE A LOUD NOISE. YOU'LL BE IN THERE FOR ABOUT TWENTY MINUTES--
TWENTY *MINUTES?* HE CAN'T STAY IN THERE THAT LONG! HE'S *SIX!*
MOMMY? IS IT GONNA HURT? C'N YOU STAY WITH ME?
IT'S NOT GOING TO HURT, SCOTTY. YOU LAY BACK LIKE THE NURSE SAYS. I'LL HOLD YOUR HAND.
DON'T LET GO, 'KAY?
OKAY.
YOU HELD MY HAND AS LONG AS YOU COULD. BUT EVENTUALLY, YOU HAD TO LET GO AS I DISAPPEARED INTO A TUNNEL OF NOISE. CRANING MY NECK TO SEE YOU AS YOU SAW ME OFF.
THE "THUMP, THUMP, THUMP" OF THE MRI MACHINE. FALLING INTO A TUNNEL OF DARKNESS.
ME BELOW. YOU ABOVE. FAR AWAY IN THE DISTANCE.
AND ALL OF THOSE MAGNETICALLY CHARGED LIGHTS.
NO ONE ELSE COULD SEE THE THINGS I SAW INSIDE THAT METAL TUNNEL.

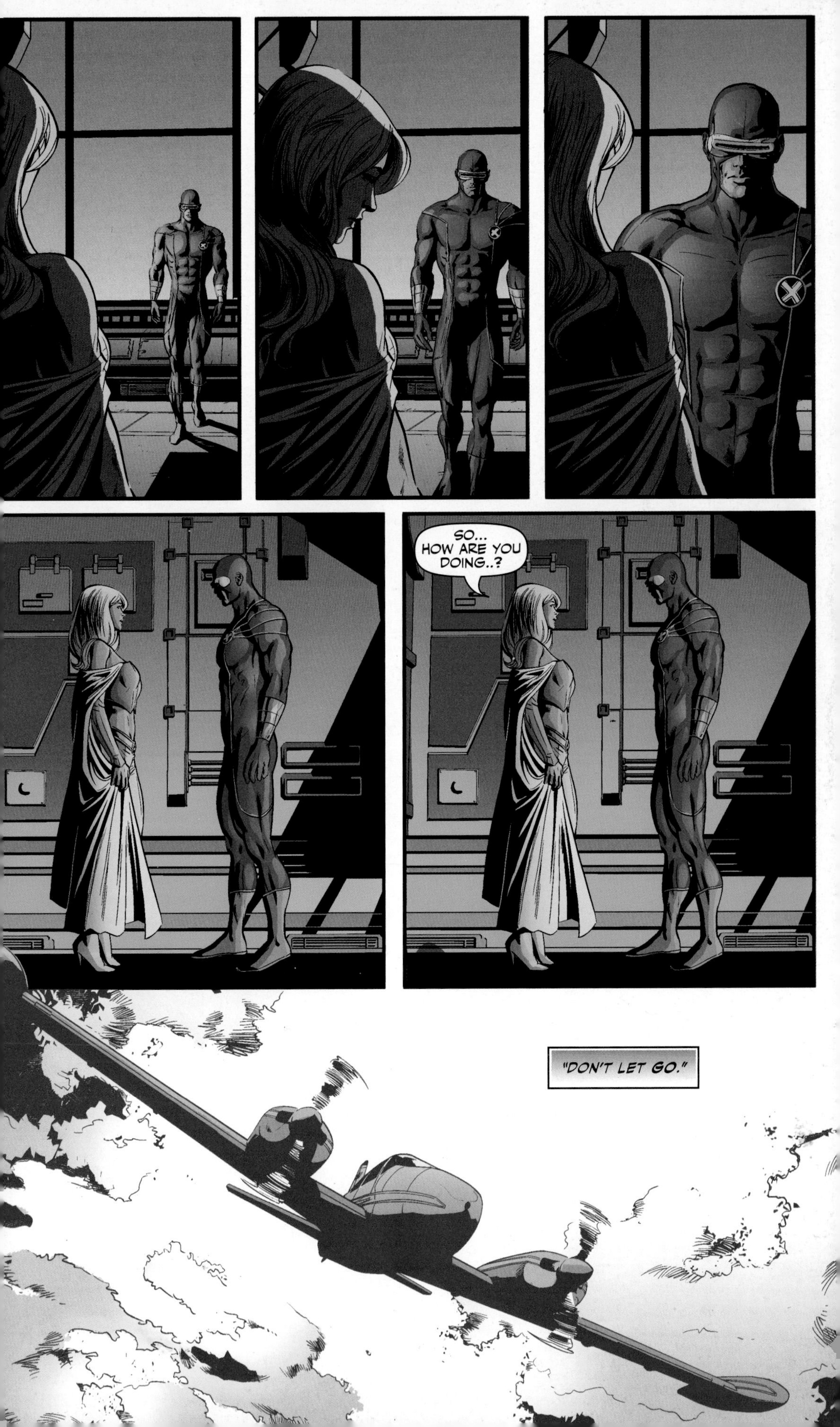
SO... HOW ARE YOU DOING..?
"DON'T LET GO."

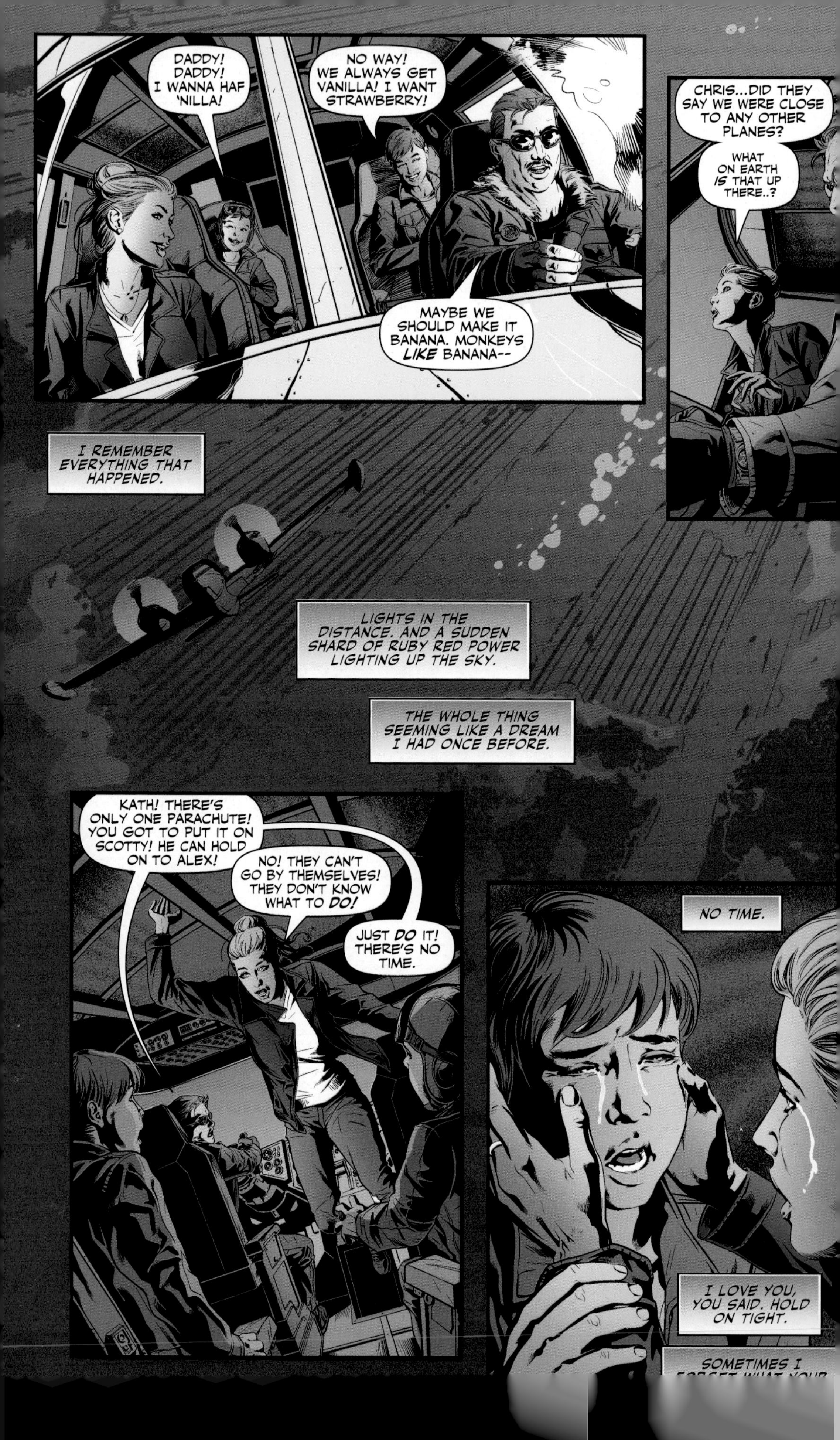
DADDY! DADDY! I WANNA HAF 'NILLA!
NO WAY! WE ALWAYS GET VANILLA! I WANT STRAWBERRY!
MAYBE WE SHOULD MAKE IT BANANA. MONKEYS LIKE BANANA--
CHRIS...DID THEY SAY WE WERE CLOSE TO ANY OTHER PLANES?
WHAT ON EARTH IS THAT UP THERE..?
I REMEMBER EVERYTHING THAT HAPPENED.
LIGHTS IN THE DISTANCE. AND A SUDDEN SHARD OF RUBY RED POWER LIGHTING UP THE SKY.
THE WHOLE THING SEEMING LIKE A DREAM I HAD ONCE BEFORE.
KATH! THERE'S ONLY ONE PARACHUTE! YOU GOT TO PUT IT ON SCOTTY! HE CAN HOLD ON TO ALEX!
NO! THEY CAN'T GO BY THEMSELVES! THEY DON'T KNOW WHAT TO DO!
JUST DO IT! THERE'S NO TIME.
NO TIME.
I LOVE YOU, YOU SAID. HOLD ON TIGHT.
SOMETIMES I

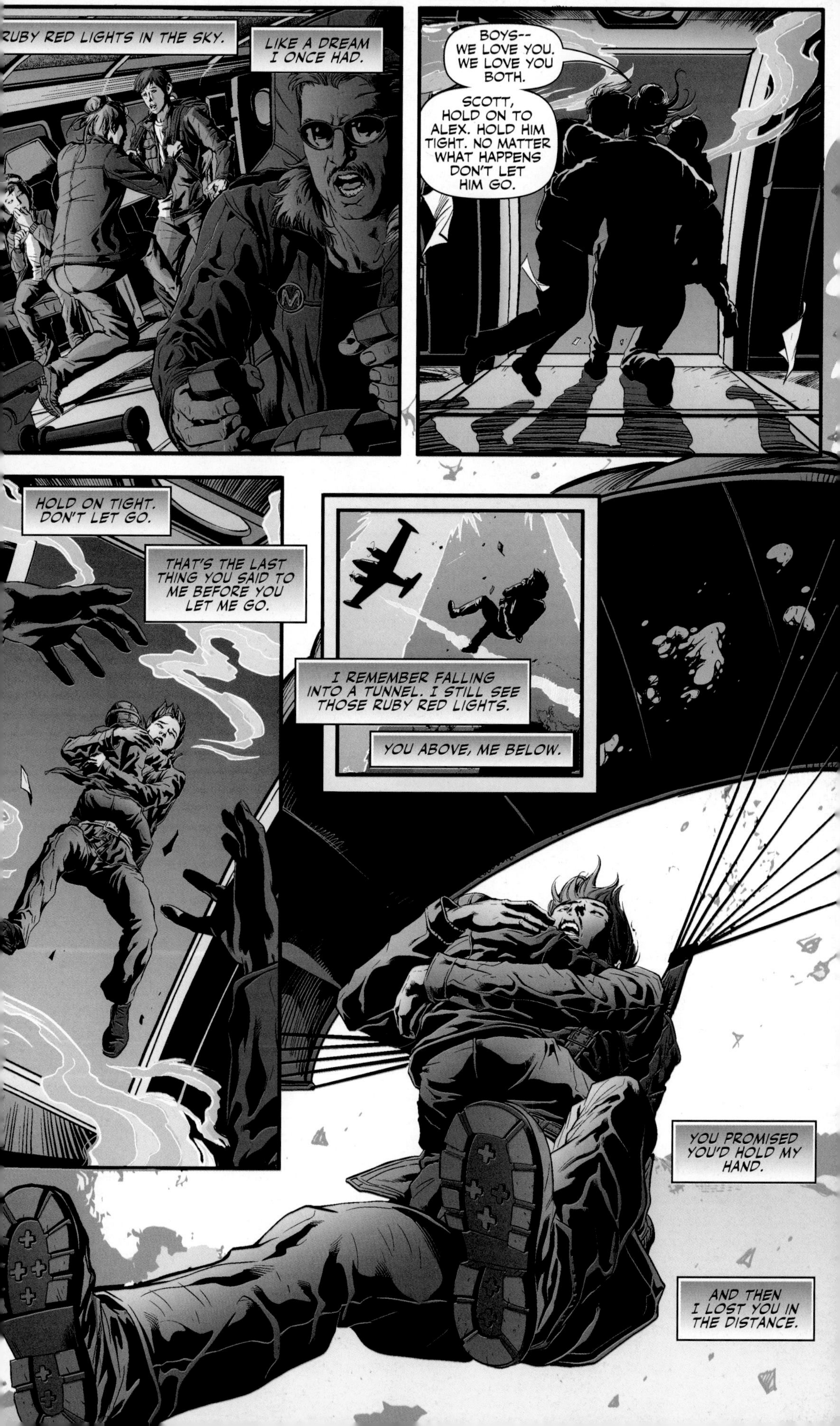

RUBY RED LIGHTS IN THE SKY.
LIKE A DREAM I ONCE HAD.
BOYS-- WE LOVE YOU. WE LOVE YOU BOTH.
SCOTT, HOLD ON TO ALEX. HOLD HIM TIGHT. NO MATTER WHAT HAPPENS DON'T LET HIM GO.
HOLD ON TIGHT. DON'T LET GO.
THAT'S THE LAST THING YOU SAID TO ME BEFORE YOU LET ME GO.
I REMEMBER FALLING INTO A TUNNEL. I STILL SEE THOSE RUBY RED LIGHTS.
YOU ABOVE, ME BELOW.
YOU PROMISED YOU'D HOLD MY HAND.
AND THEN I LOST YOU IN THE DISTANCE.

HOLD ON TIGHT.

DON'T LET GO.

EVENTUALLY, YOU ALWAYS HAVE TO LET GO.

AS I LAY THERE ON MY BACK, STUNNED AND CONFUSED. HOW COULD I HAVE KNOWN THAT MOMENT WOULD HAVE HAD SUCH AN IMPACT.

THAT ONCE MY POWERS MANIFESTED, I'D NEVER BE ABLE TO CONTROL THEM BECAUSE OF THAT CONCUSSION.

ALL I COULD SEE WAS THE BRILLIANT BLUE SKY.

ALL I COULD THINK OF WAS BEING UP THERE. WITH YOU.

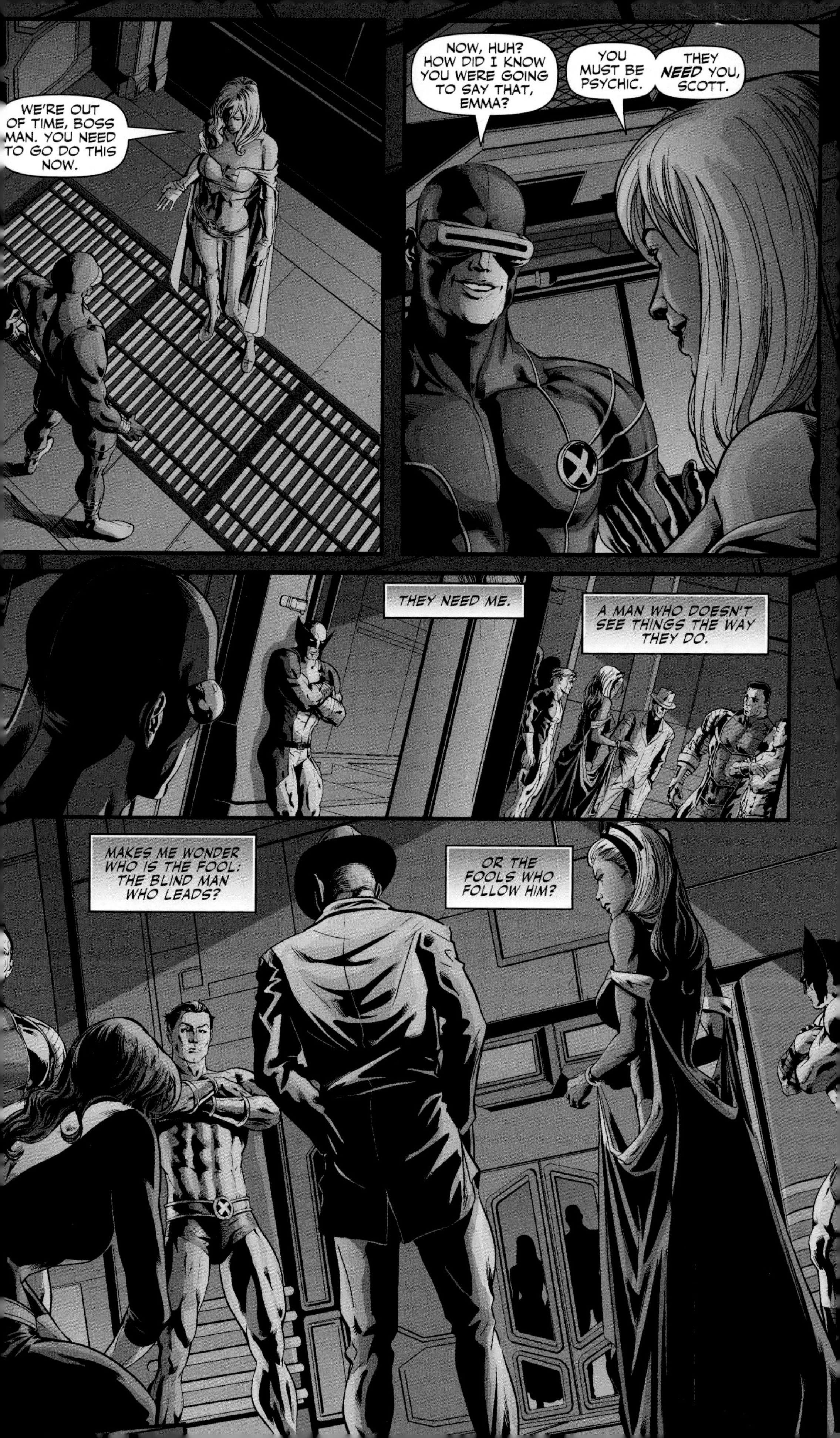

WE'RE OUT OF TIME, BOSS MAN. YOU NEED TO GO DO THIS NOW.
NOW, HUH? HOW DID I KNOW YOU WERE GOING TO SAY THAT, EMMA?
YOU MUST BE PSYCHIC.
THEY NEED YOU, SCOTT.
THEY NEED ME.
A MAN WHO DOESN'T SEE THINGS THE WAY THEY DO.
MAKES ME WONDER WHO IS THE FOOL: THE BLIND MAN WHO LEADS?
OR THE FOOLS WHO FOLLOW HIM?

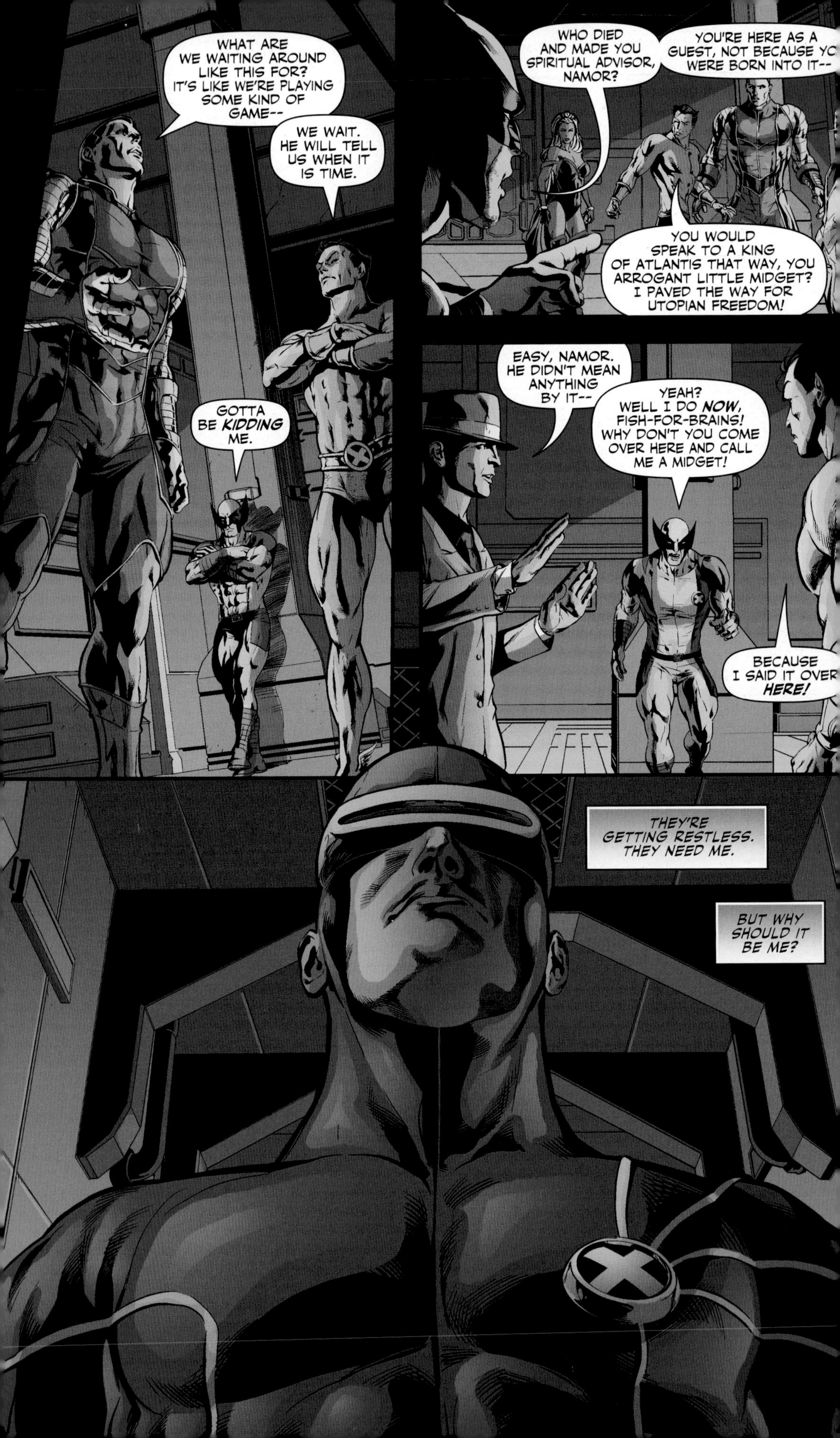
WHAT ARE WE WAITING AROUND LIKE THIS FOR? IT'S LIKE WE'RE PLAYING SOME KIND OF GAME--
WE WAIT. HE WILL TELL US WHEN IT IS TIME.
GOTTA BE *KIDDING* ME.
WHO DIED AND MADE YOU SPIRITUAL ADVISOR, NAMOR?
YOU'RE HERE AS A GUEST, NOT BECAUSE YO WERE BORN INTO IT--
YOU WOULD SPEAK TO A KING OF ATLANTIS THAT WAY, YOU ARROGANT LITTLE MIDGET? I PAVED THE WAY FOR UTOPIAN FREEDOM!
EASY, NAMOR. HE DIDN'T MEAN ANYTHING BY IT--
YEAH? WELL I DO *NOW*, FISH-FOR-BRAINS! WHY DON'T YOU COME OVER HERE AND CALL ME A MIDGET!
BECAUSE I SAID IT OVER *HERE!*
THEY'RE GETTING RESTLESS. THEY NEED ME.
BUT WHY SHOULD IT BE ME?

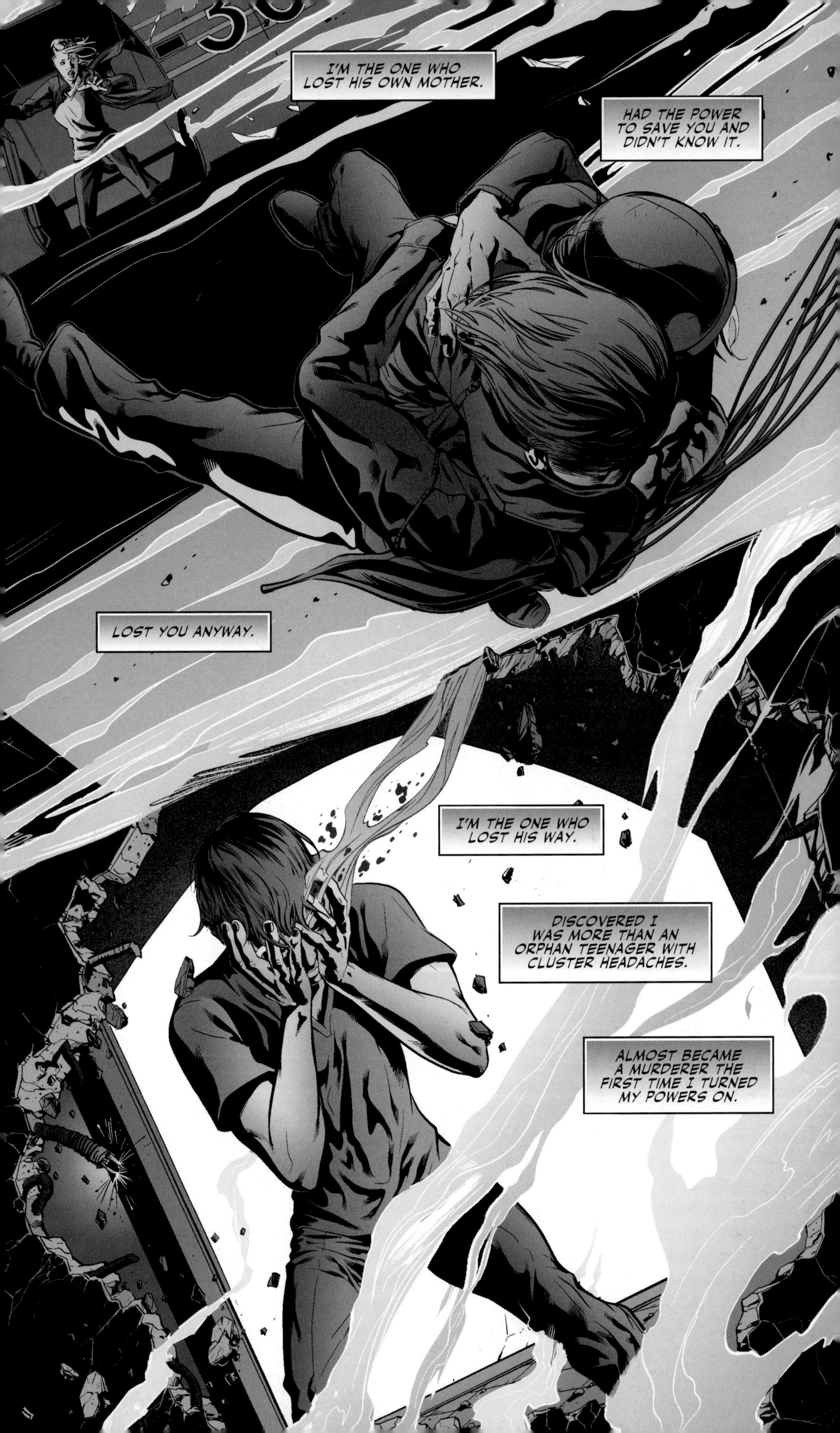
I'M THE ONE WHO LOST HIS OWN MOTHER.
HAD THE POWER TO SAVE YOU AND DIDN'T KNOW IT.
LOST YOU ANYWAY.
I'M THE ONE WHO LOST HIS WAY.
DISCOVERED I WAS MORE THAN AN ORPHAN TEENAGER WITH CLUSTER HEADACHES.
ALMOST BECAME A MURDERER THE FIRST TIME I TURNED MY POWERS ON.

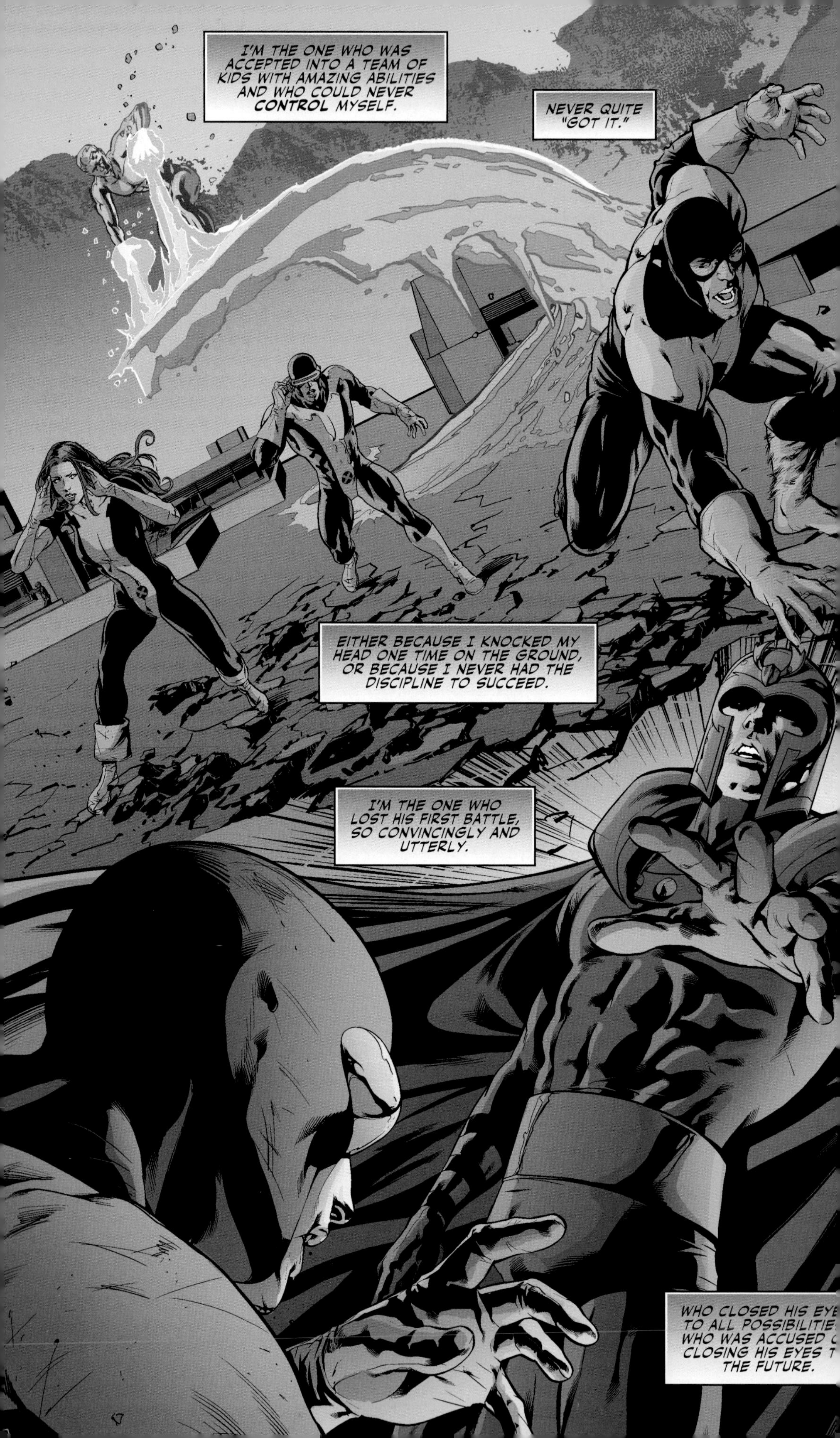
I'M THE ONE WHO WAS ACCEPTED INTO A TEAM OF KIDS WITH AMAZING ABILITIES AND WHO COULD NEVER CONTROL MYSELF.
NEVER QUITE "GOT IT."
EITHER BECAUSE I KNOCKED MY HEAD ONE TIME ON THE GROUND, OR BECAUSE I NEVER HAD THE DISCIPLINE TO SUCCEED.
I'M THE ONE WHO LOST HIS FIRST BATTLE, SO CONVINCINGLY AND UTTERLY.
WHO CLOSED HIS EYE TO ALL POSSIBILITIE WHO WAS ACCUSED C CLOSING HIS EYES T THE FUTURE.

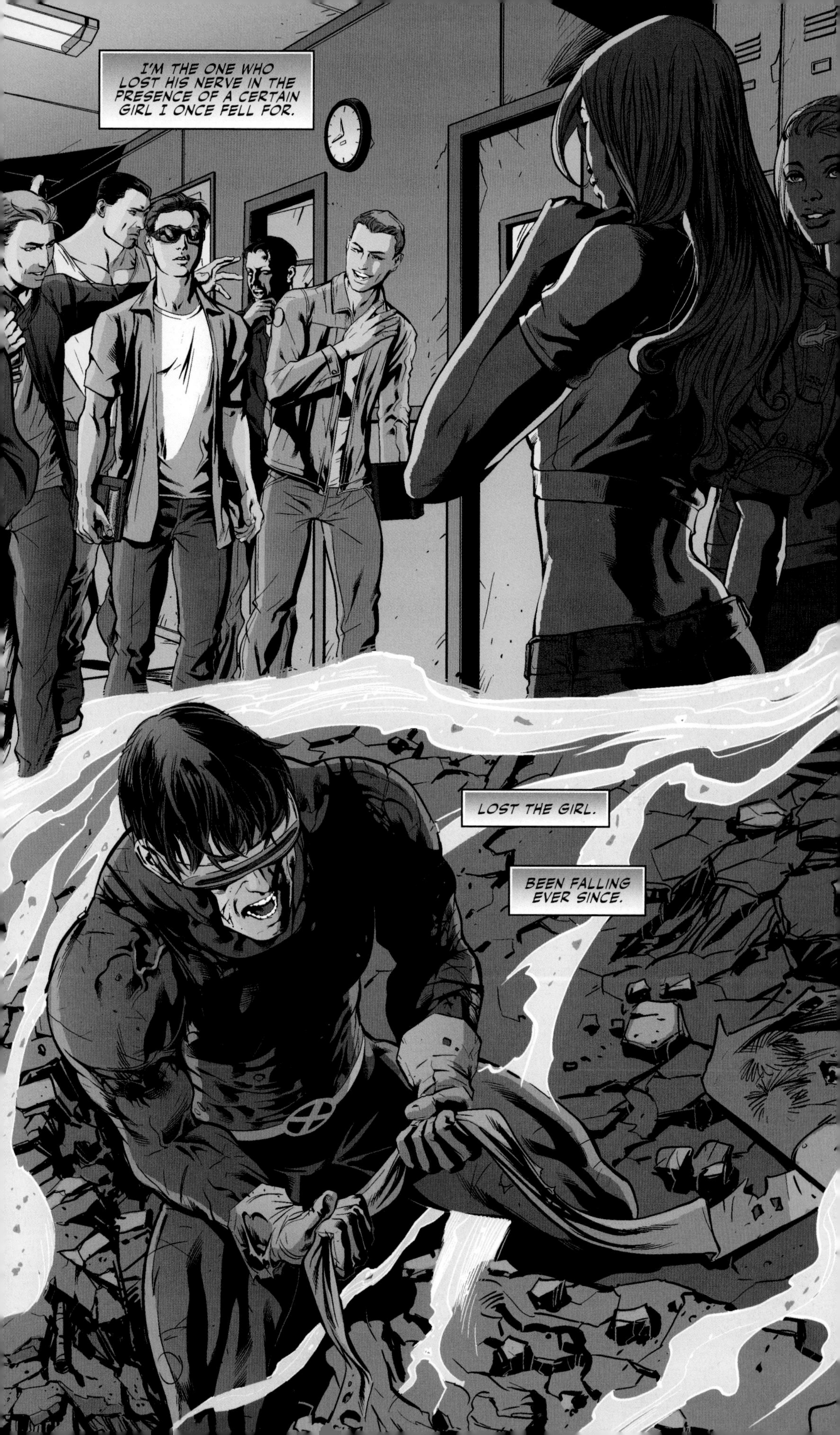
I'M THE ONE WHO LOST HIS NERVE IN THE PRESENCE OF A CERTAIN GIRL I ONCE FELL FOR.
LOST THE GIRL.
BEEN FALLING EVER SINCE.

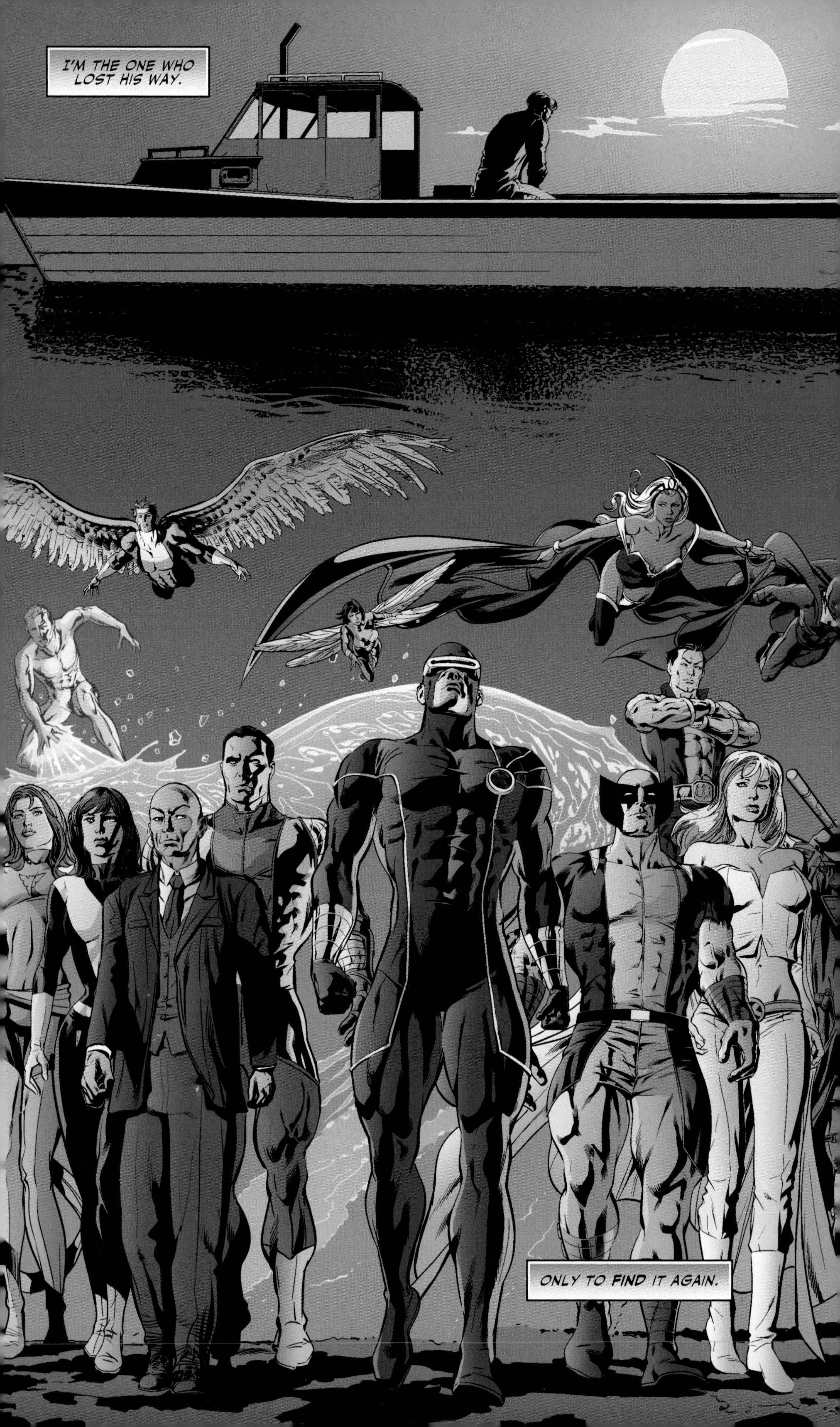
I'M THE ONE WHO LOST HIS WAY.
ONLY TO FIND IT AGAIN.

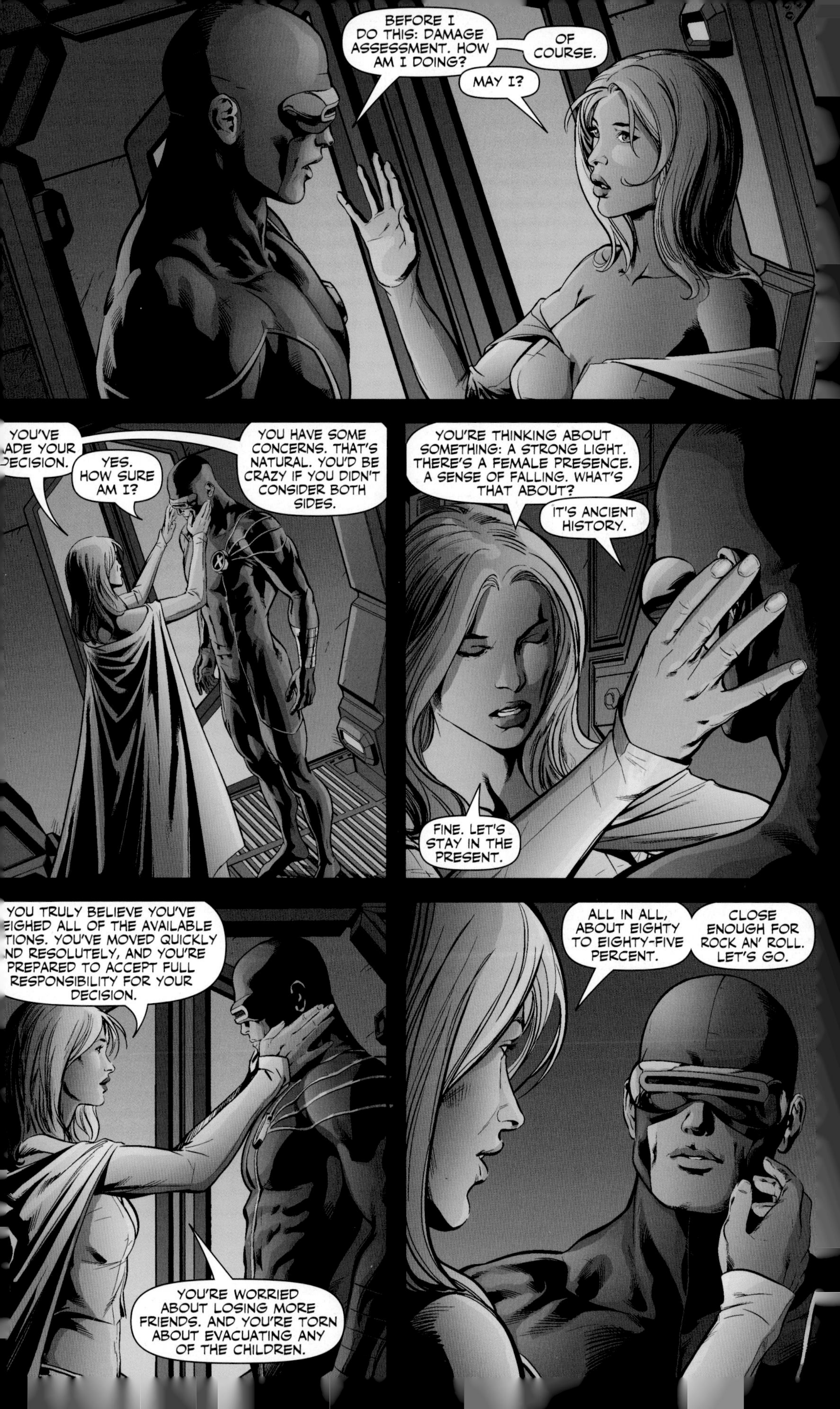
BEFORE I DO THIS: DAMAGE ASSESSMENT. HOW AM I DOING?
OF COURSE.
MAY I?
YOU'VE ADE YOUR ECISION.
YES. HOW SURE AM I?
YOU HAVE SOME CONCERNS. THAT'S NATURAL. YOU'D BE CRAZY IF YOU DIDN'T CONSIDER BOTH SIDES.
YOU'RE THINKING ABOUT SOMETHING: A STRONG LIGHT. THERE'S A FEMALE PRESENCE. A SENSE OF FALLING. WHAT'S THAT ABOUT?
IT'S ANCIENT HISTORY.
FINE. LET'S STAY IN THE PRESENT.
YOU TRULY BELIEVE YOU'VE EIGHED ALL OF THE AVAILABLE TIONS. YOU'VE MOVED QUICKLY ND RESOLUTELY, AND YOU'RE PREPARED TO ACCEPT FULL RESPONSIBILITY FOR YOUR DECISION.
YOU'RE WORRIED ABOUT LOSING MORE FRIENDS. AND YOU'RE TORN ABOUT EVACUATING ANY OF THE CHILDREN.
ALL IN ALL, ABOUT EIGHTY TO EIGHTY-FIVE PERCENT.
CLOSE ENOUGH FOR ROCK AN' ROLL. LET'S GO.

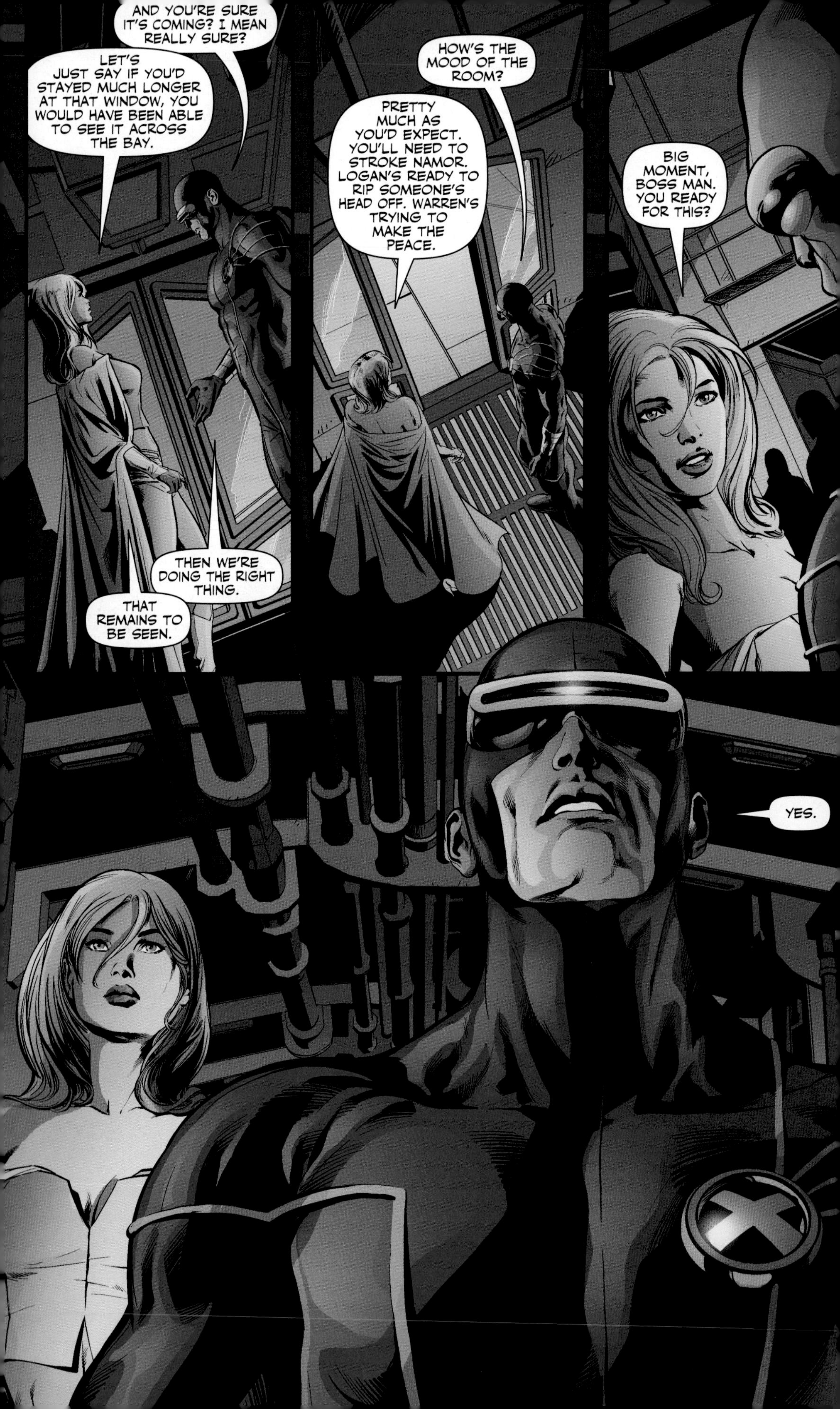

AND YOU'RE SURE IT'S COMING? I MEAN REALLY SURE?
LET'S JUST SAY IF YOU'D STAYED MUCH LONGER AT THAT WINDOW, YOU WOULD HAVE BEEN ABLE TO SEE IT ACROSS THE BAY.
THEN WE'RE DOING THE RIGHT THING.
THAT REMAINS TO BE SEEN.
HOW'S THE MOOD OF THE ROOM?
PRETTY MUCH AS YOU'D EXPECT. YOU'LL NEED TO STROKE NAMOR. LOGAN'S READY TO RIP SOMEONE'S HEAD OFF. WARREN'S TRYING TO MAKE THE PEACE.
BIG MOMENT, BOSS MAN. YOU READY FOR THIS?
YES.

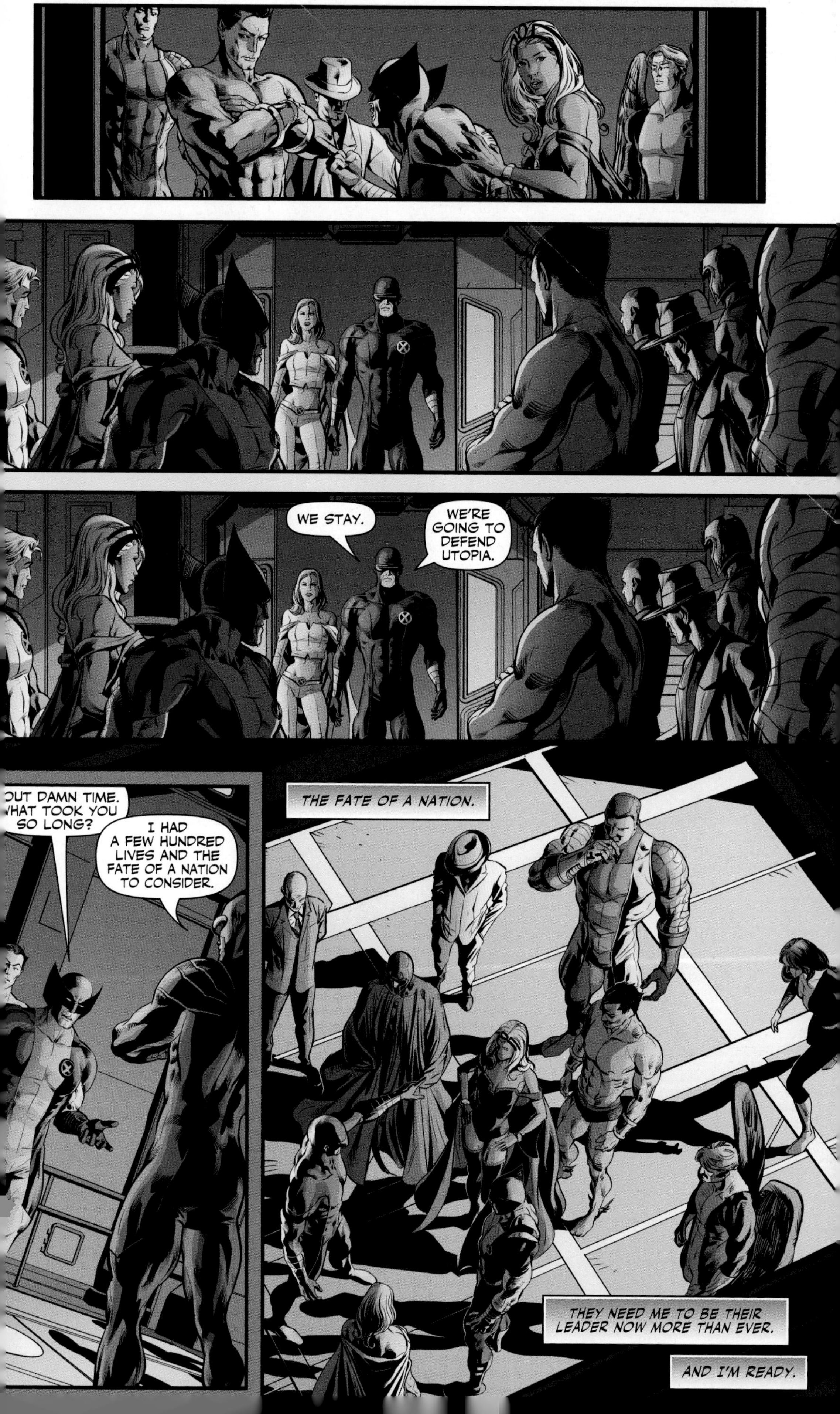
WE STAY.
WE'RE GOING TO DEFEND UTOPIA.
OUT DAMN TIME. WHAT TOOK YOU SO LONG?
I HAD A FEW HUNDRED LIVES AND THE FATE OF A NATION TO CONSIDER.
THE FATE OF A NATION.
THEY NEED ME TO BE THEIR LEADER NOW MORE THAN EVER.
AND I'M READY.

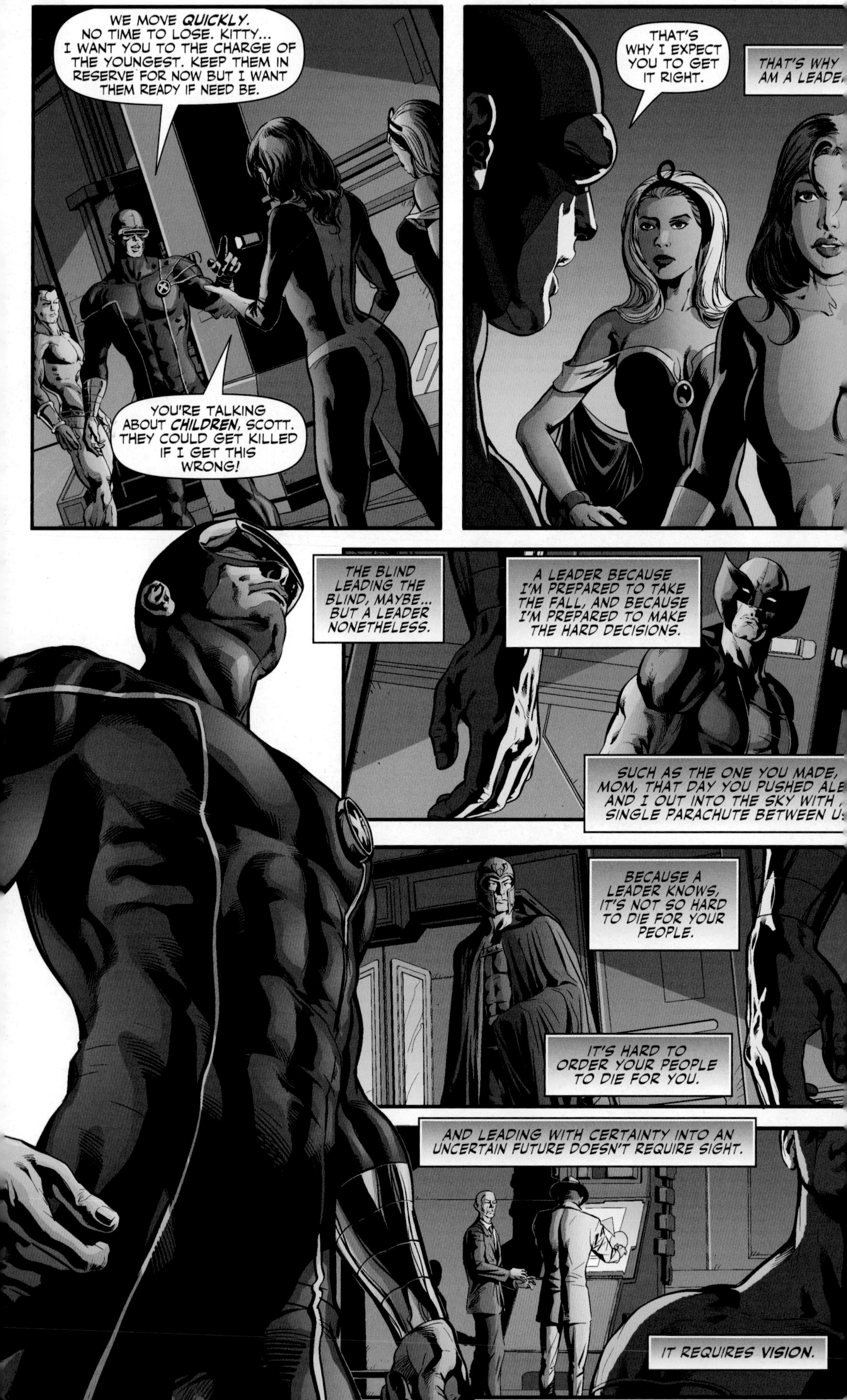
WE MOVE QUICKLY. NO TIME TO LOSE. KITTY... I WANT YOU TO THE CHARGE OF THE YOUNGEST. KEEP THEM IN RESERVE FOR NOW BUT I WANT THEM READY IF NEED BE.
YOU'RE TALKING ABOUT CHILDREN, SCOTT. THEY COULD GET KILLED IF I GET THIS WRONG!
THAT'S WHY I EXPECT YOU TO GET IT RIGHT.
THAT'S WHY AM A LEADE
THE BLIND LEADING THE BLIND, MAYBE... BUT A LEADER NONETHELESS.
A LEADER BECAUSE I'M PREPARED TO TAKE THE FALL, AND BECAUSE I'M PREPARED TO MAKE THE HARD DECISIONS.
SUCH AS THE ONE YOU MADE, MOM, THAT DAY YOU PUSHED ALE AND I OUT INTO THE SKY WITH SINGLE PARACHUTE BETWEEN U
BECAUSE A LEADER KNOWS, IT'S NOT SO HARD TO DIE FOR YOUR PEOPLE.
IT'S HARD TO ORDER YOUR PEOPLE TO DIE FOR YOU.
AND LEADING WITH CERTAINTY INTO AN UNCERTAIN FUTURE DOESN'T REQUIRE SIGHT.
IT REQUIRES VISION.

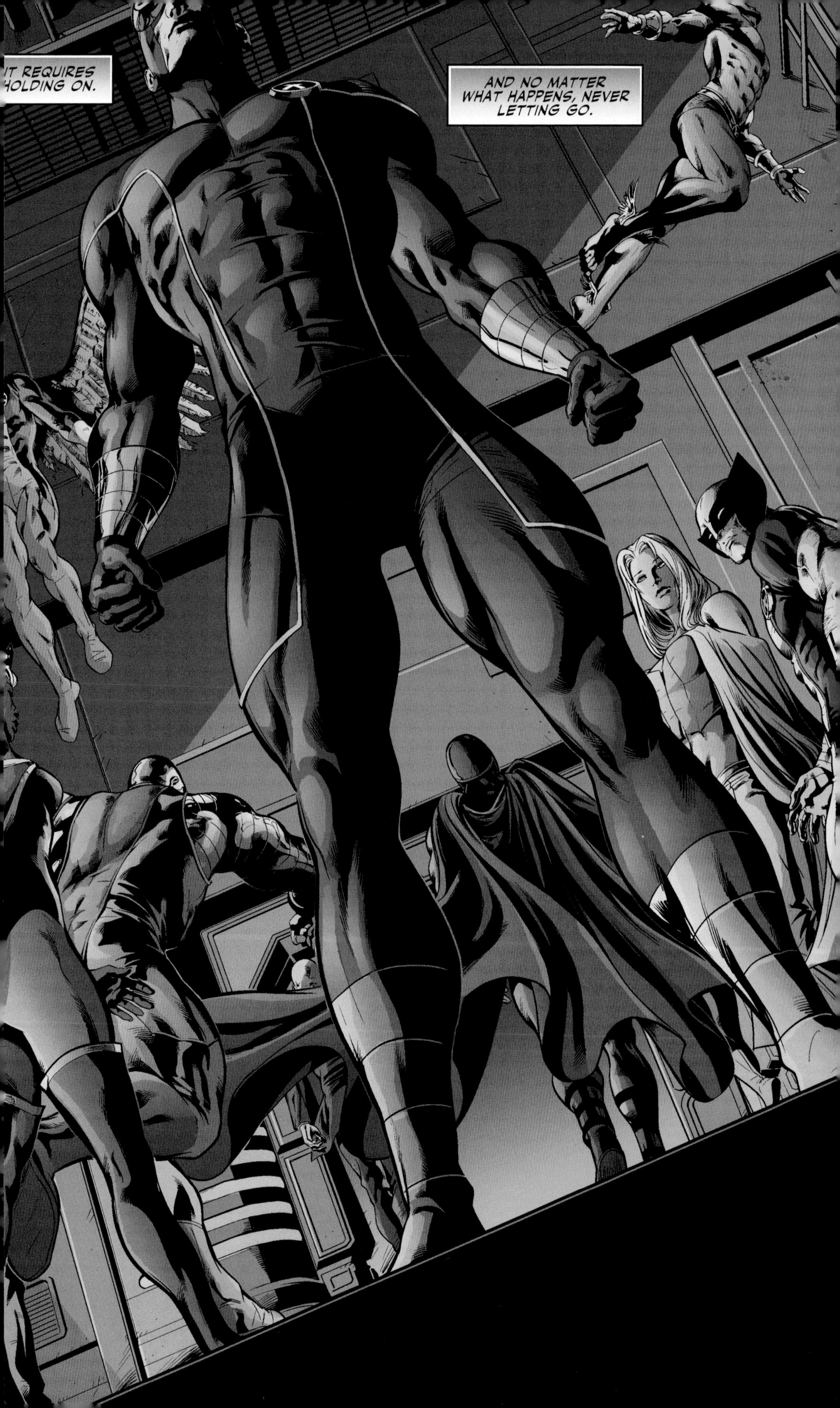
IT REQUIRES HOLDING ON.
AND NO MATTER WHAT HAPPENS, NEVER LETTING GO.

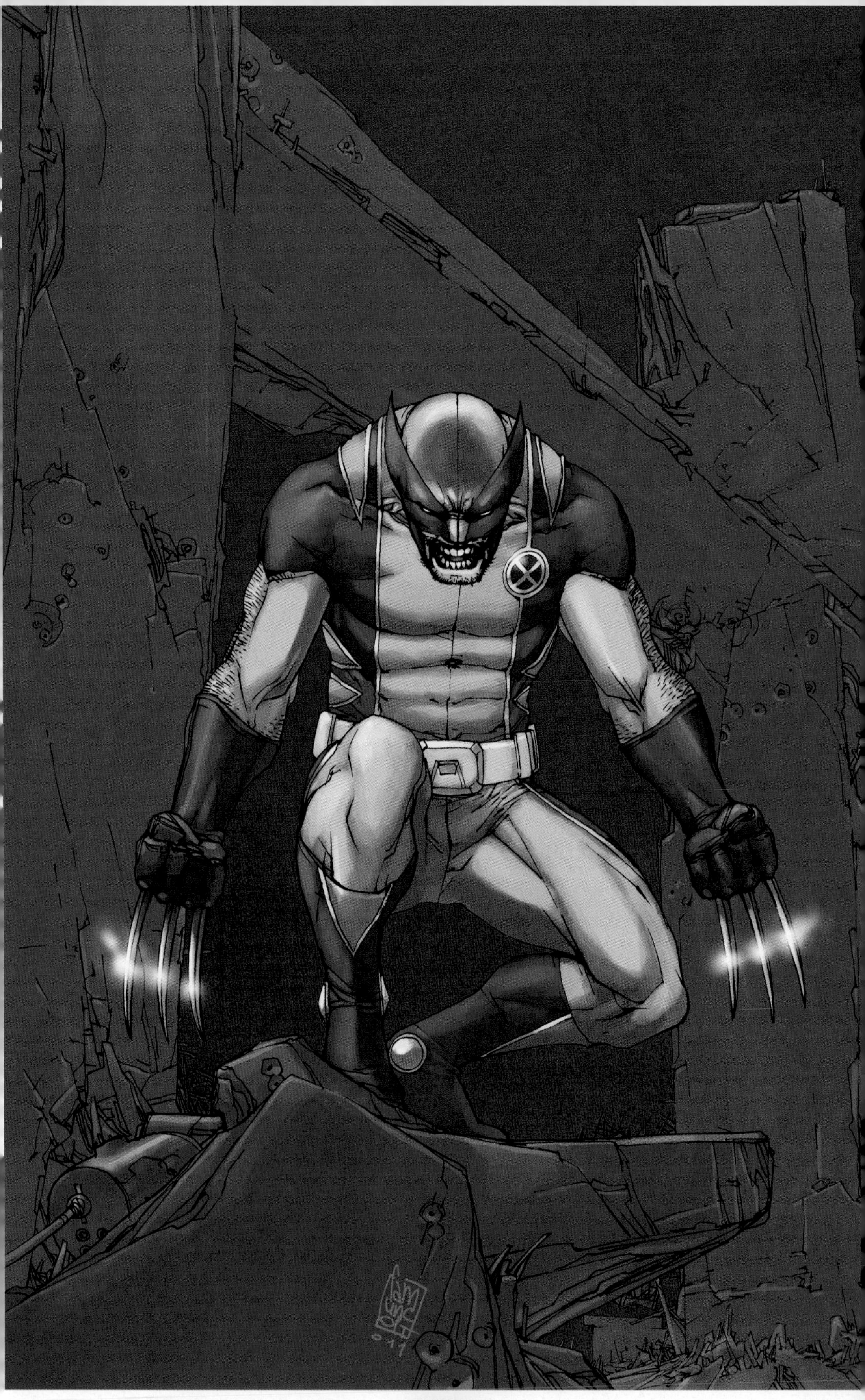

4

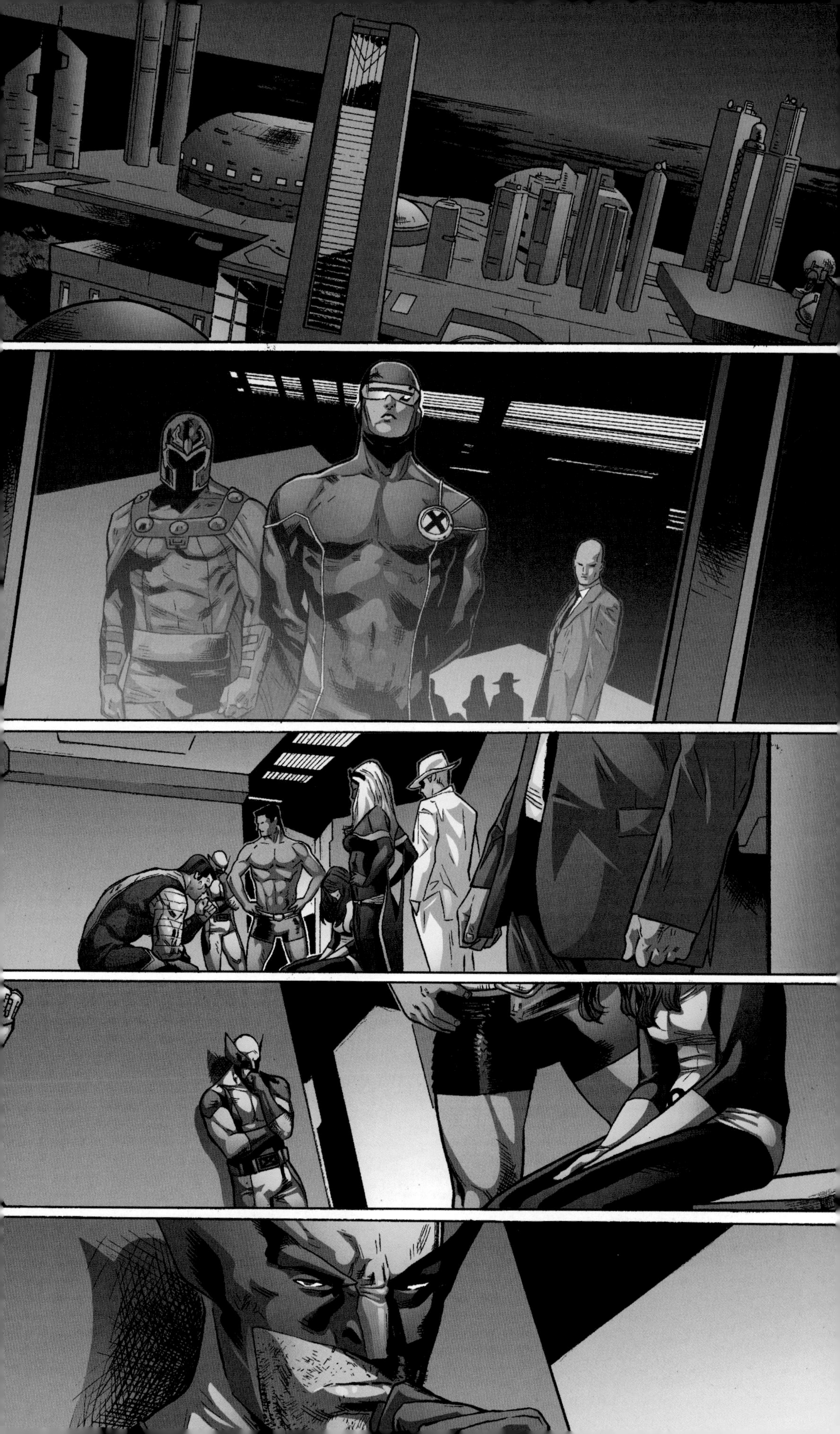

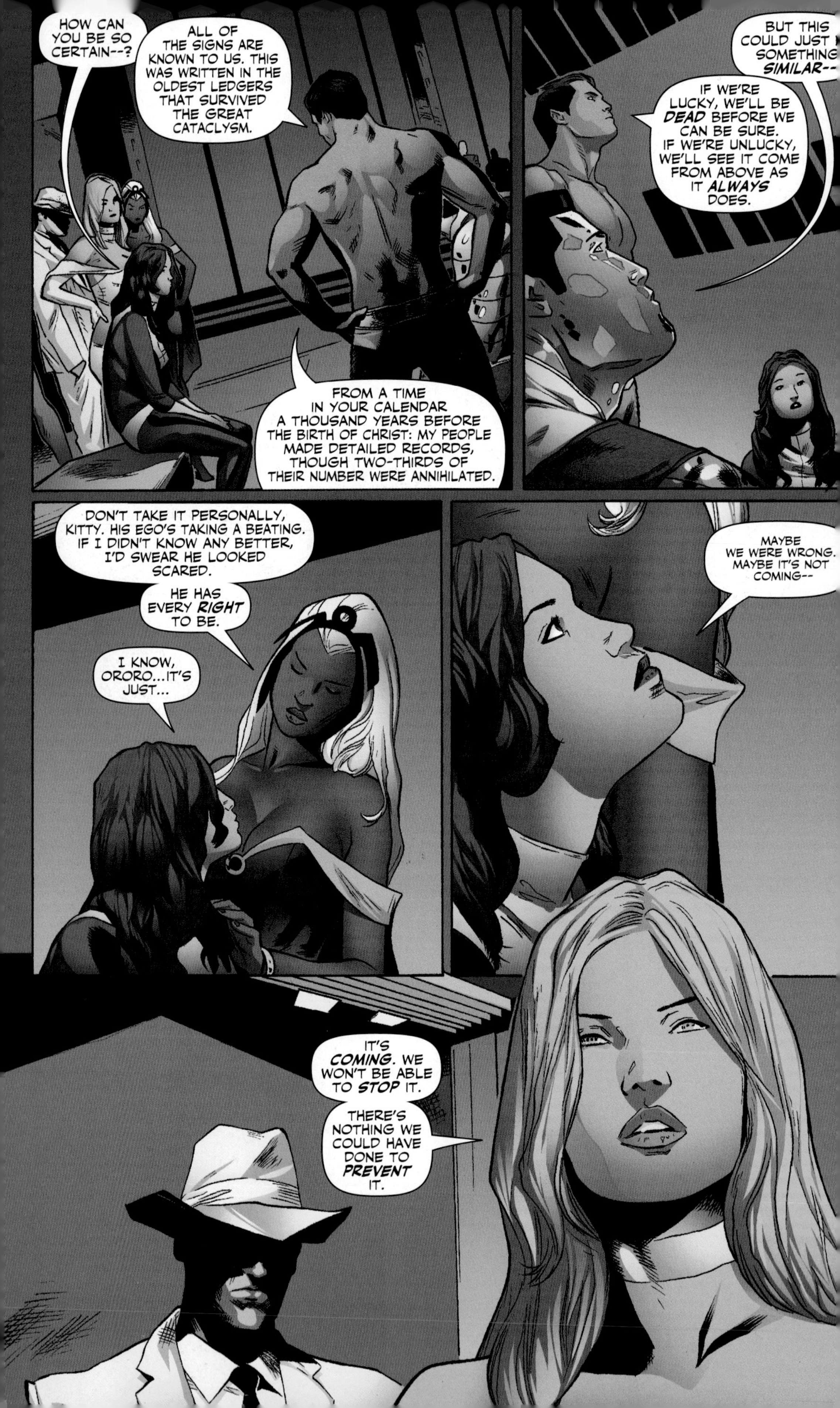
HOW CAN YOU BE SO CERTAIN--?
ALL OF THE SIGNS ARE KNOWN TO US. THIS WAS WRITTEN IN THE OLDEST LEDGERS THAT SURVIVED THE GREAT CATACLYSM.
FROM A TIME IN YOUR CALENDAR A THOUSAND YEARS BEFORE THE BIRTH OF CHRIST: MY PEOPLE MADE DETAILED RECORDS, THOUGH TWO-THIRDS OF THEIR NUMBER WERE ANNIHILATED.
BUT THIS COULD JUST SOMETHING SIMILAR--
IF WE'RE LUCKY, WE'LL BE DEAD BEFORE WE CAN BE SURE. IF WE'RE UNLUCKY, WE'LL SEE IT COME FROM ABOVE AS IT ALWAYS DOES.
DON'T TAKE IT PERSONALLY, KITTY. HIS EGO'S TAKING A BEATING. IF I DIDN'T KNOW ANY BETTER, I'D SWEAR HE LOOKED SCARED.
HE HAS EVERY RIGHT TO BE.
I KNOW, ORORO...IT'S JUST...
MAYBE WE WERE WRONG. MAYBE IT'S NOT COMING--
IT'S COMING. WE WON'T BE ABLE TO STOP IT.
THERE'S NOTHING WE COULD HAVE DONE TO PREVENT IT.

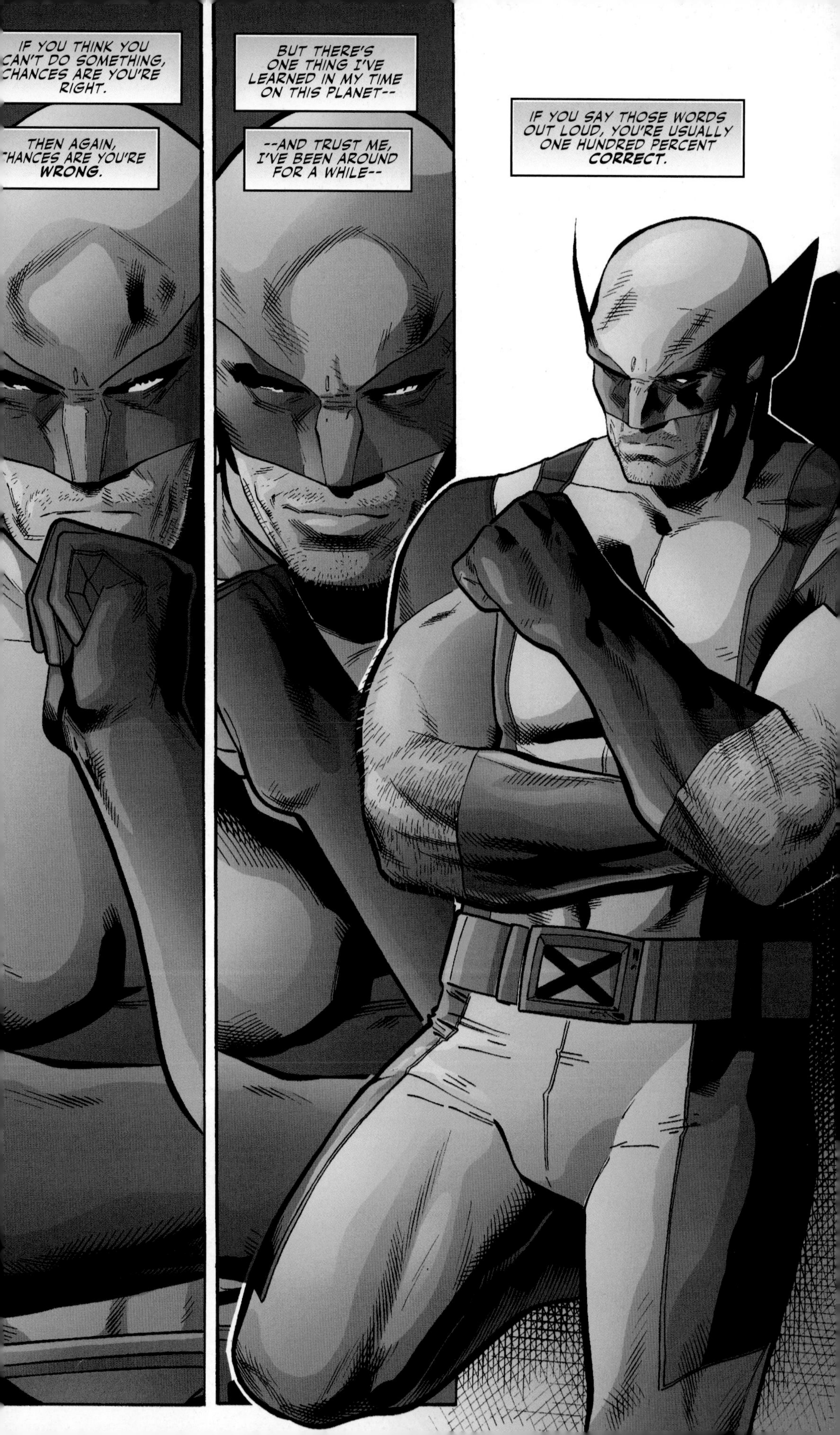
IF YOU THINK YOU CAN'T DO SOMETHING, CHANCES ARE YOU'RE RIGHT.
THEN AGAIN, CHANCES ARE YOU'RE WRONG.
BUT THERE'S ONE THING I'VE LEARNED IN MY TIME ON THIS PLANET--
--AND TRUST ME, I'VE BEEN AROUND FOR A WHILE--
IF YOU SAY THOSE WORDS OUT LOUD, YOU'RE USUALLY ONE HUNDRED PERCENT CORRECT.

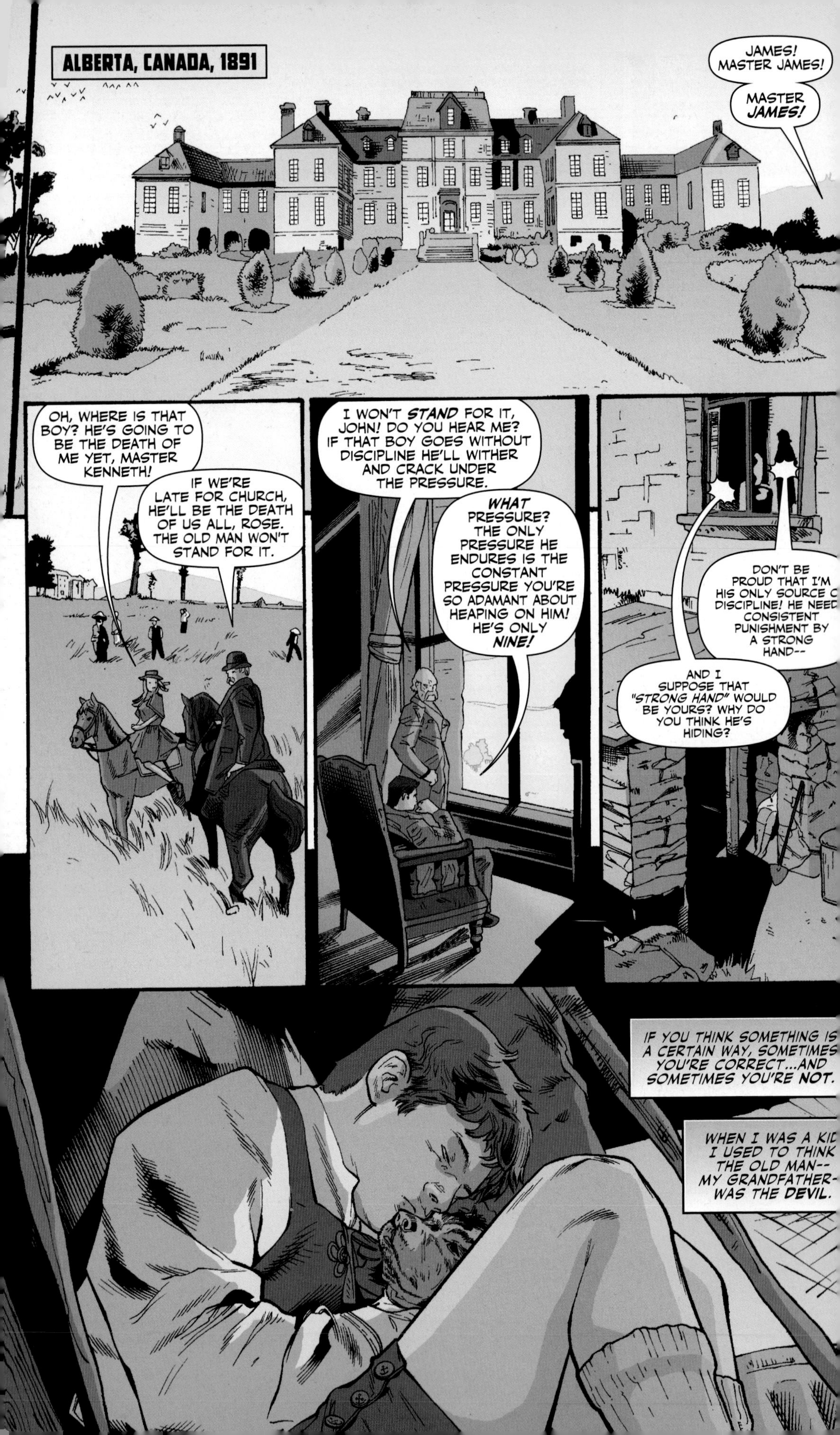
ALBERTA, CANADA, 1891
JAMES! MASTER JAMES!
MASTER JAMES!
OH, WHERE IS THAT BOY? HE'S GOING TO BE THE DEATH OF ME YET, MASTER KENNETH!
IF WE'RE LATE FOR CHURCH, HE'LL BE THE DEATH OF US ALL, ROSE. THE OLD MAN WON'T STAND FOR IT.
I WON'T STAND FOR IT, JOHN! DO YOU HEAR ME? IF THAT BOY GOES WITHOUT DISCIPLINE HE'LL WITHER AND CRACK UNDER THE PRESSURE.
WHAT PRESSURE? THE ONLY PRESSURE HE ENDURES IS THE CONSTANT PRESSURE YOU'RE SO ADAMANT ABOUT HEAPING ON HIM! HE'S ONLY NINE!
DON'T BE PROUD THAT I'M HIS ONLY SOURCE O DISCIPLINE! HE NEED CONSISTENT PUNISHMENT BY A STRONG HAND--
AND I SUPPOSE THAT "STRONG HAND" WOULD BE YOURS? WHY DO YOU THINK HE'S HIDING?
IF YOU THINK SOMETHING IS A CERTAIN WAY, SOMETIMES YOU'RE CORRECT...AND SOMETIMES YOU'RE NOT.
WHEN I WAS A KID I USED TO THINK THE OLD MAN-- MY GRANDFATHER- WAS THE DEVIL.

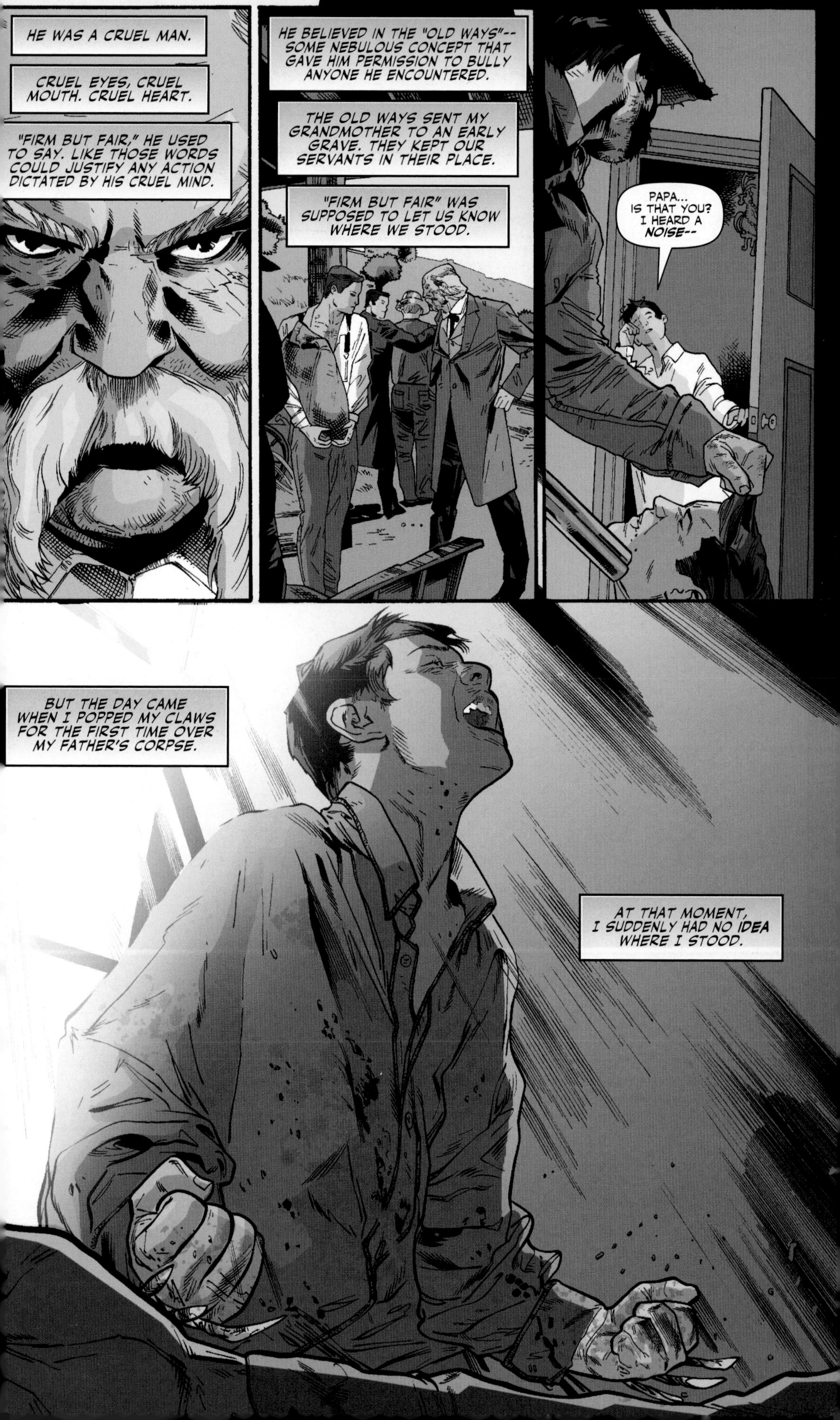
HE WAS A CRUEL MAN.
CRUEL EYES, CRUEL MOUTH. CRUEL HEART.
"FIRM BUT FAIR," HE USED TO SAY. LIKE THOSE WORDS COULD JUSTIFY ANY ACTION DICTATED BY HIS CRUEL MIND.
HE BELIEVED IN THE "OLD WAYS"-- SOME NEBULOUS CONCEPT THAT GAVE HIM PERMISSION TO BULLY ANYONE HE ENCOUNTERED.
THE OLD WAYS SENT MY GRANDMOTHER TO AN EARLY GRAVE. THEY KEPT OUR SERVANTS IN THEIR PLACE.
"FIRM BUT FAIR" WAS SUPPOSED TO LET US KNOW WHERE WE STOOD.
PAPA... IS THAT YOU? I HEARD A NOISE--
BUT THE DAY CAME WHEN I POPPED MY CLAWS FOR THE FIRST TIME OVER MY FATHER'S CORPSE.
AT THAT MOMENT, I SUDDENLY HAD NO IDEA WHERE I STOOD.

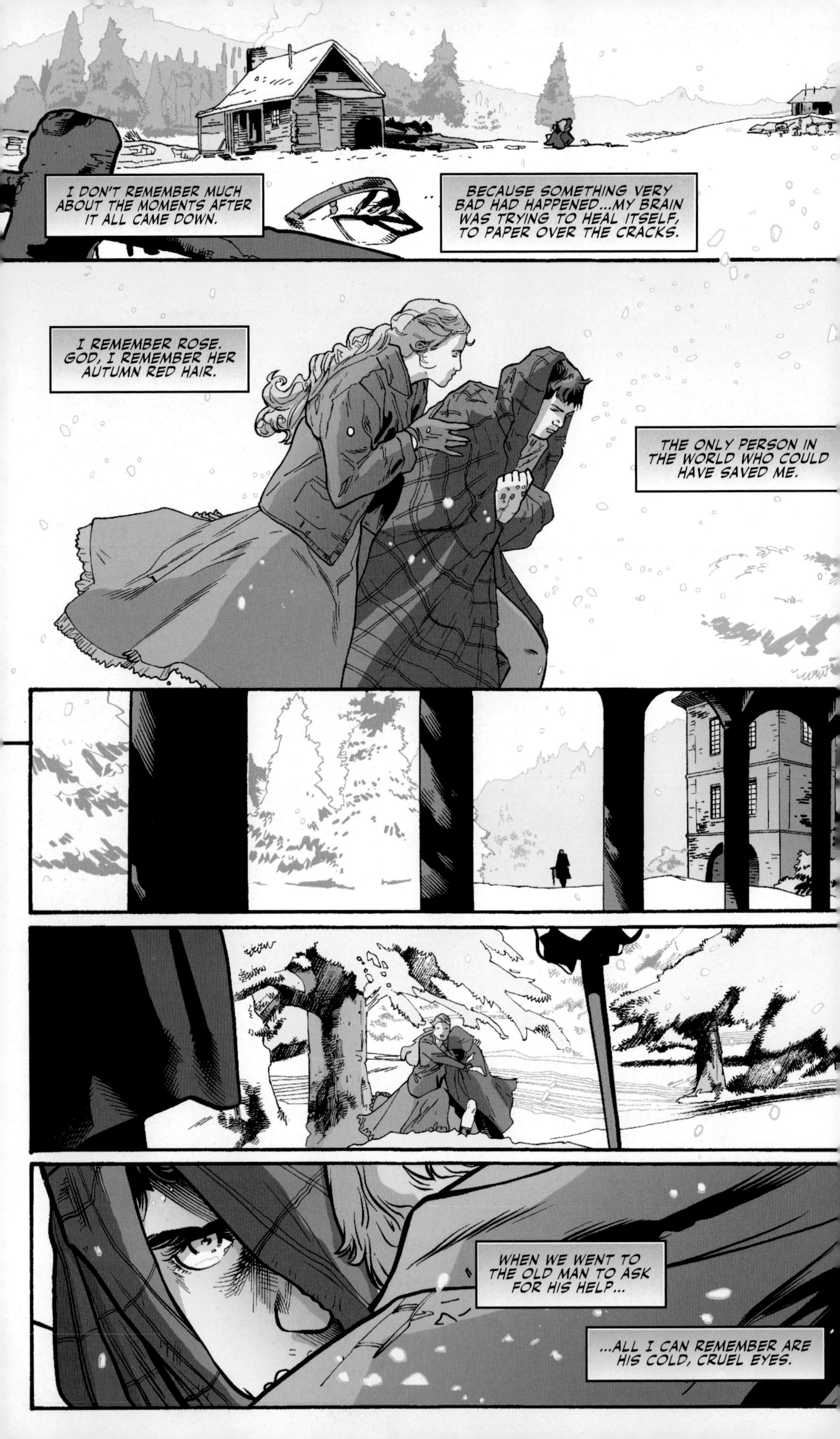
I DON'T REMEMBER MUCH ABOUT THE MOMENTS AFTER IT ALL CAME DOWN.
BECAUSE SOMETHING VERY BAD HAD HAPPENED...MY BRAIN WAS TRYING TO HEAL ITSELF, TO PAPER OVER THE CRACKS.
I REMEMBER ROSE. GOD, I REMEMBER HER AUTUMN RED HAIR.
THE ONLY PERSON IN THE WORLD WHO COULD HAVE SAVED ME.
WHEN WE WENT TO THE OLD MAN TO ASK FOR HIS HELP...
...ALL I CAN REMEMBER ARE HIS COLD, CRUEL EYES.

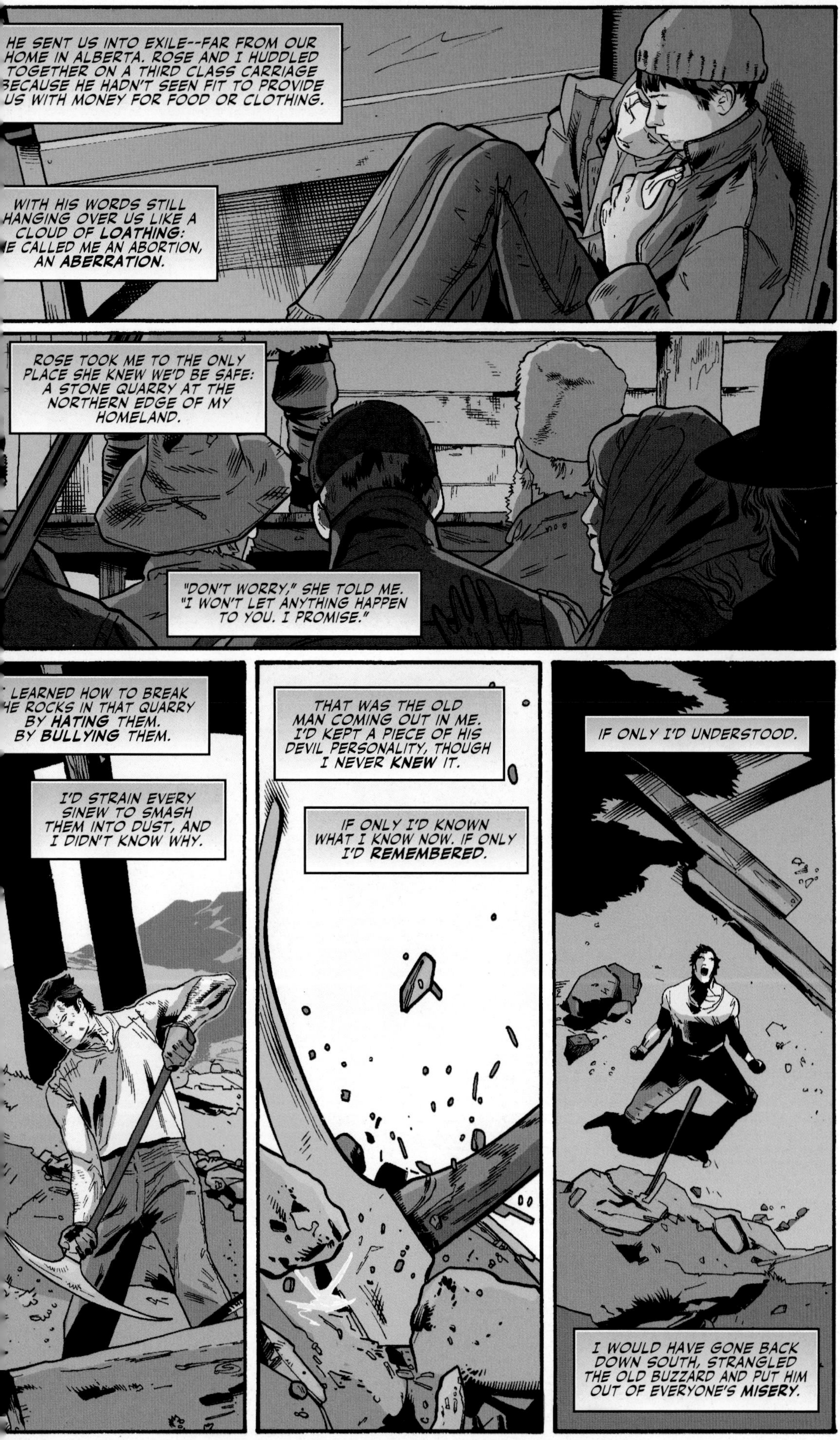

HE SENT US INTO EXILE--FAR FROM OUR HOME IN ALBERTA. ROSE AND I HUDDLED TOGETHER ON A THIRD CLASS CARRIAGE ECAUSE HE HADN'T SEEN FIT TO PROVIDE US WITH MONEY FOR FOOD OR CLOTHING.
WITH HIS WORDS STILL HANGING OVER US LIKE A CLOUD OF LOATHING: E CALLED ME AN ABORTION, AN ABERRATION.
ROSE TOOK ME TO THE ONLY PLACE SHE KNEW WE'D BE SAFE: A STONE QUARRY AT THE NORTHERN EDGE OF MY HOMELAND.
"DON'T WORRY," SHE TOLD ME. "I WON'T LET ANYTHING HAPPEN TO YOU. I PROMISE."
LEARNED HOW TO BREAK HE ROCKS IN THAT QUARRY BY HATING THEM. BY BULLYING THEM.
I'D STRAIN EVERY SINEW TO SMASH THEM INTO DUST, AND I DIDN'T KNOW WHY.
THAT WAS THE OLD MAN COMING OUT IN ME. I'D KEPT A PIECE OF HIS DEVIL PERSONALITY, THOUGH I NEVER KNEW IT.
IF ONLY I'D KNOWN WHAT I KNOW NOW. IF ONLY I'D REMEMBERED.
IF ONLY I'D UNDERSTOOD.
I WOULD HAVE GONE BACK DOWN SOUTH, STRANGLED THE OLD BUZZARD AND PUT HIM OUT OF EVERYONE'S MISERY.

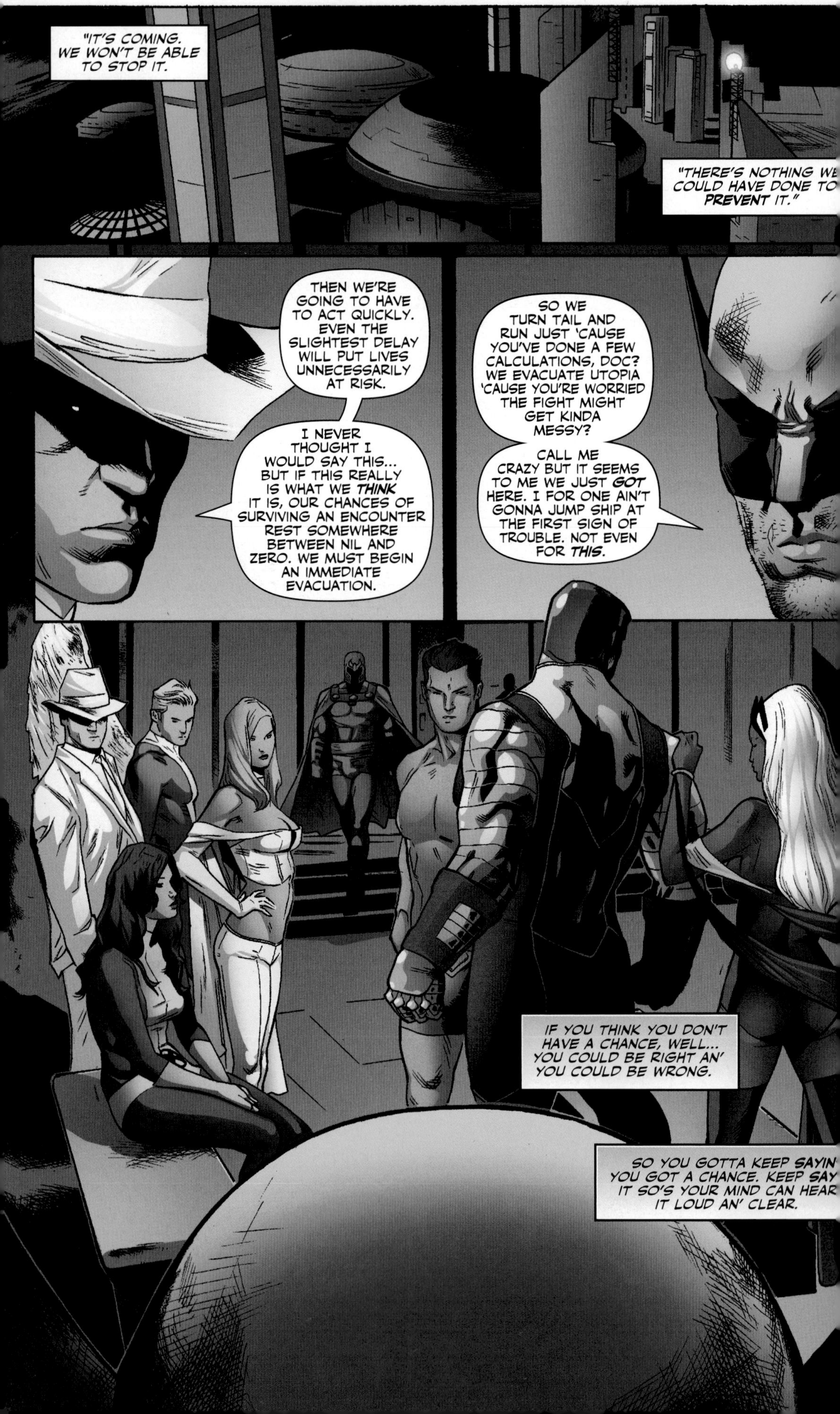
"IT'S COMING. WE WON'T BE ABLE TO STOP IT.
"THERE'S NOTHING WE COULD HAVE DONE TO PREVENT IT."
THEN WE'RE GOING TO HAVE TO ACT QUICKLY. EVEN THE SLIGHTEST DELAY WILL PUT LIVES UNNECESSARILY AT RISK.
I NEVER THOUGHT I WOULD SAY THIS... BUT IF THIS REALLY IS WHAT WE THINK IT IS, OUR CHANCES OF SURVIVING AN ENCOUNTER REST SOMEWHERE BETWEEN NIL AND ZERO. WE MUST BEGIN AN IMMEDIATE EVACUATION.
SO WE TURN TAIL AND RUN JUST 'CAUSE YOU'VE DONE A FEW CALCULATIONS, DOC? WE EVACUATE UTOPIA 'CAUSE YOU'RE WORRIED THE FIGHT MIGHT GET KINDA MESSY?
CALL ME CRAZY BUT IT SEEMS TO ME WE JUST GOT HERE. I FOR ONE AIN'T GONNA JUMP SHIP AT THE FIRST SIGN OF TROUBLE. NOT EVEN FOR THIS.
IF YOU THINK YOU DON'T HAVE A CHANCE, WELL... YOU COULD BE RIGHT AN' YOU COULD BE WRONG.
SO YOU GOTTA KEEP SAYIN YOU GOT A CHANCE. KEEP SAY IT SO'S YOUR MIND CAN HEAR IT LOUD AN' CLEAR.

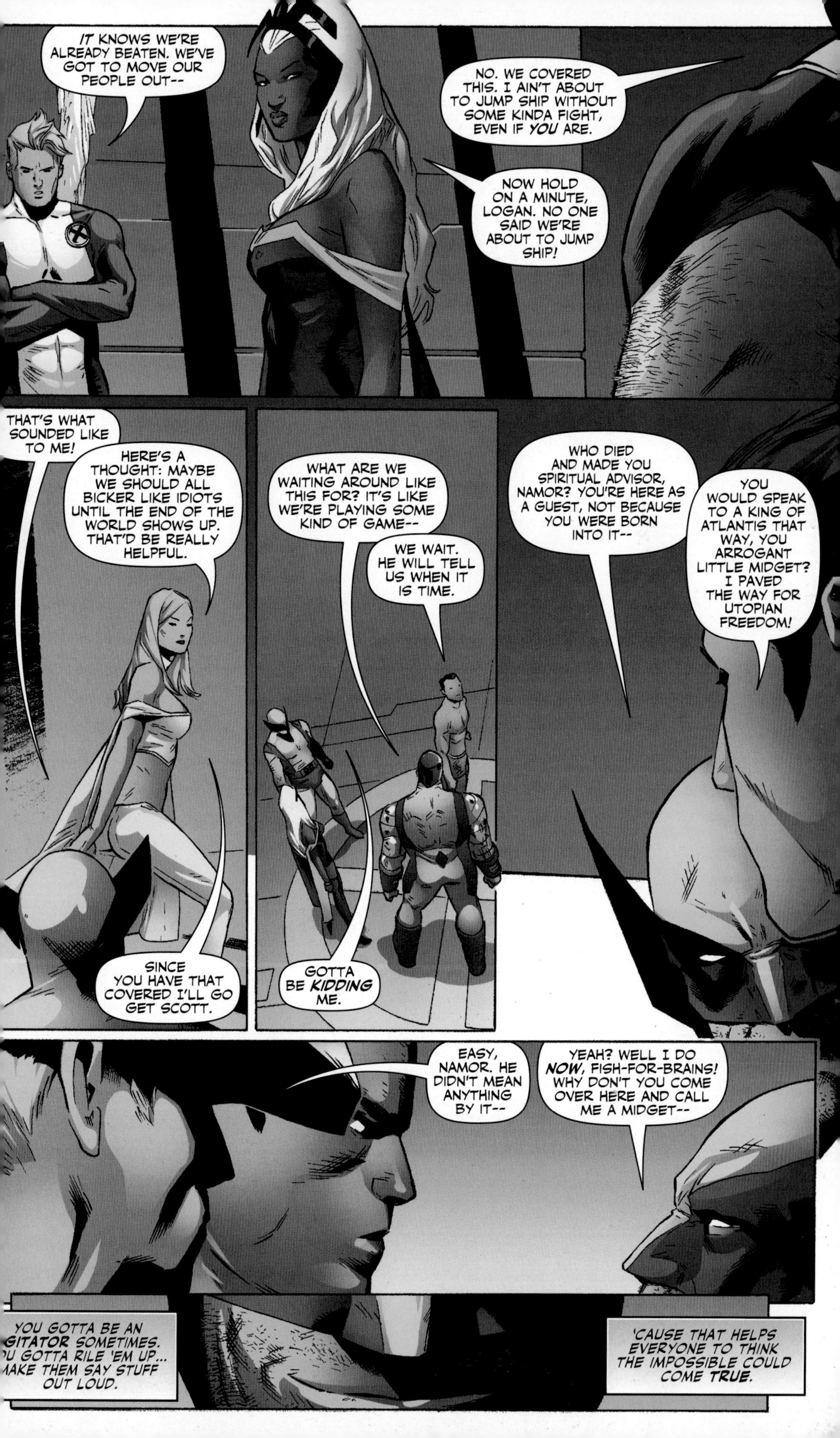
IT KNOWS WE'RE ALREADY BEATEN. WE'VE GOT TO MOVE OUR PEOPLE OUT--
NO. WE COVERED THIS. I AIN'T ABOUT TO JUMP SHIP WITHOUT SOME KINDA FIGHT, EVEN IF YOU ARE.
NOW HOLD ON A MINUTE, LOGAN. NO ONE SAID WE'RE ABOUT TO JUMP SHIP!
THAT'S WHAT SOUNDED LIKE TO ME!
HERE'S A THOUGHT: MAYBE WE SHOULD ALL BICKER LIKE IDIOTS UNTIL THE END OF THE WORLD SHOWS UP. THAT'D BE REALLY HELPFUL.
SINCE YOU HAVE THAT COVERED I'LL GO GET SCOTT.
WHAT ARE WE WAITING AROUND LIKE THIS FOR? IT'S LIKE WE'RE PLAYING SOME KIND OF GAME--
WE WAIT. HE WILL TELL US WHEN IT IS TIME.
GOTTA BE KIDDING ME.
WHO DIED AND MADE YOU SPIRITUAL ADVISOR, NAMOR? YOU'RE HERE AS A GUEST, NOT BECAUSE YOU WERE BORN INTO IT--
YOU WOULD SPEAK TO A KING OF ATLANTIS THAT WAY, YOU ARROGANT LITTLE MIDGET? I PAVED THE WAY FOR UTOPIAN FREEDOM!
EASY, NAMOR. HE DIDN'T MEAN ANYTHING BY IT--
YEAH? WELL I DO NOW, FISH-FOR-BRAINS! WHY DON'T YOU COME OVER HERE AND CALL ME A MIDGET--
YOU GOTTA BE AN GITATOR SOMETIMES. U GOTTA RILE 'EM UP... MAKE THEM SAY STUFF OUT LOUD.
'CAUSE THAT HELPS EVERYONE TO THINK THE IMPOSSIBLE COULD COME TRUE.

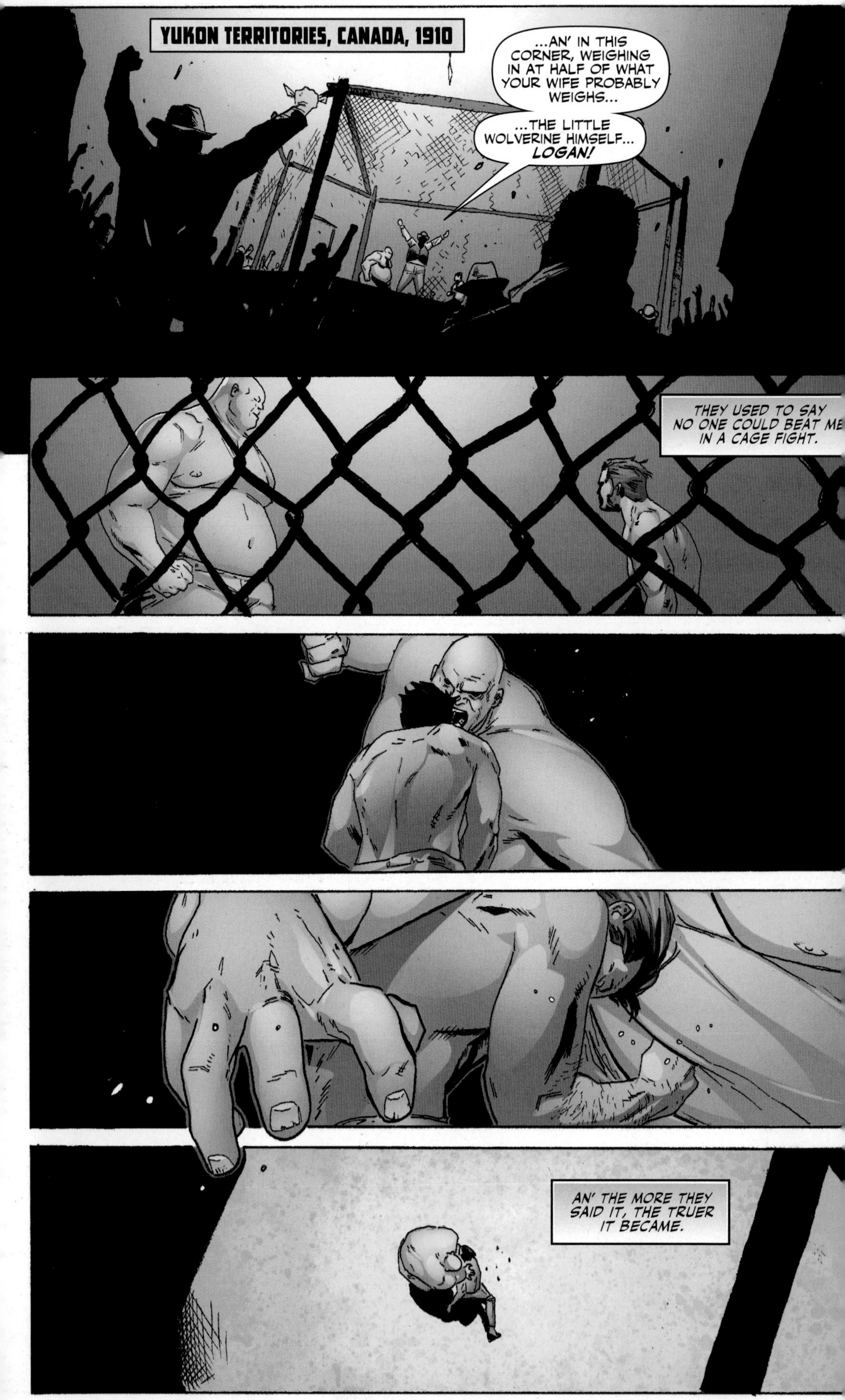
YUKON TERRITORIES, CANADA, 1910
...AN' IN THIS CORNER, WEIGHING IN AT HALF OF WHAT YOUR WIFE PROBABLY WEIGHS...
...THE LITTLE WOLVERINE HIMSELF... LOGAN!
THEY USED TO SAY NO ONE COULD BEAT ME IN A CAGE FIGHT.
AN' THE MORE THEY SAID IT, THE TRUER IT BECAME.

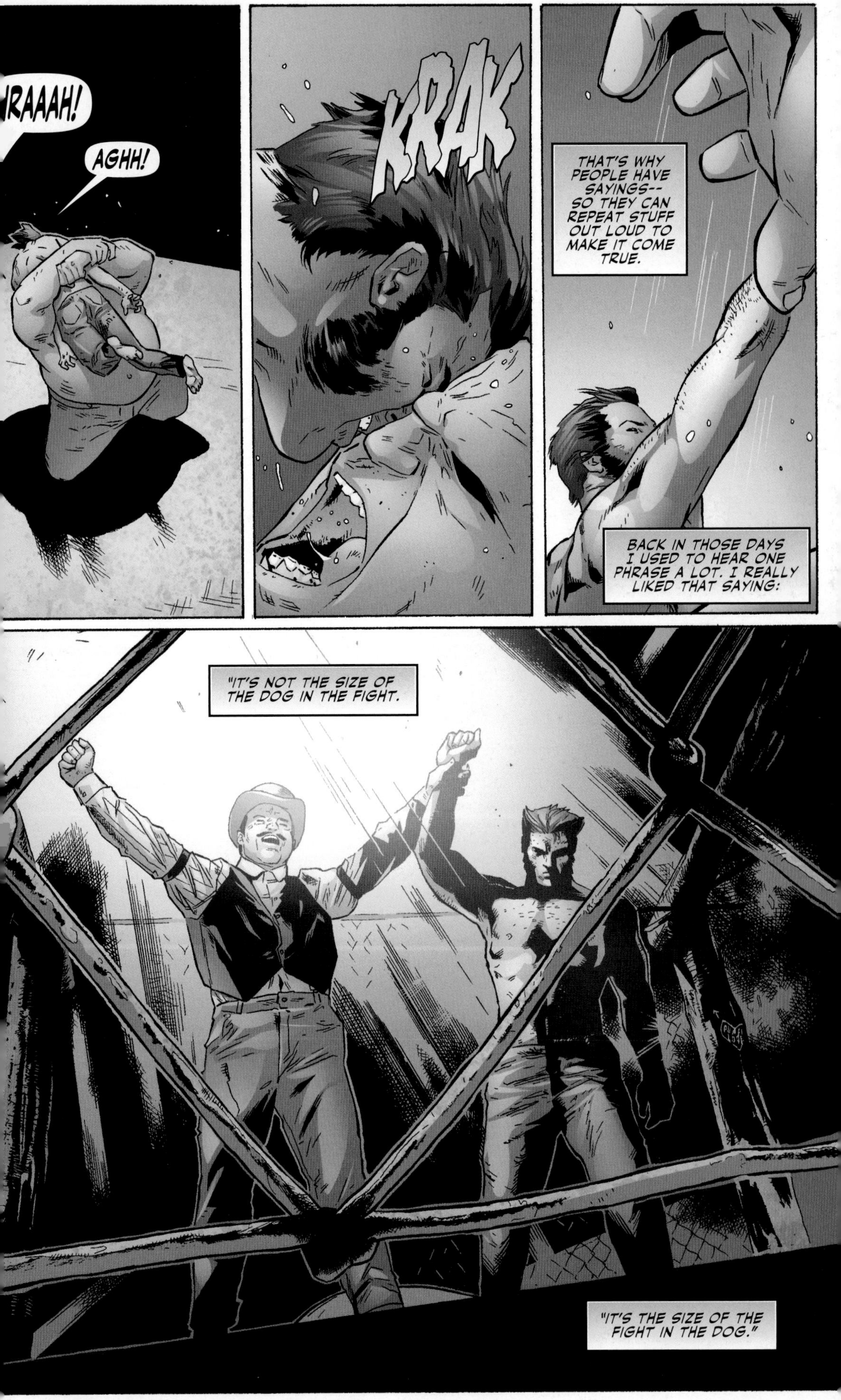

RAAAH!
AGHH!
KRAK
THAT'S WHY PEOPLE HAVE SAYINGS-- SO THEY CAN REPEAT STUFF OUT LOUD TO MAKE IT COME TRUE.
BACK IN THOSE DAYS I USED TO HEAR ONE PHRASE A LOT. I REALLY LIKED THAT SAYING:
"IT'S NOT THE SIZE OF THE DOG IN THE FIGHT.
"IT'S THE SIZE OF THE FIGHT IN THE DOG."

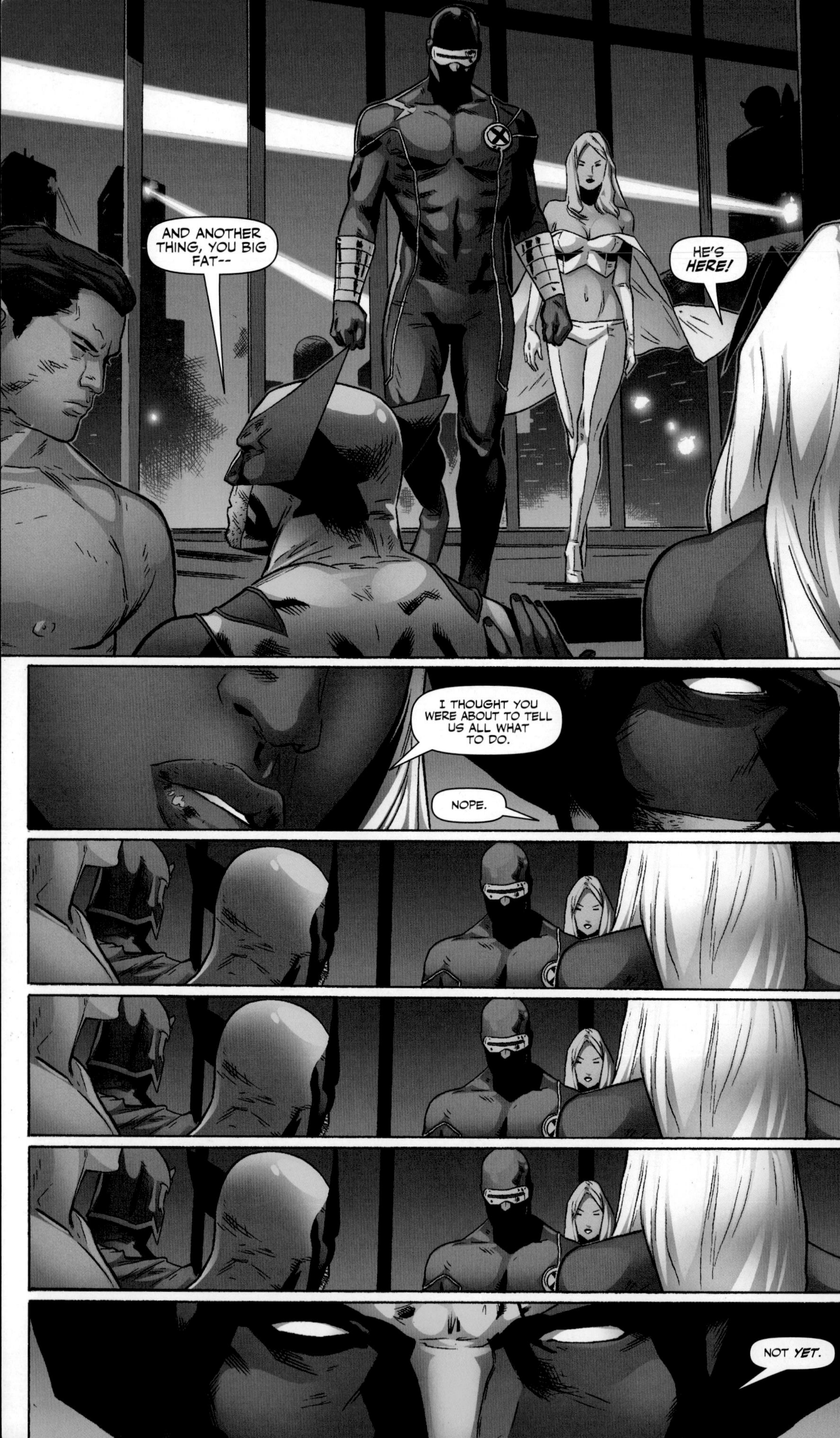
AND ANOTHER THING, YOU BIG FAT--
HE'S *HERE!*
I THOUGHT YOU WERE ABOUT TO TELL US ALL WHAT TO DO.
NOPE.
NOT *YET*.

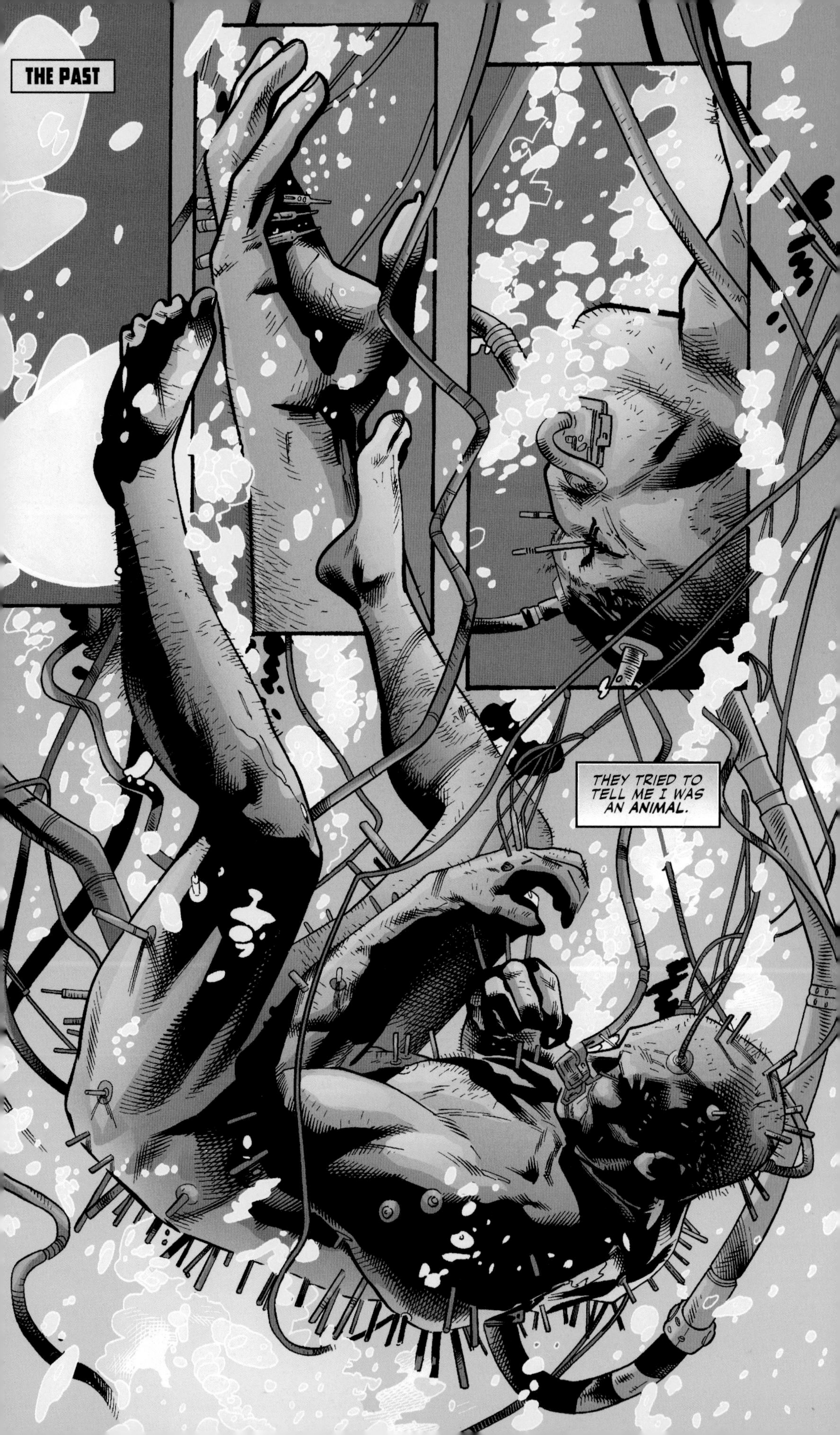
THE PAST
THEY TRIED TO TELL ME I WAS AN ANIMAL.

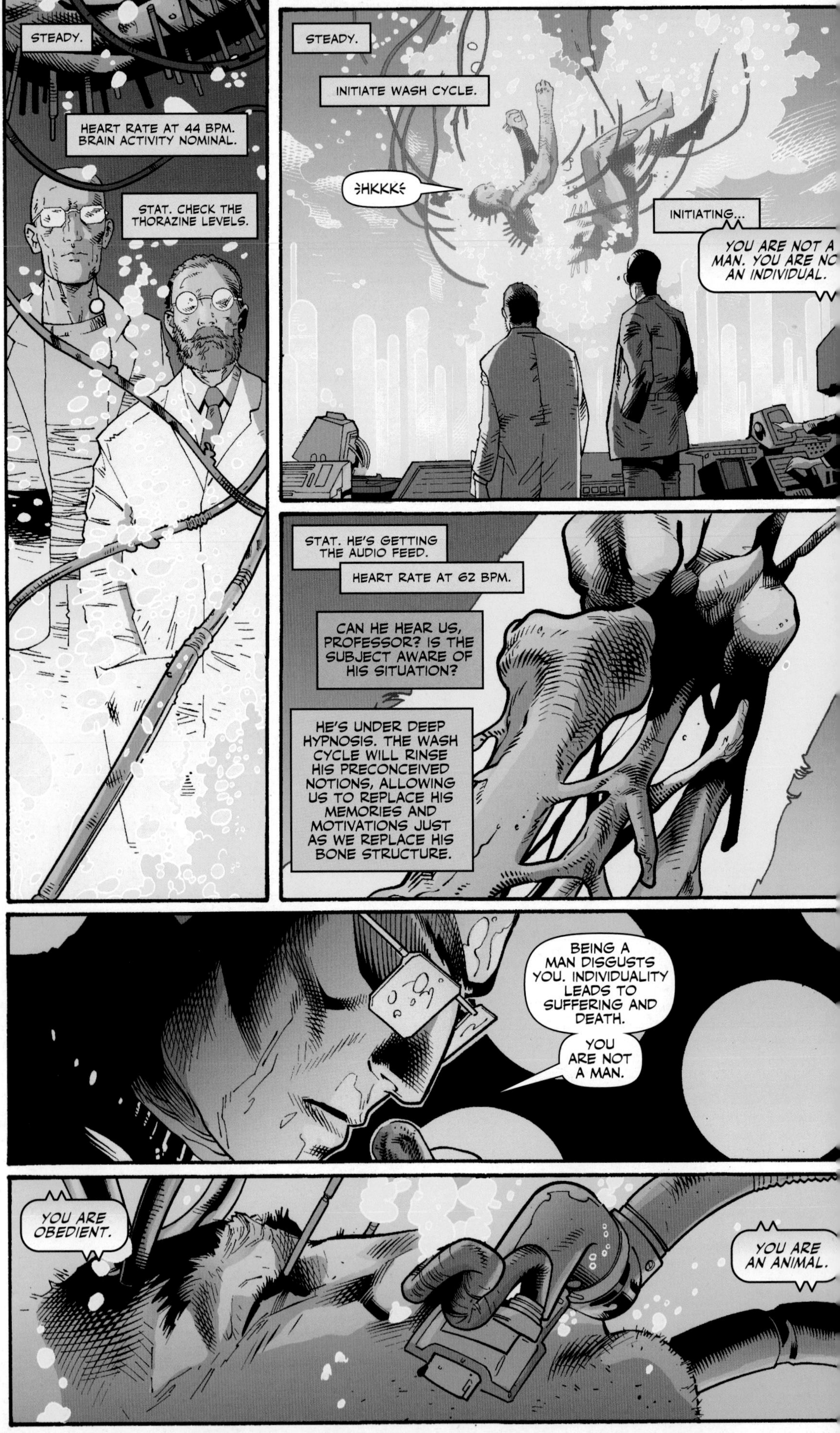
STEADY.
HEART RATE AT 44 BPM. BRAIN ACTIVITY NOMINAL.
STAT. CHECK THE THORAZINE LEVELS.
STEADY.
INITIATE WASH CYCLE.
HKKK
INITIATING...
YOU ARE NOT A MAN. YOU ARE NO AN INDIVIDUAL.
STAT. HE'S GETTING THE AUDIO FEED.
HEART RATE AT 62 BPM.
CAN HE HEAR US, PROFESSOR? IS THE SUBJECT AWARE OF HIS SITUATION?
HE'S UNDER DEEP HYPNOSIS. THE WASH CYCLE WILL RINSE HIS PRECONCEIVED NOTIONS, ALLOWING US TO REPLACE HIS MEMORIES AND MOTIVATIONS JUST AS WE REPLACE HIS BONE STRUCTURE.
BEING A MAN DISGUSTS YOU. INDIVIDUALITY LEADS TO SUFFERING AND DEATH.
YOU ARE NOT A MAN.
YOU ARE OBEDIENT.
YOU ARE AN ANIMAL.

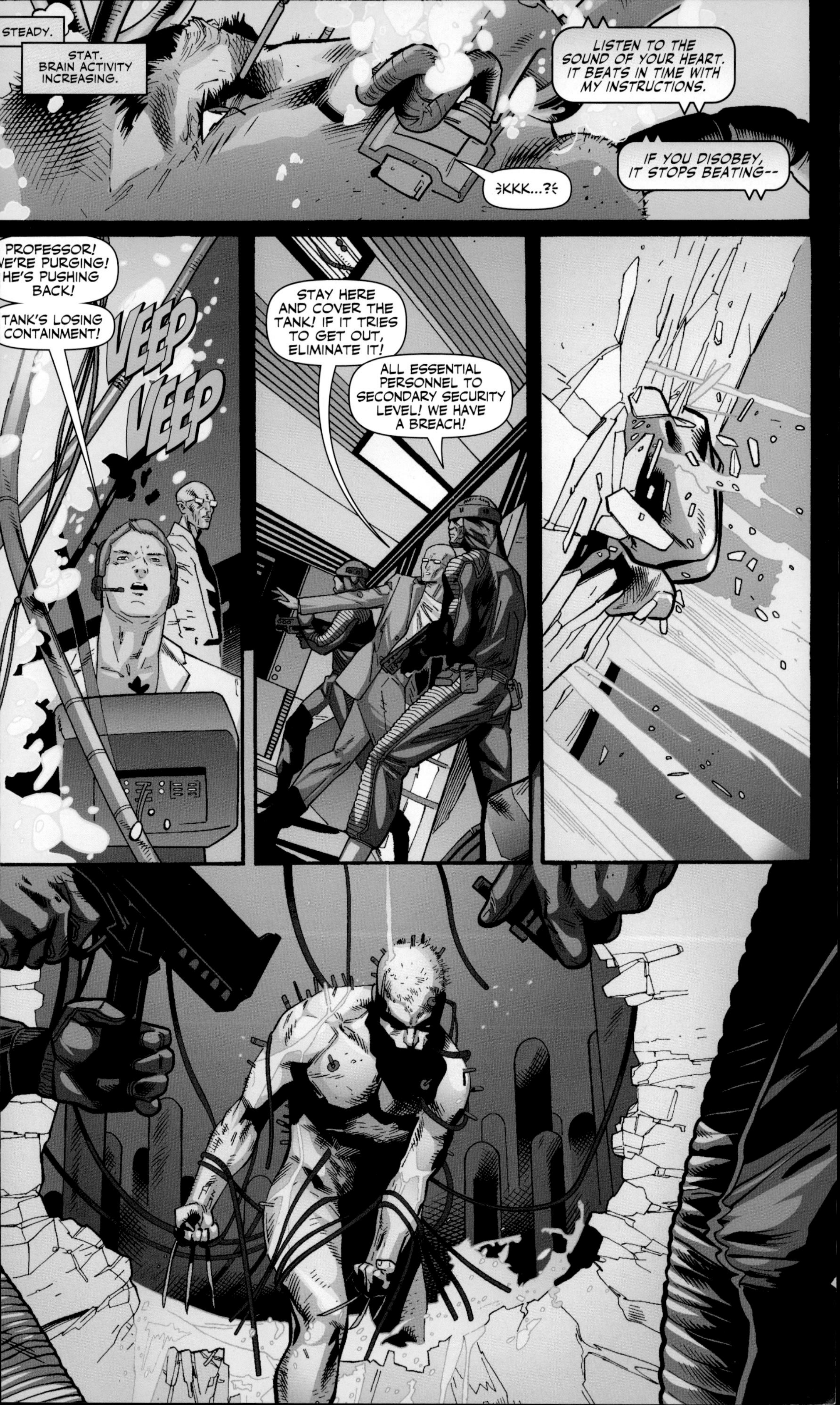
STEADY.
STAT. BRAIN ACTIVITY INCREASING.
LISTEN TO THE SOUND OF YOUR HEART. IT BEATS IN TIME WITH MY INSTRUCTIONS.
IF YOU DISOBEY, IT STOPS BEATING--
KKK...?
PROFESSOR! WE'RE PURGING! HE'S PUSHING BACK!
TANK'S LOSING CONTAINMENT!
VEEP VEEP
STAY HERE AND COVER THE TANK! IF IT TRIES TO GET OUT, ELIMINATE IT!
ALL ESSENTIAL PERSONNEL TO SECONDARY SECURITY LEVEL! WE HAVE A BREACH!

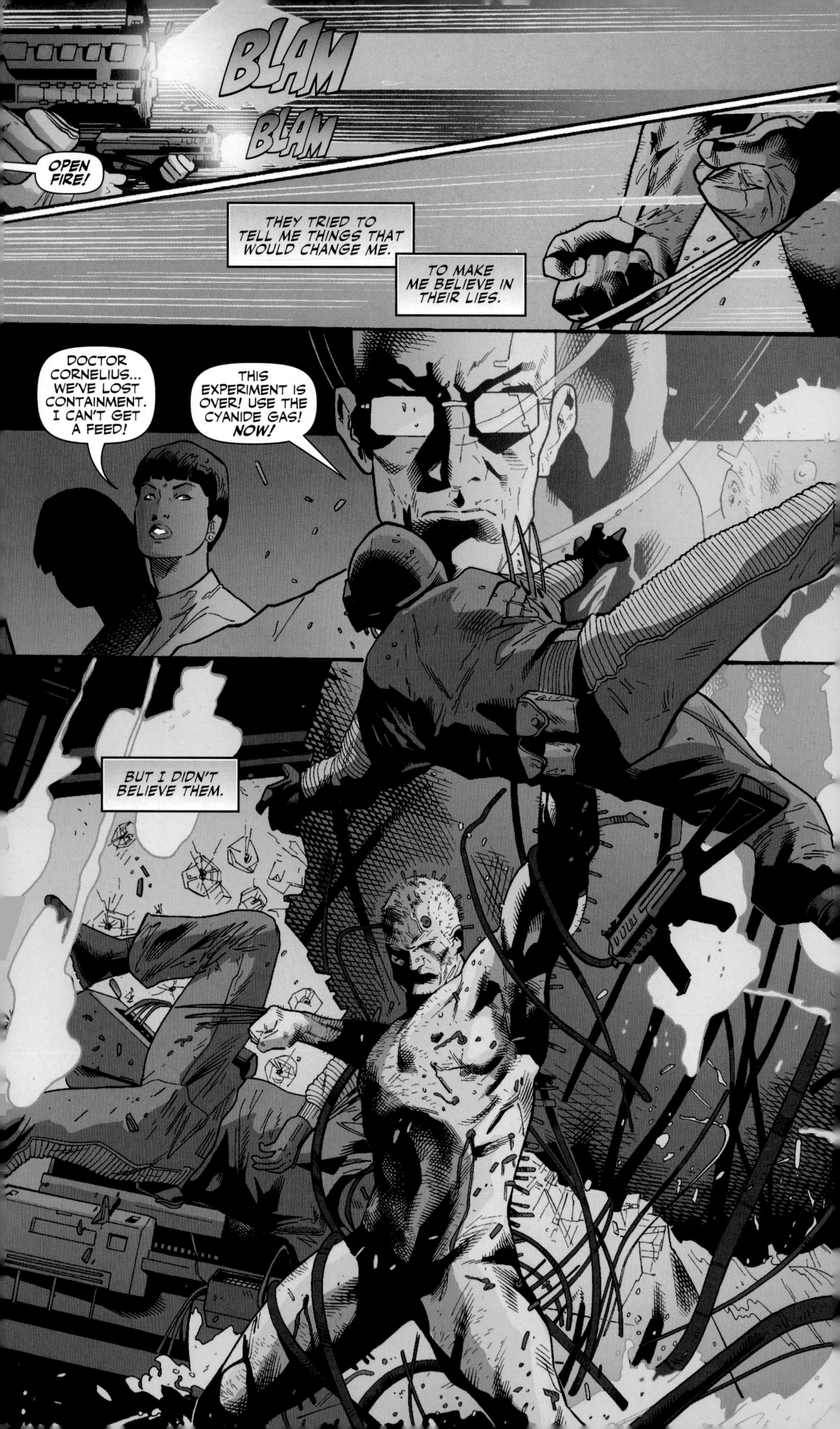
OPEN FIRE!
BLAM
BLAM
THEY TRIED TO TELL ME THINGS THAT WOULD CHANGE ME.
TO MAKE ME BELIEVE IN THEIR LIES.
DOCTOR CORNELIUS... WE'VE LOST CONTAINMENT. I CAN'T GET A FEED!
THIS EXPERIMENT IS OVER! USE THE CYANIDE GAS! NOW!
BUT I DIDN'T BELIEVE THEM.

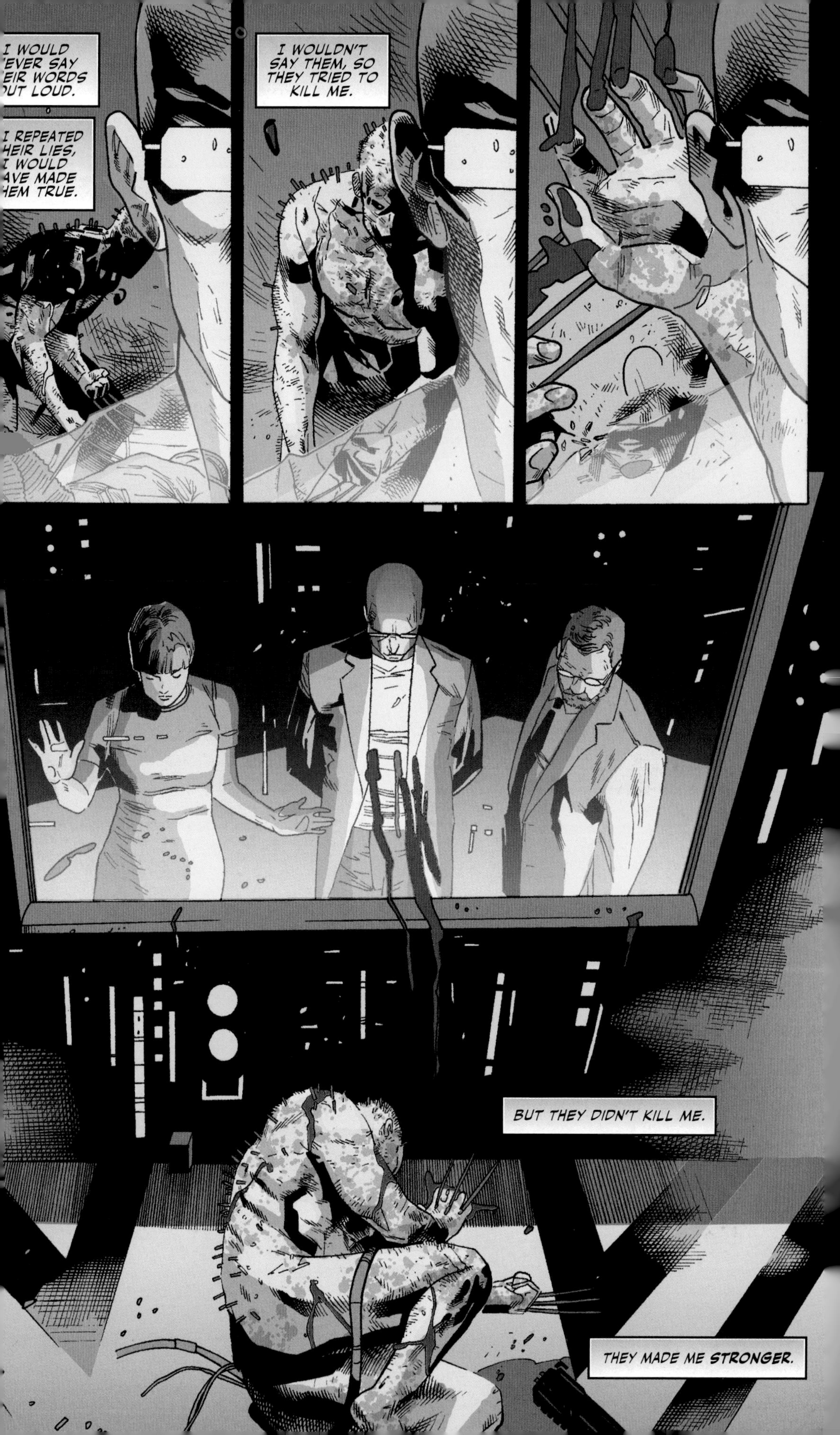

I WOULD NEVER SAY THEIR WORDS OUT LOUD.
IF I REPEATED THEIR LIES, I WOULD HAVE MADE THEM TRUE.
I WOULDN'T SAY THEM, SO THEY TRIED TO KILL ME.
BUT THEY DIDN'T KILL ME.
THEY MADE ME STRONGER.

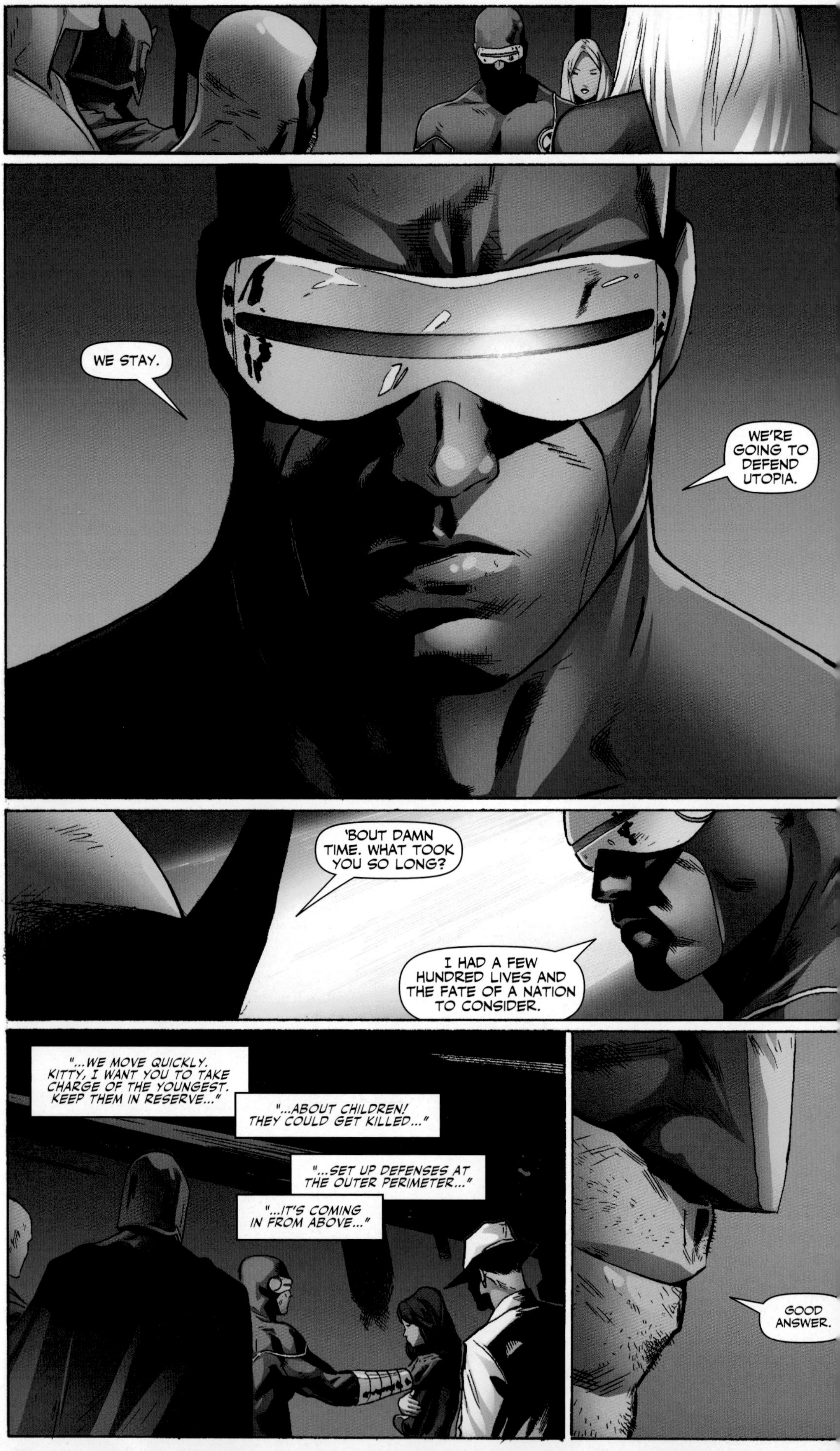
WE STAY.
WE'RE GOING TO DEFEND UTOPIA.
'BOUT DAMN TIME. WHAT TOOK YOU SO LONG?
I HAD A FEW HUNDRED LIVES AND THE FATE OF A NATION TO CONSIDER.
"...WE MOVE QUICKLY. KITTY, I WANT YOU TO TAKE CHARGE OF THE YOUNGEST. KEEP THEM IN RESERVE..."
"...ABOUT CHILDREN! THEY COULD GET KILLED..."
"...SET UP DEFENSES AT THE OUTER PERIMETER..."
"...IT'S COMING IN FROM ABOVE..."
GOOD ANSWER.

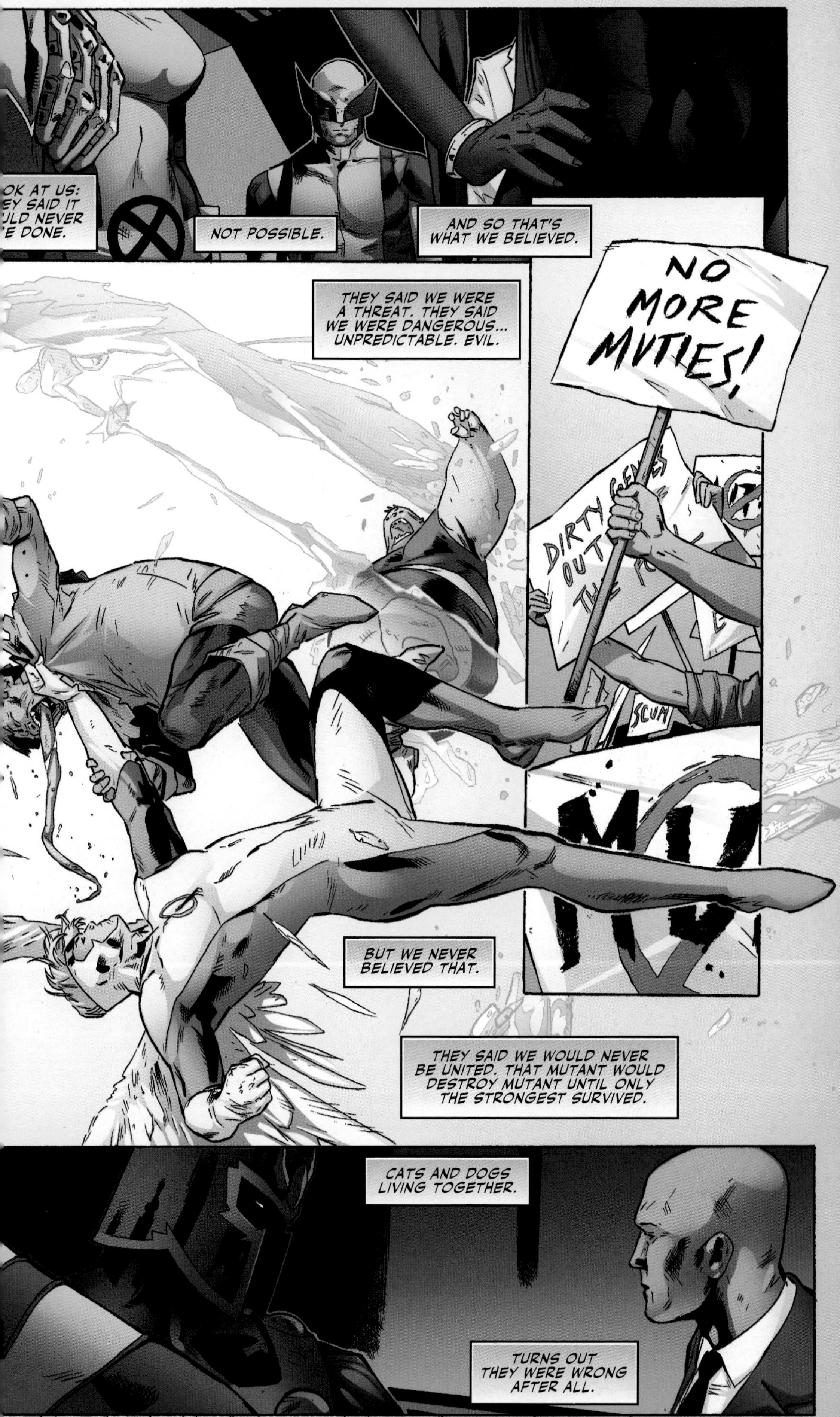
OK AT US:
EY SAID IT
ULD NEVER
'E DONE.
NOT POSSIBLE.
AND SO THAT'S
WHAT WE BELIEVED.
THEY SAID WE WERE
A THREAT. THEY SAID
WE WERE DANGEROUS...
UNPREDICTABLE. EVIL.
NO MORE MUTIES!
DIRTY
OUT
SCUM
BUT WE NEVER
BELIEVED THAT.
THEY SAID WE WOULD NEVER
BE UNITED. THAT MUTANT WOULD
DESTROY MUTANT UNTIL ONLY
THE STRONGEST SURVIVED.
CATS AND DOGS
LIVING TOGETHER.
TURNS OUT
THEY WERE WRONG
AFTER ALL.

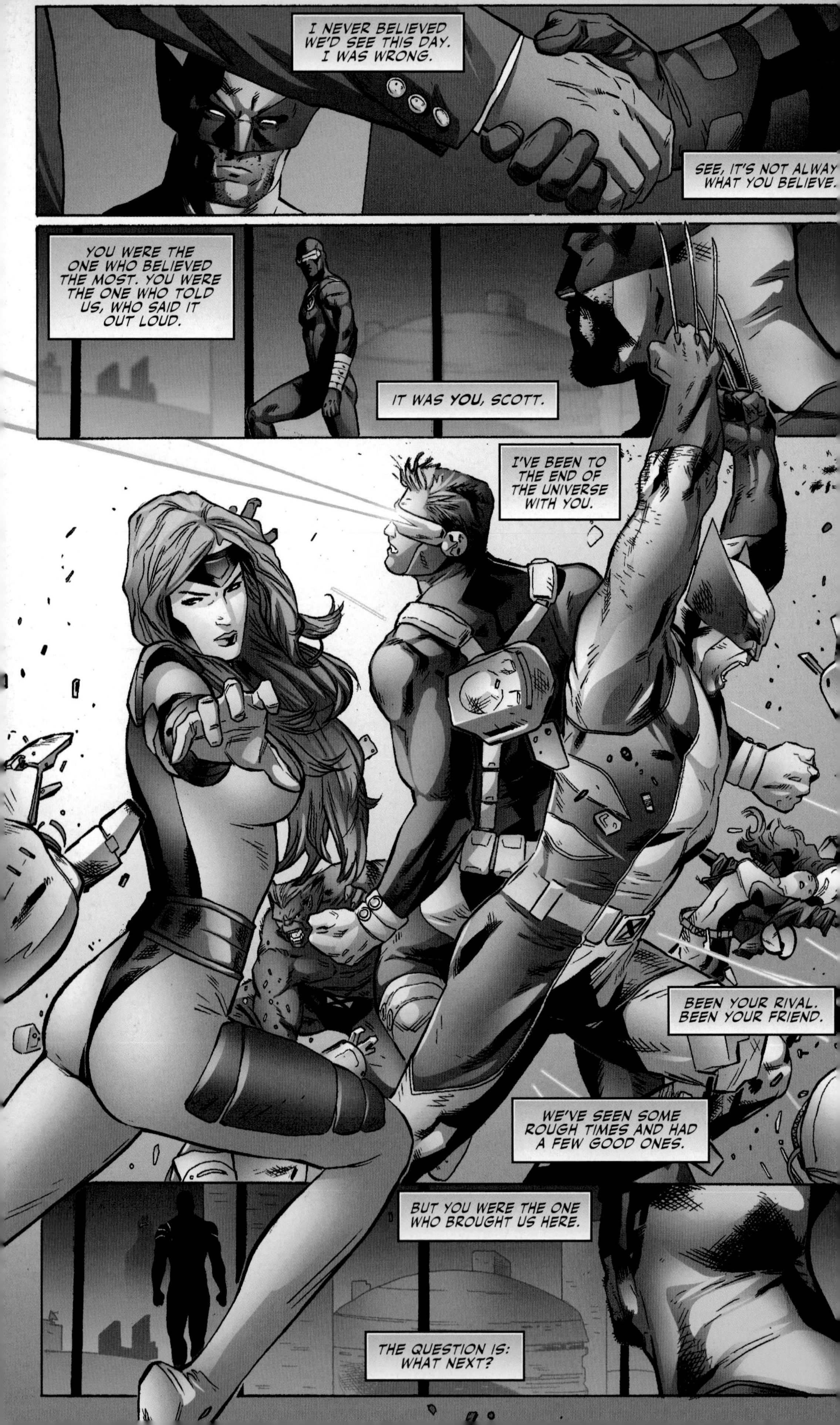
I NEVER BELIEVED WE'D SEE THIS DAY. I WAS WRONG.
SEE, IT'S NOT ALWAY WHAT YOU BELIEVE.
YOU WERE THE ONE WHO BELIEVED THE MOST. YOU WERE THE ONE WHO TOLD US, WHO SAID IT OUT LOUD.
IT WAS YOU, SCOTT.
I'VE BEEN TO THE END OF THE UNIVERSE WITH YOU.
BEEN YOUR RIVAL. BEEN YOUR FRIEND.
WE'VE SEEN SOME ROUGH TIMES AND HAD A FEW GOOD ONES.
BUT YOU WERE THE ONE WHO BROUGHT US HERE.
THE QUESTION IS: WHAT NEXT?

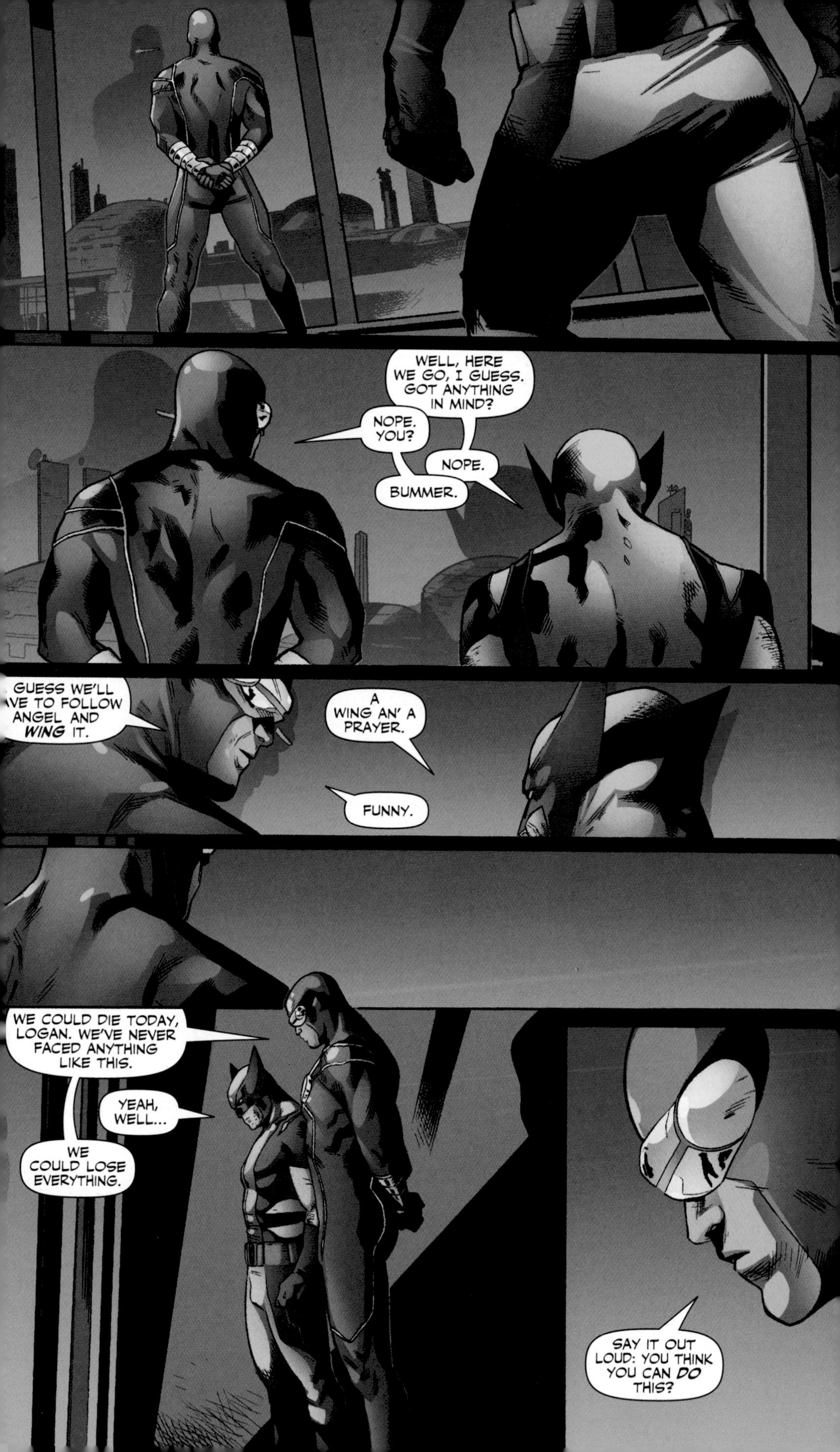
WELL, HERE WE GO, I GUESS. GOT ANYTHING IN MIND?
NOPE. YOU?
NOPE.
BUMMER.
GUESS WE'LL ...VE TO FOLLOW ANGEL AND *WING* IT.
A WING AN' A PRAYER.
FUNNY.
WE COULD DIE TODAY, LOGAN. WE'VE NEVER FACED ANYTHING LIKE THIS.
YEAH, WELL...
WE COULD LOSE EVERYTHING.
SAY IT OUT LOUD: YOU THINK YOU CAN *DO* THIS?

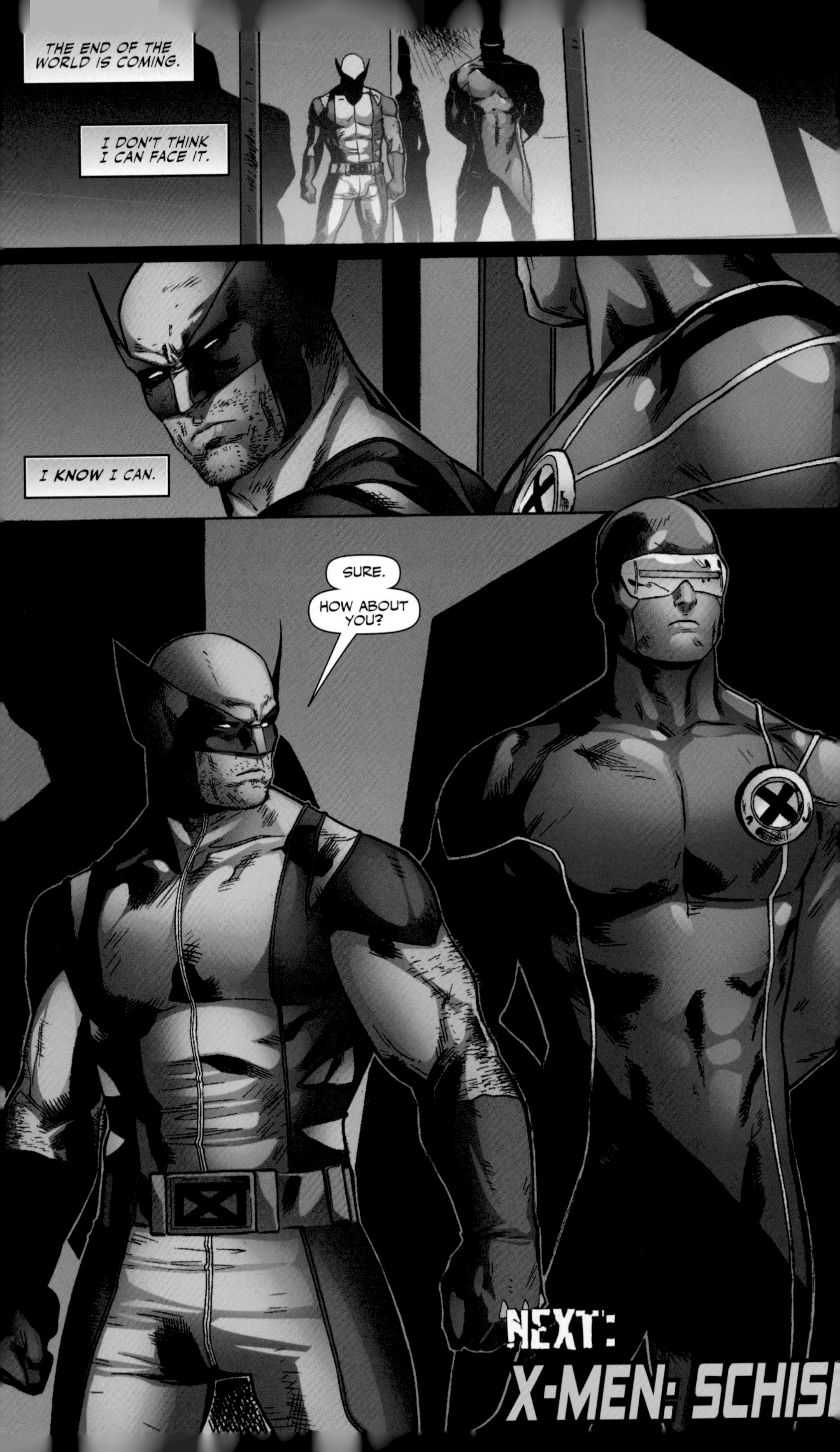
THE END OF THE WORLD IS COMING.
I DON'T THINK I CAN FACE IT.
I KNOW I CAN.
SURE.
HOW ABOUT YOU?
NEXT:
X-MEN: SCHIS

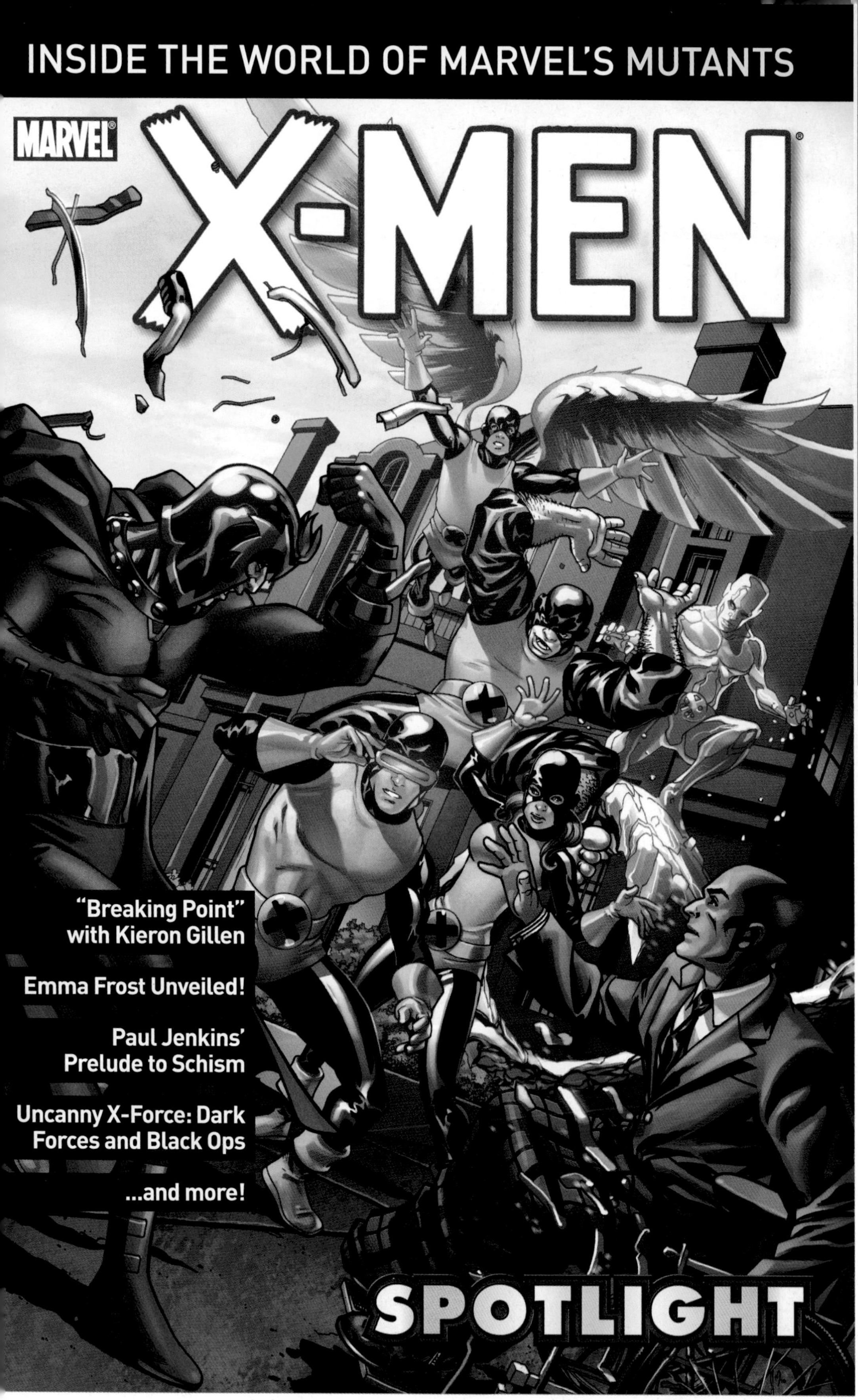
INSIDE THE WORLD OF MARVEL'S MUTANTS
MARVEL
X-MEN
"Breaking Point" with Kieron Gillen
Emma Frost Unveiled!
Paul Jenkins' Prelude to Schism
Uncanny X-Force: Dark Forces and Black Ops
...and more!
SPOTLIGHT

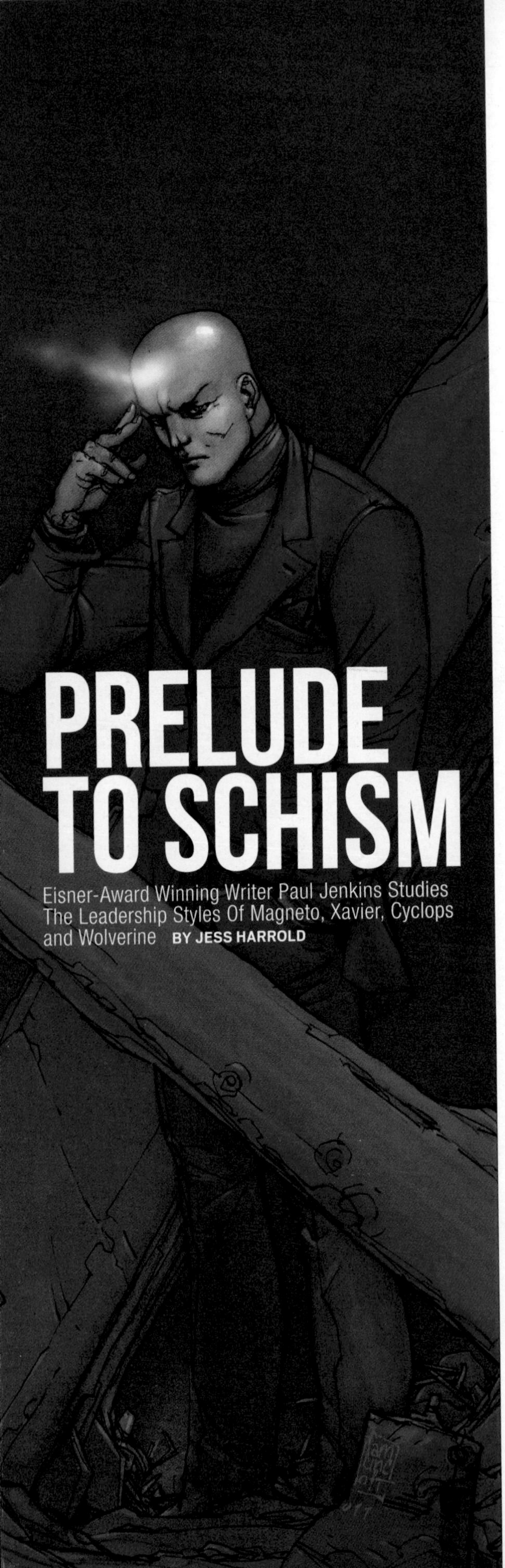

Cover to *X-Men: Prelude to Schism #1* by Giuseppe Camuncoli.

# PRELUDE TO SCHISM

Eisner-Award Winning Writer Paul Jenkins Studies The Leadership Styles Of Magneto, Xavier, Cyclops and Wolverine **BY JESS HARROLD**

The future of the X-Men starts with Paul Jenk
The man who ten years ago penned the s
they said could never be told in the page
*Wolverine: Origin* has returned to rock
world of Marvel's Merry Mutants once ag
A "Schism" is coming – and in a series
plays to his strengths as a master of chara
Paul gets deep inside the heads of four pivotal figures in
X-firmament as they stand on the precipice of the seis
shift set to tear Utopia asunder. *Spotlight* caught up
the always-engaging, Eisner Award-winning writer du
the calm before the storm to chat about the four-i
*Prelude to Schism*, as well as a couple other projects he
in the pipeline.

**What can you tell us about *Prelude to Schism*?**

We are looking at a major event that is going to occu
the Marvel Universe. There's going to be some turn
some stuff going on. Something big is coming. And *Pre*
is a precursor to the event, really setting up the pe
involved. Over my career with Marvel, I've spent a lo
time getting into the meat of the characters. I really
doing that. So we're taking the four core X-Men leaders
examining who they are, what their differences are. W
doing it *Rashomon* style, taking the situation and loo
at it from four different vantage points. We're lookin
Magneto, Xavier, Cyclops and Wolverine because they
all leader mentalities. We're examining what they feel a
leadership and why.

**Sounds good. You haven't written much X-Men, with a notable exceptions like *Origin* and the X-Men *Mythos* b What drew you to this project?**

The thing that attracted me to this project is the same t
that makes it difficult for me to get into the X-Men pr
I'm not really a soap-opera kind of guy. I've never r
been a guy interested in doing the weekly, monthly
opera. When I wrote Spider-Man monthly, I was al
doing single-issue stories because I really like that ki
book and think I'm pretty good at it. Even looking

R'S STORY: Roberto de la Torre pencils Paul Jenkins' first issue of *X-Men: Prelude to Schism*.

*ude* was more of a character study. This was about the people involved. One of the things Marvel has done is chosen artists that care more about the
*ive*. We don't care about the fight if we don't care about the people involved in the fight, and I think that's well-reflected in Roberto's artwork."

---

*humans*, we did lots of single-issue stories that had
es and tied them into one overarching story. I'm very
a character-study kind of guy, and that's the way I'm
ng *Prelude*. We are leading into something big that's
ening, but the good news is I get to write single-issue
acter studies.

**writer, you now seem to be more interested in self-
ained stories like this, rather than getting involved in a
thly series. Is that fair to say?**
nd no. That seems to have been the discussion I have
with some of the editors at Marvel. I haven't done a
thly book in a long time, but I love doing single-issue
es, which I think have such tremendous value to our
stry. Print publishing is suffering. We have a finite au-
ce that seems to be abandoning us slowly. I always feel
you can do single-issue stories that could potentially
g in new members to your audience. I'd love to do a
thly book — but I would want to do it my way, and I
k that doesn't really fit the model these days, where
vel likes things that tie in to each other. It's not that I
t know how to do the tie-ins, or how to work with other
le. It's just that I don't really gravitate to that.

**e you're not as involved as some writers in the monthly
gs-on at Marvel, how do you go about conducting re-
ch when you take on a project like this?**
, blimey, that is tough! It's a pain. I constantly
omething that I think has real value in terms of
telling, and then I'll send it in and the editor will say,
y Paul, I feel really bad about this, but we just killed

him." I just wrote the whole issue centering on the guy,
and he's dead. So it is difficult to stay on top. But I tend to
communicate with the editors pretty well and hopefully not
misstep too much.

**Your approach in *Prelude* seems to include looking back
on past events to explore what brought each character to
where they are now.**
I think that's a very good way of putting it. I remember
when I wrote my very last issue of *Spectacular Spider-Man*
with Bucky [*Artist Mark Buckingham — Ed.*], one of the
things I was really so proud of is that we wrote about what
I felt was his real reason for being Spider-Man, in the sense
that he was always going to be that person because he had
lost his parents before he had a chance to prove himself
worthwhile. So this was his actual reason for doing it. He
knew it, his Uncle Ben always knew it, but he had never
really admitted it to himself. I thought that really added
value to the character, that there was some important stuff
in his past that dictated where he is now.

Magneto is obviously like that. He's a man who had the
experience of living through the extermination of seven
and a half million people, where a lot of those kids would
actually be in charge of turning on the gas ovens or picking
up the bodies. They made the Jews kill the Jews. We're
looking at his feelings of why you must lead a certain way;
why you must never abandon a portion of your people. He
has very strong feelings about that. He feels that, to be a
leader, you must never make the mistakes of the past. But
also, here's a guy whose world has been turned upside-down
because Scott Summers has done the one thing that he and

Xavier always wanted to do. He's kind of drunk the Kool-Aid and has tremendous admiration for Cyclops. I think we have something in the Magneto book very similar to my last issue of *Spectacular Spider-Man*. When readers realize what Magneto is saying — and why he's so proud of Scott — they might say, "Oh, yeah, that makes a lot of sense."

**What are your thoughts on the other key figures in *Prelude*?**
Xavier is very proud of Scott because he sees him almost as a son. But Xavier has this myopic mentality where you can't put people at risk. He's been a bit misguided in my opinion. I think he's done his best to make a cohesive world for the X-Men, but he hasn't executed it properly. He has a bit of remorse. His view of leadership is you must be prepared to accept all possibilities. But in my opinion, his view is the one that's proven to be faulty. Cyclops, on the other hand, has a very strong idea about how to be in control, because he has always had to struggle to control his powers. His struggle to control himself has taught him how to exert control over other people, and over a situation. I know that editor Nick Lowe is very, very excited about the Cyclops issue. He thinks we've done something in that story that really opens up a view of Cyclops that people haven't seen before. Finally, you've got Logan, and his view is very much, "The world is a wolf pack; the strongest wolf is the one who

gets to lead." So leadership is always up for review, sense. He very much admires what Scott has done, but a little wary. He wants to make sure that it's done prop He certainly is not a power-hungry guy. He's never that profile. But he is a guy who wants to make sure strongest is always in a leadership position.

**Speaking of Wolverine — you revealed the character's hidden origin, but this must be the first time you've wr him with the benefit of his memories.**
That's absolutely true! (*Laughs.*) Since I did *Origin*, y looking at ten years of movement. It's one of the rea why we were right to do it. We said at the time that it c reenergize the character. Now, they've had years of b able to tell, "Oh, I remember this, I remember that." bit complex in some ways, but I'm taking a relatively si approach. I like to get to the core — what led him to be and what taught him to think this way.

**It's great to see you busy at Marvel again, with a few projects on the way beyond *Prelude*. Seeing as though a longtime friend of the X-Men, what can you tell us a your upcoming *Ka-Zar* series?**
One of the things I was given the task of, when I first to Marvel, was fixing a character. The Inhumans had r

---

MAGNETO BY MUTTI: Pencils by Andrea Mutti from *X-Men: Prelude to Schism* featuring Magneto.

"The core of the Magneto issue was that we were trying to get into the gravity of a man's tormented past. I was a bit nervous about whether that wou carried. But I've got to say — and this is not blowing smoke; it's not talking the Marvel line — wow, I was so impressed that the gravity of the materi were talking about was not glossed over. It's totally in there, and I love it for that."

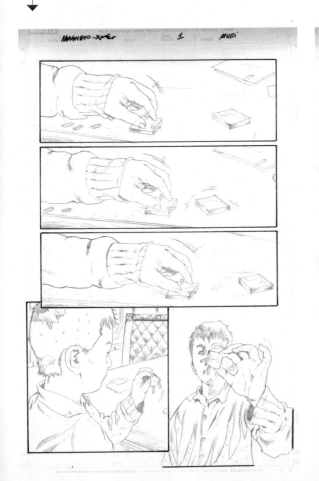

·n successful, but Jae Lee and I seemed to do quite well. *ıe series won Paul his Eisner! — Ed.*] We were able to Spider-Man, who was in the doldrums a bit at the time, l Bucky and I did very simple stories that righted the p a bit. So I talked with Tom Brevoort about a couple of ıracters that aren't being successful right now, and one :hem was Ka-Zar. I started working on it, and I came up h this very *Inhumans* kind of vibe with the Savage Land l the tribes. I thought the idea of the zebra tribe was ıolutely brilliant. They have these people that, if they're ite, they draw black stripes upon themselves, and if ·y're black they draw white stripes — so they have no e at all. I thought that was a beautiful idea, and they've /er done anything with it. So I started looking, and y have all these crazy tribes, and I thought, "Wow, it's : *Inhumans*. We can do really cool things with them." *'nhumans* was about the United States, then *Ka-Zar* is ›ut the world.

**;t question: You've got an *All-Winners Squad* miniseries tap. Any chance of a Logan cameo?**

*ughs.*) Blimey, I can't remember if we did! I've actually tten all eight issues. I prefer to call that *Band of Heroes*. ıt's like my favorite title in years. It just tells the story, now? So I think it's *All-Winners Squad: Band of Heroes*.

That one is a massive labor of love for me. I love Second World War stuff. What *Band of Heroes* is about is that back in the day, Timely Comics was publishing all these crummy old characters. One seven-page story of "Davy and the Demon," and he would just disappear! So the premise I came up with was that Timely was actually printing propaganda leaflets for the U.S. military. Those Timely comics were actually propaganda, so the people in them were actually real. So why did people like Davey and the Demon only have one seven-page story printed? Because they went to foreign lands and lost their lives in service of their country. So it's really poignant, and everyone will cry.

*We're tearing up already! Look out for Paul tugging at your heartstrings in the pages of* X-Men: Prelude to Schism, Ka-Zar *and* All-Winners Squad: Band of Heroes. ■

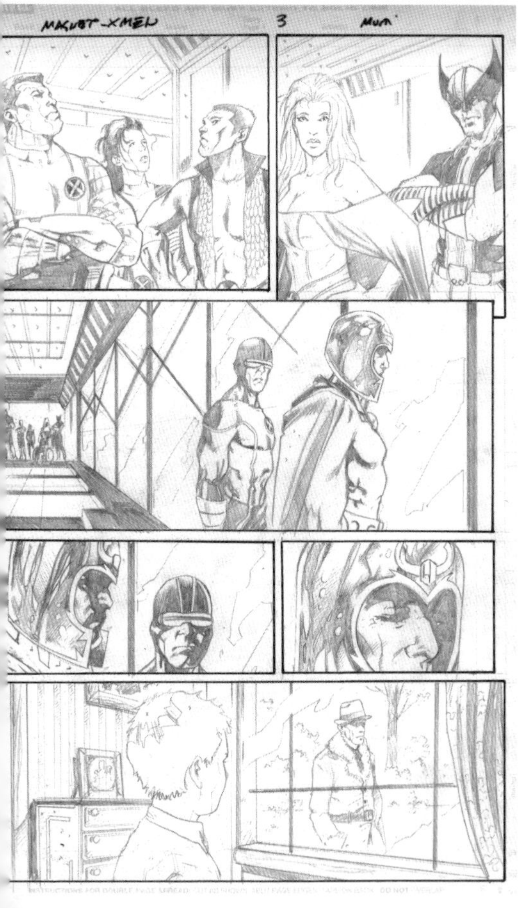

Cover to *X-Men: Prelude to Schism #3* by Camuncoli.

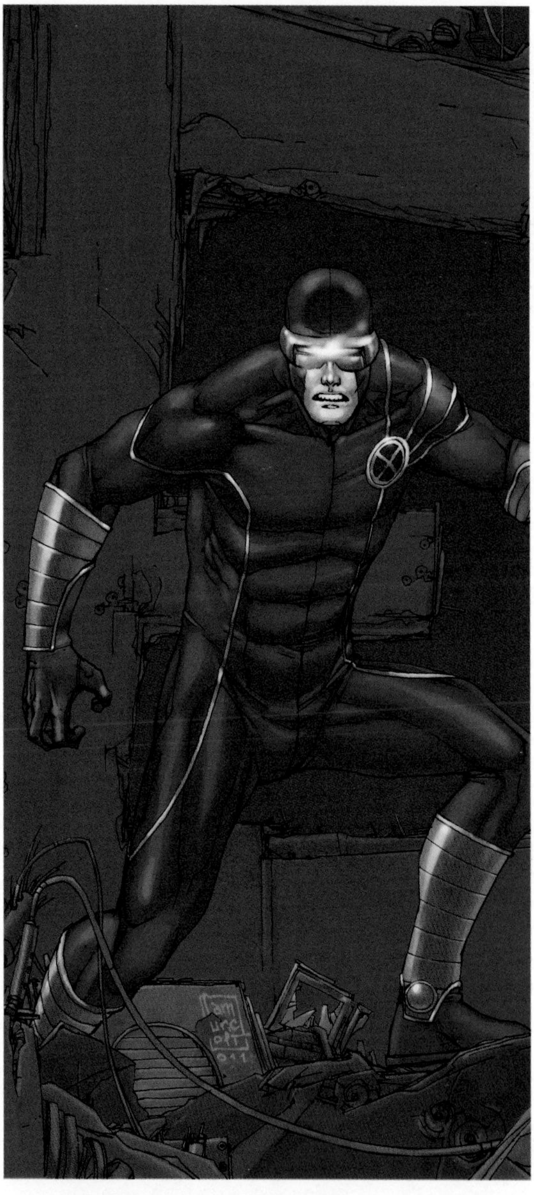

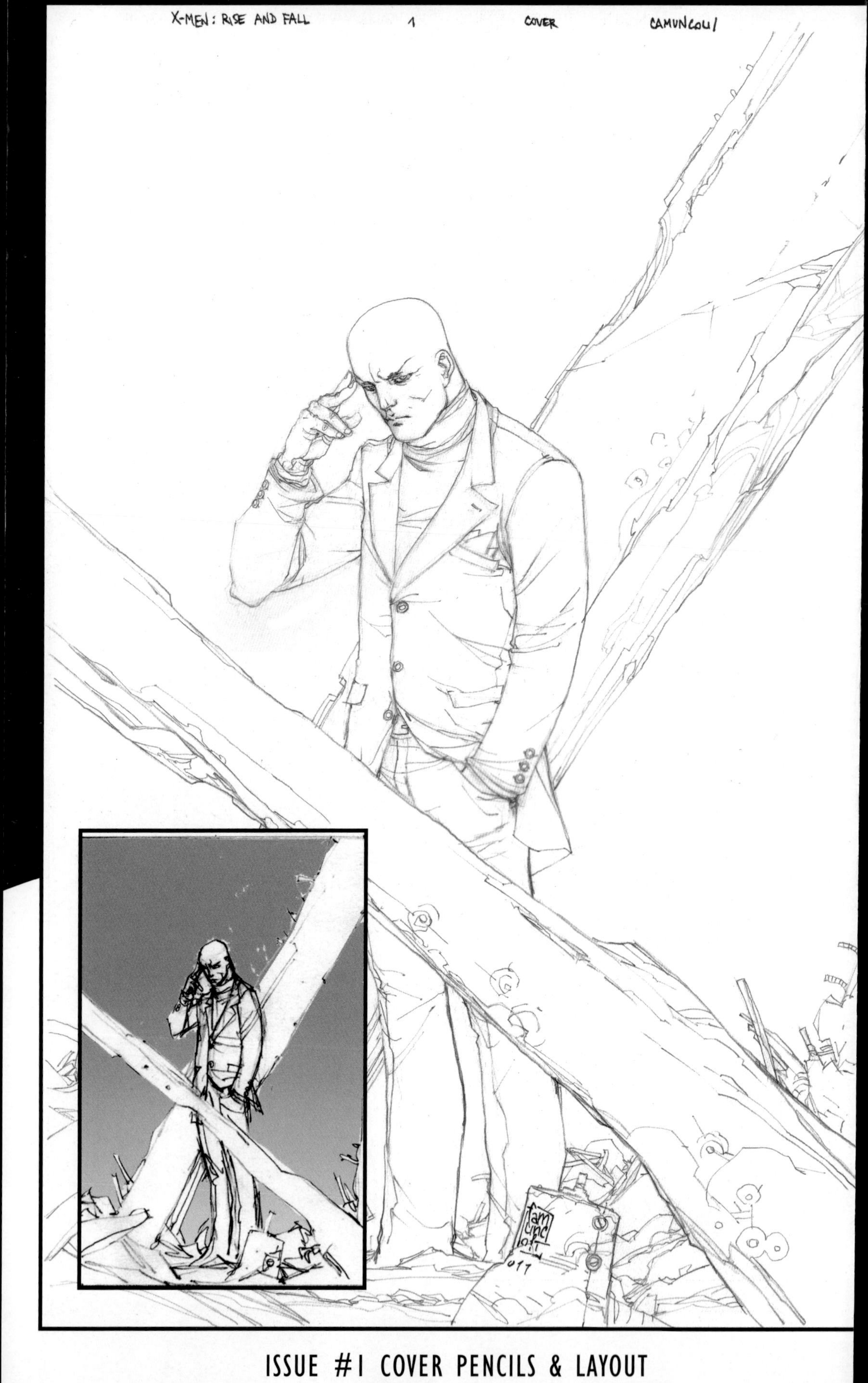
X-MEN: RISE AND FALL
1
COVER
CAMUNCOLI

ISSUE #1 COVER PENCILS & LAYOUT

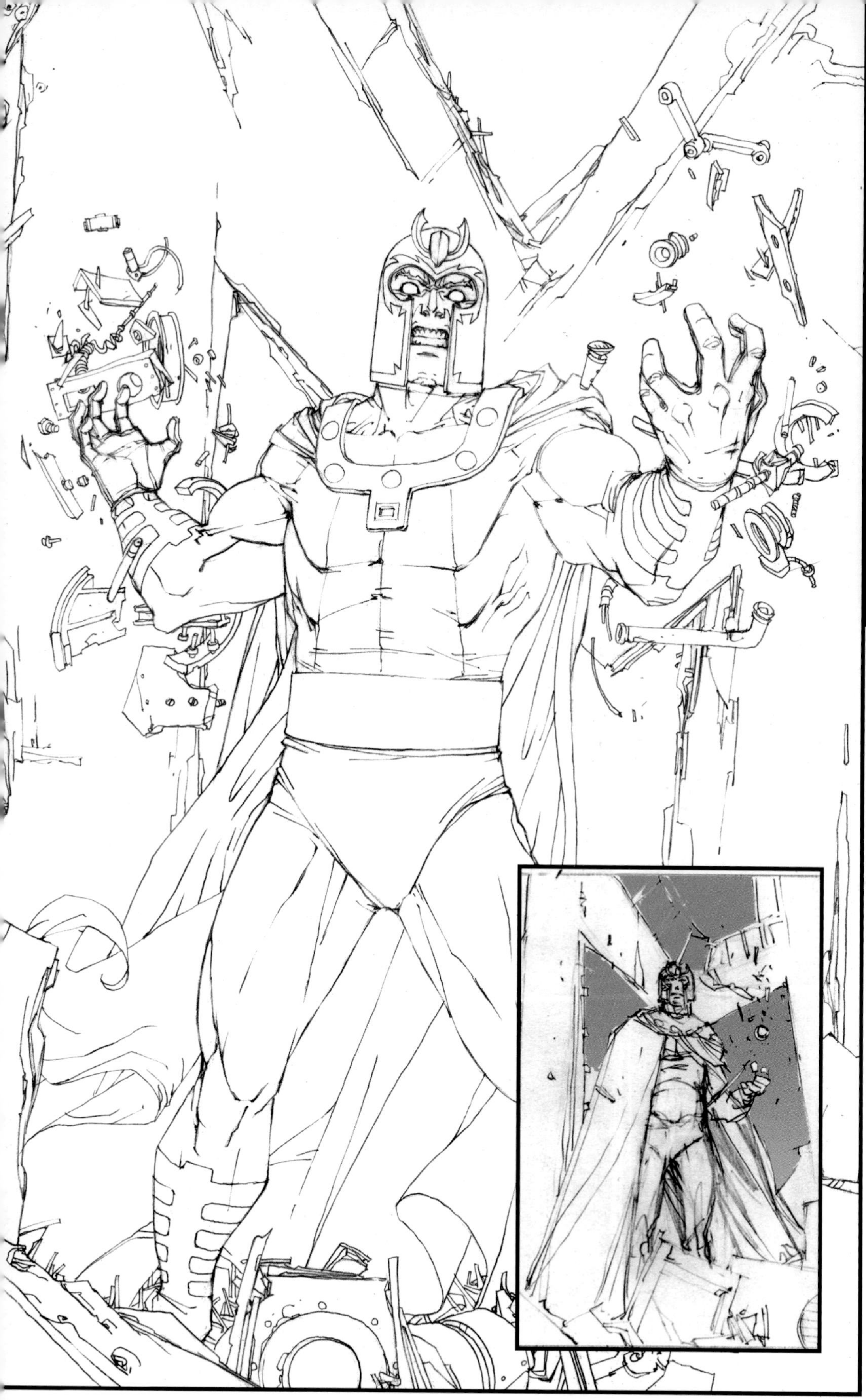

ISSUE #2 COVER PENCILS & LAYOUT

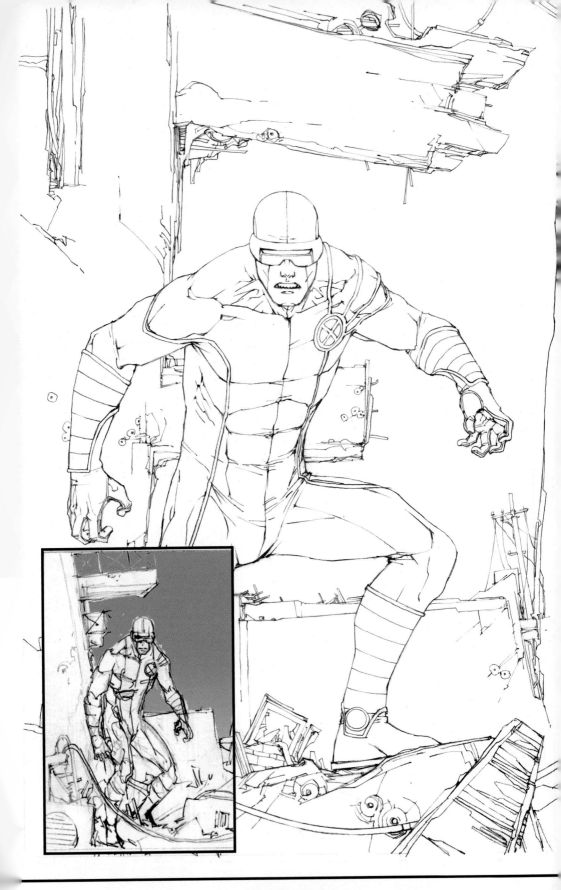

ISSUE #3 COVER PENCILS & LAYOUT

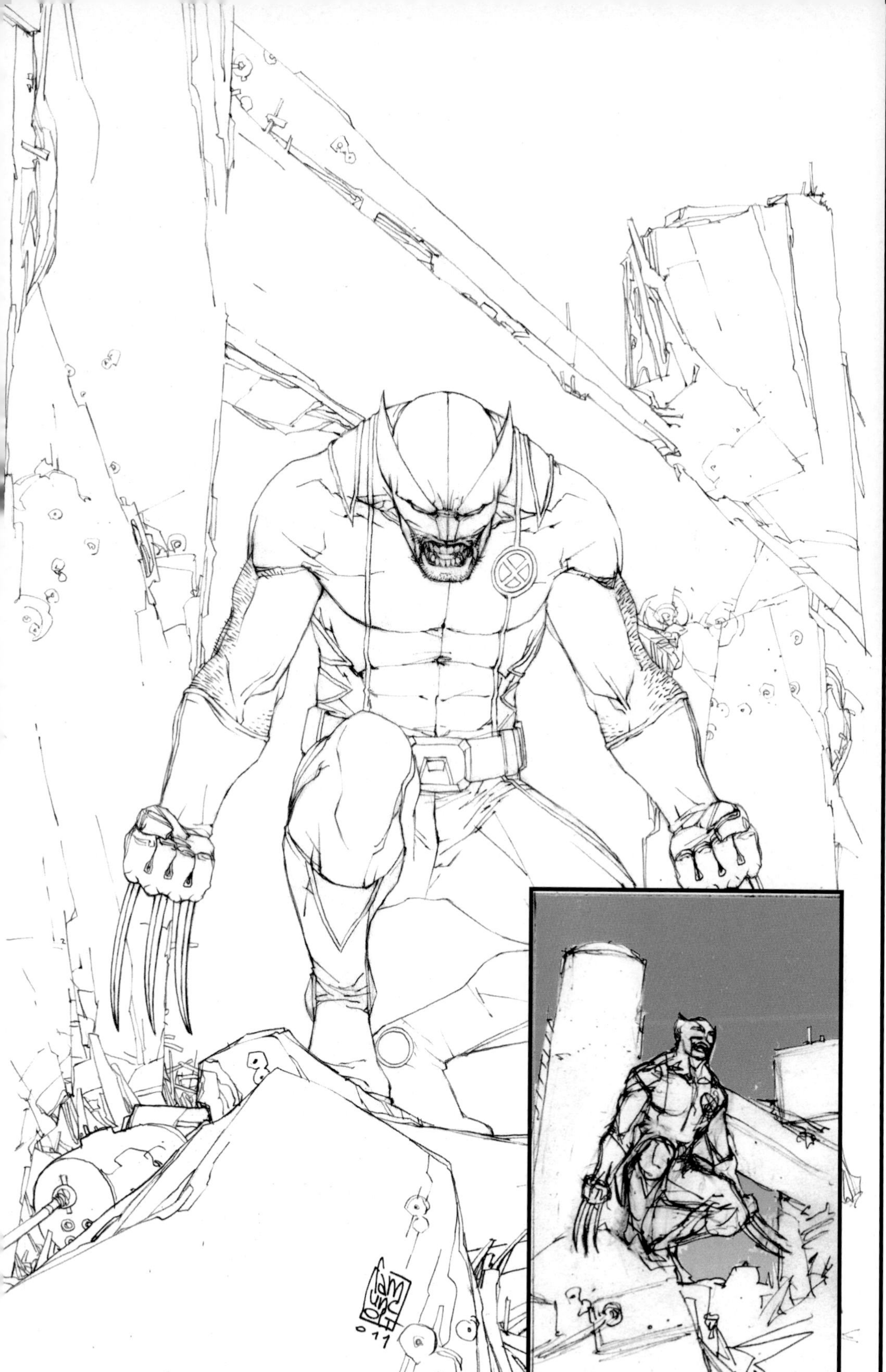

ISSUE #4 COVER PENCILS & LAYOUT

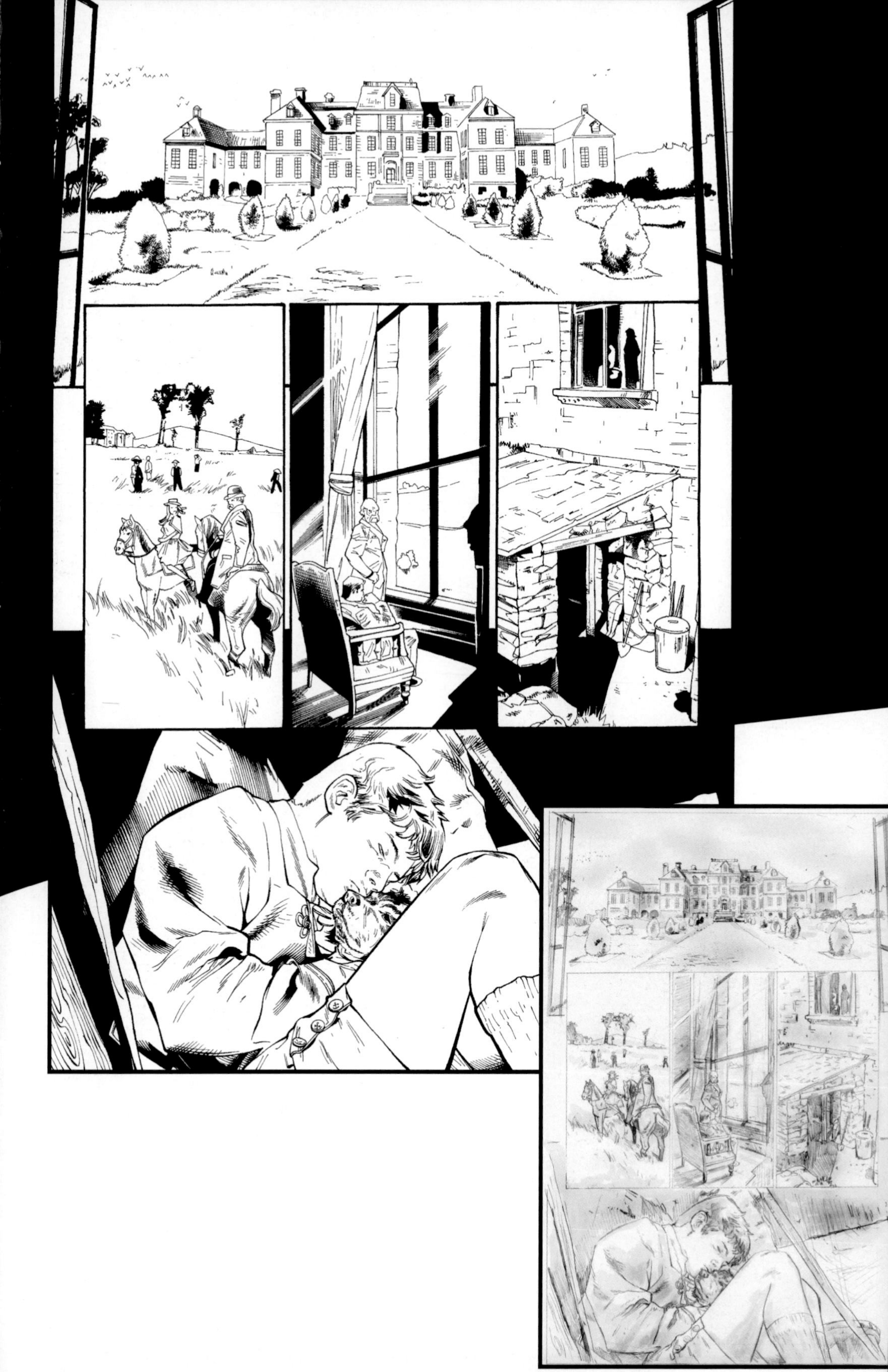

ISSUE #4 PAGE 4 PENCILS & INKS

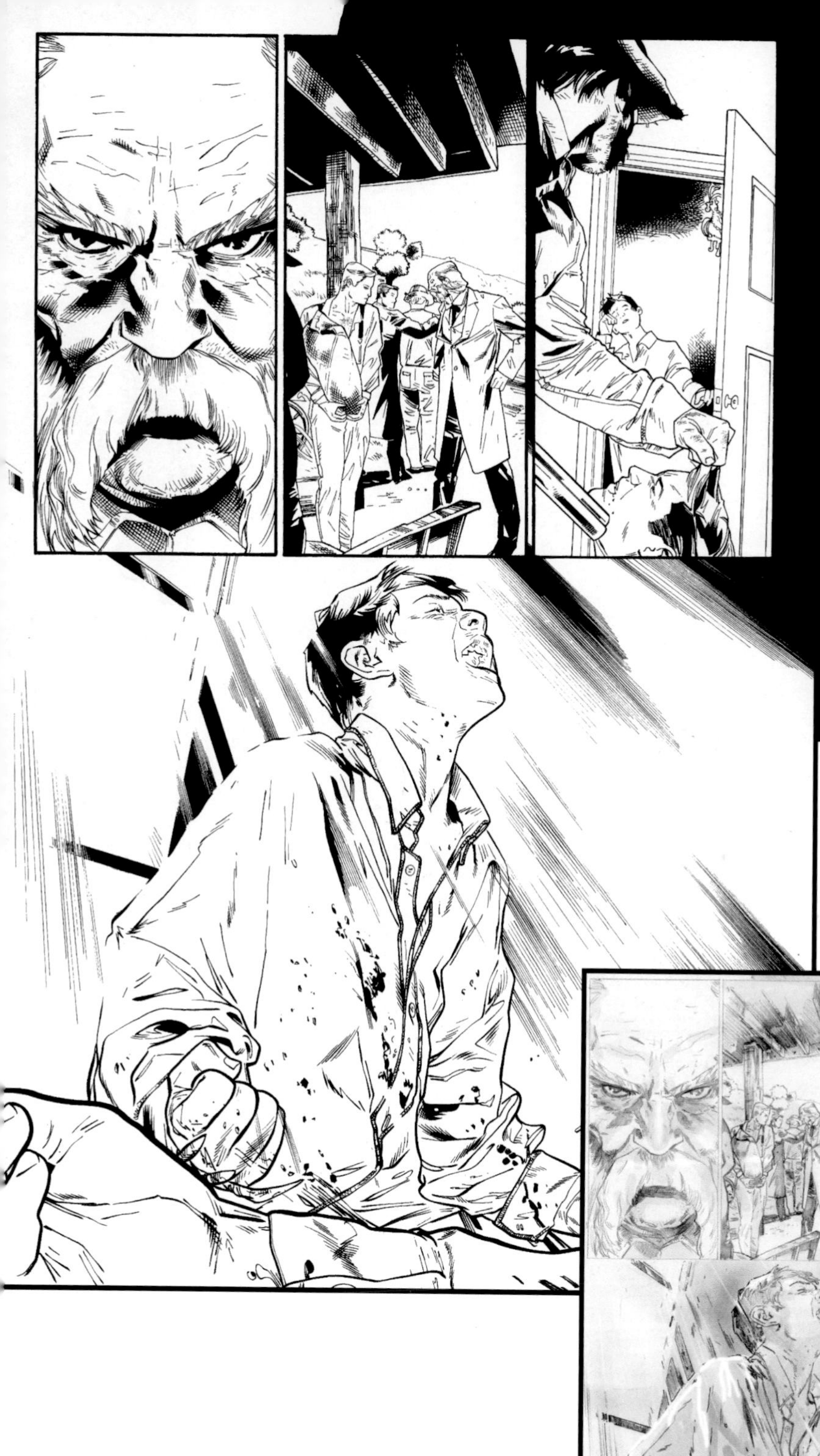

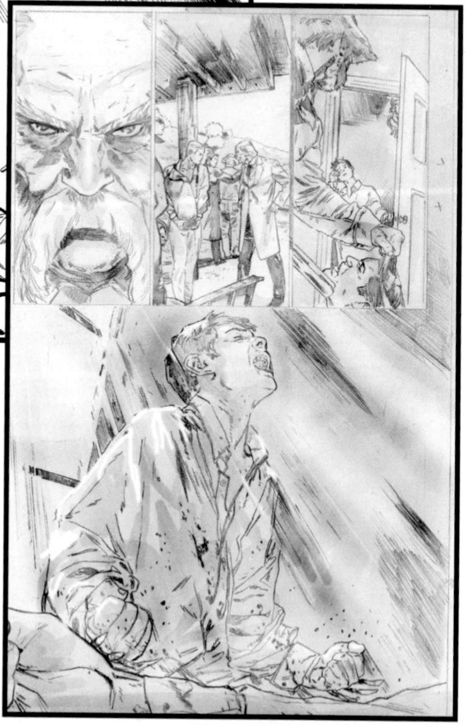

ISSUE #4 PAGE 5 PENCILS & INKS

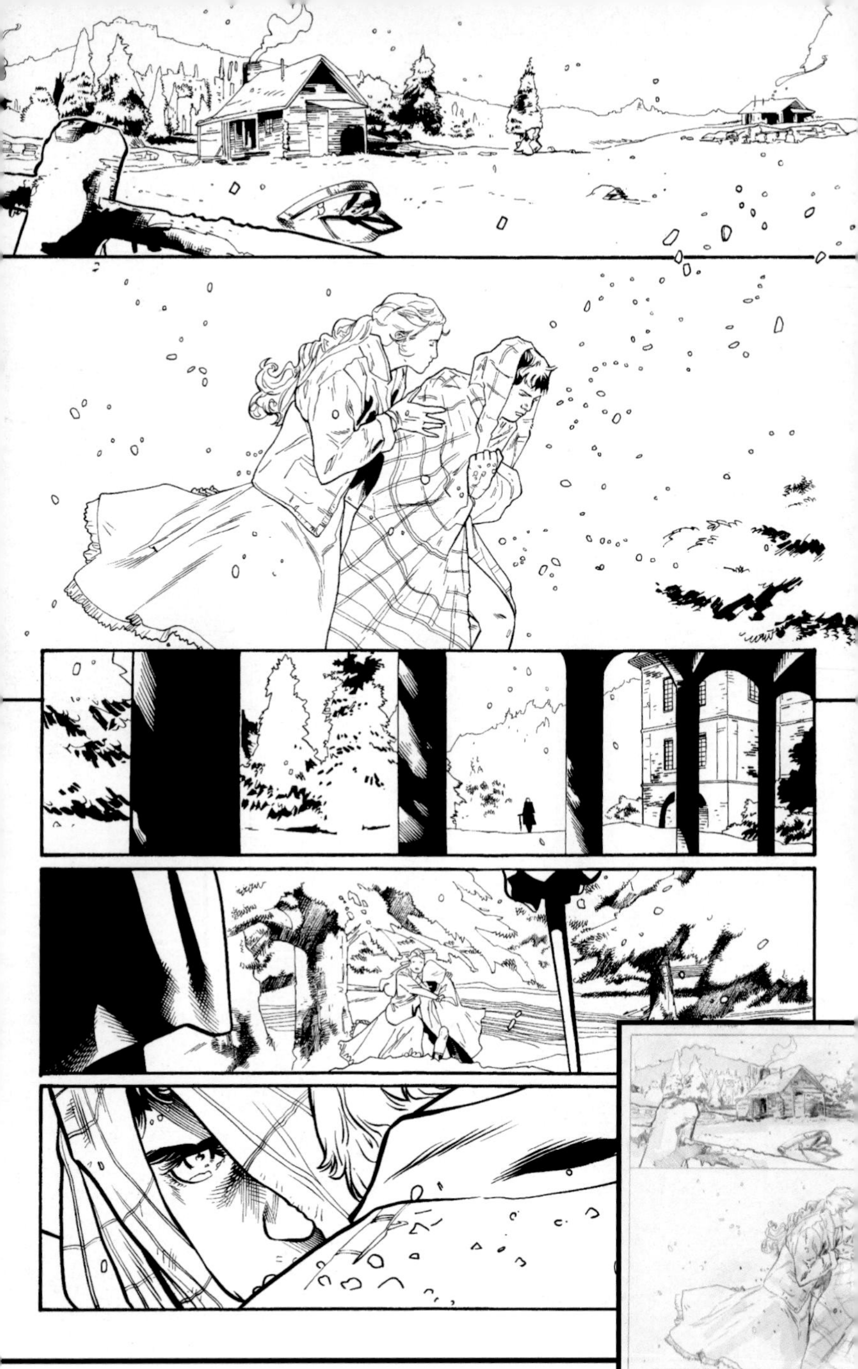

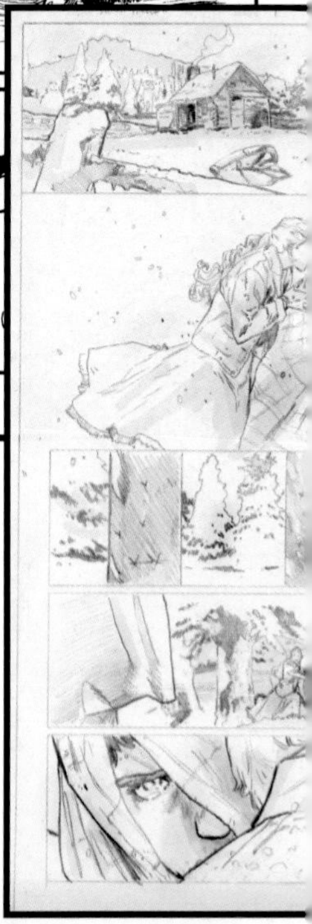

ISSUE #4 PAGE 6 PENCILS & INKS

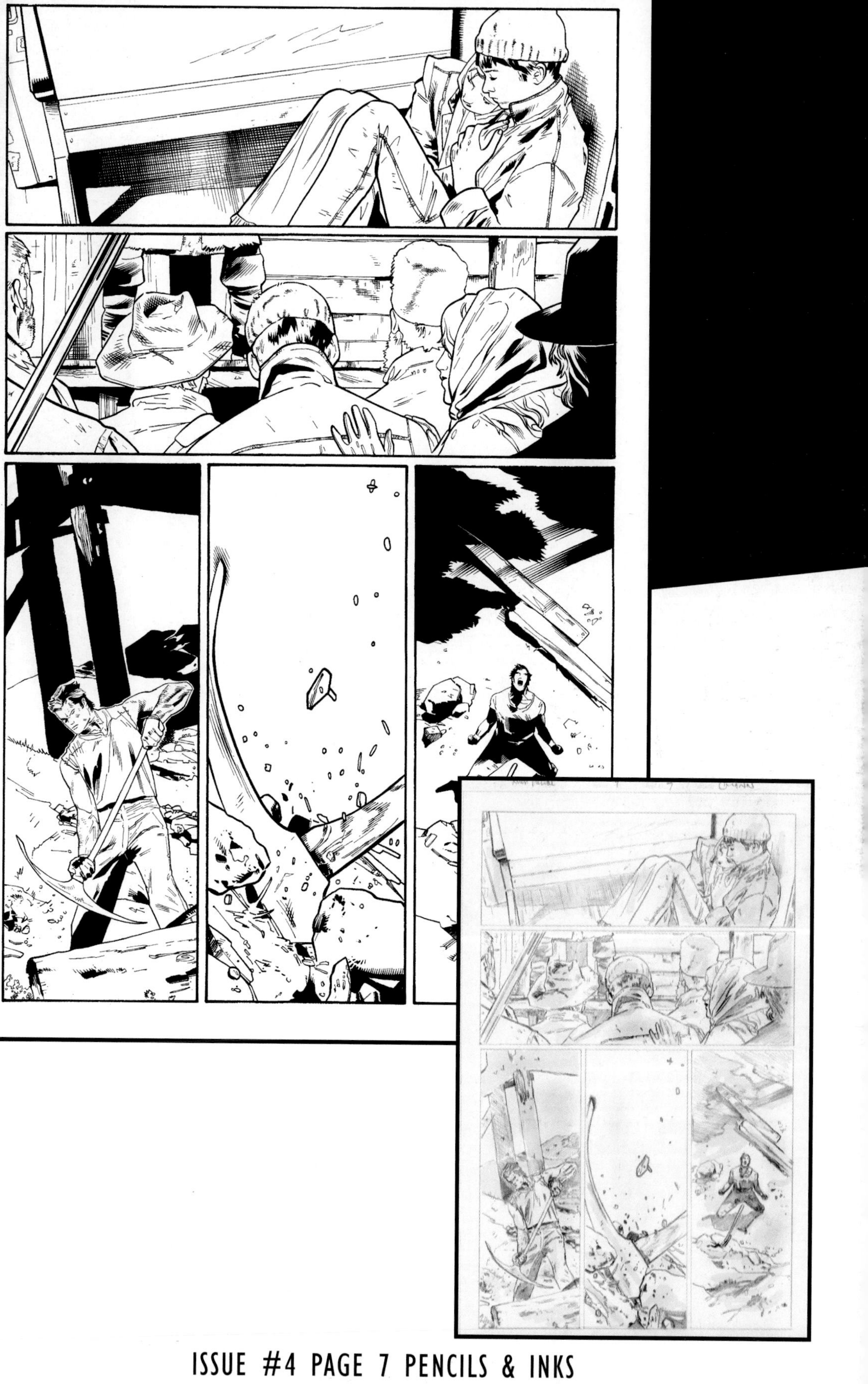

ISSUE #4 PAGE 7 PENCILS & INKS

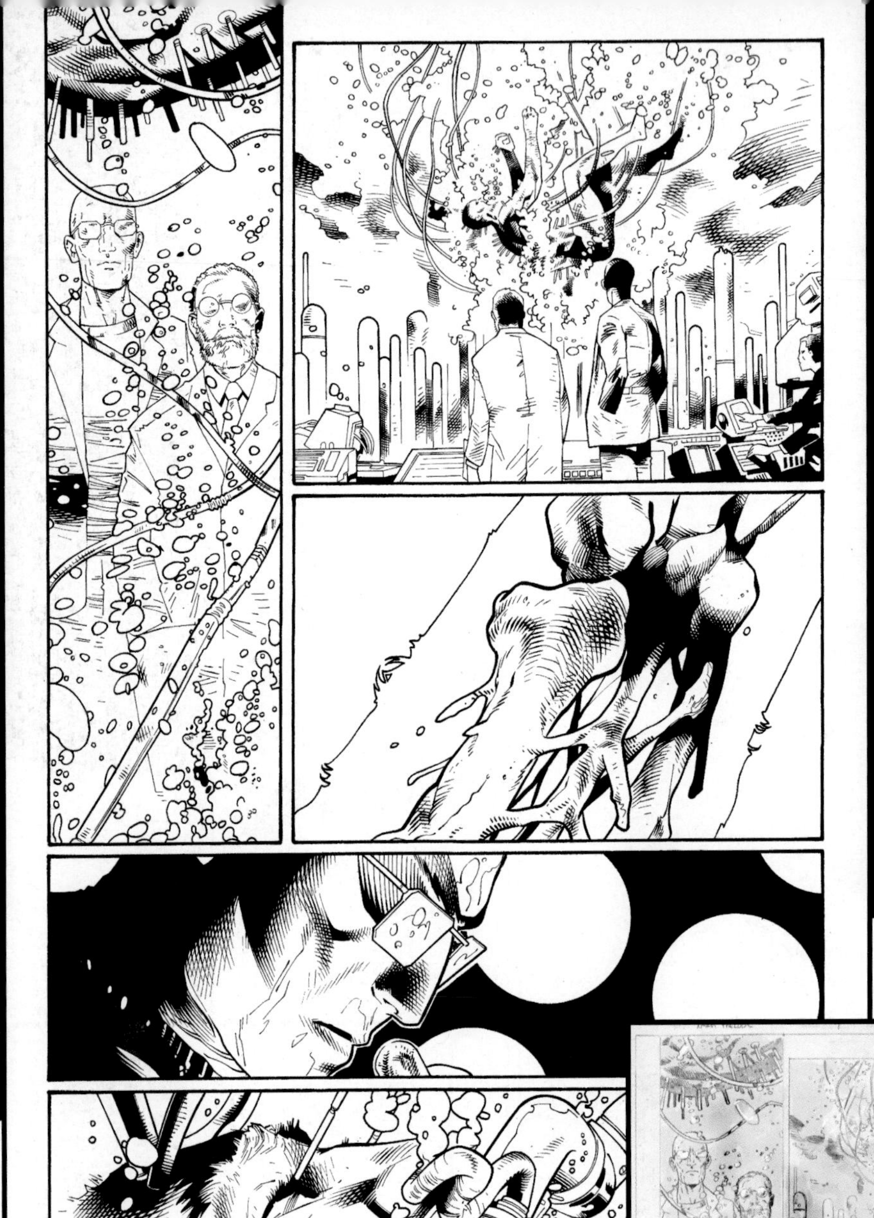

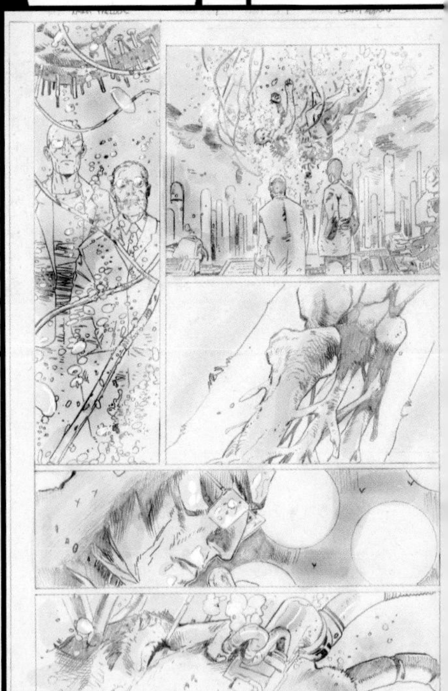

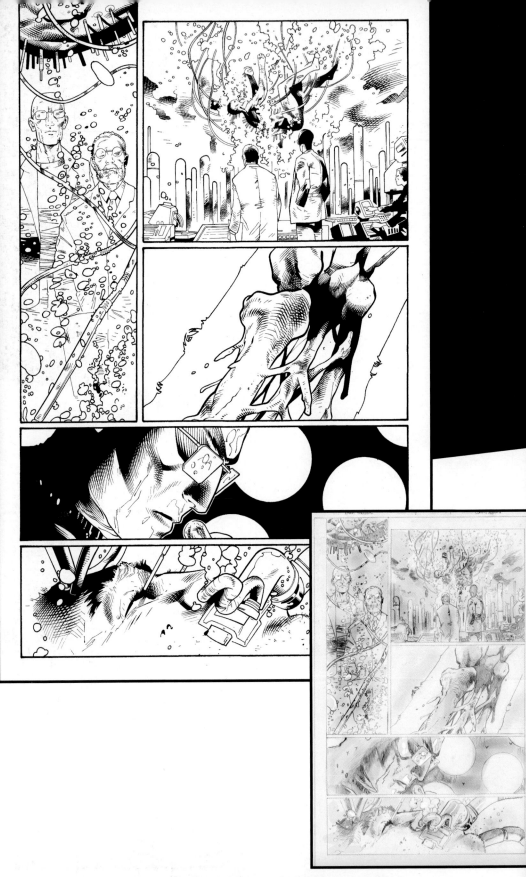

ISSUE #4 PAGE 14 PENCILS & INKS

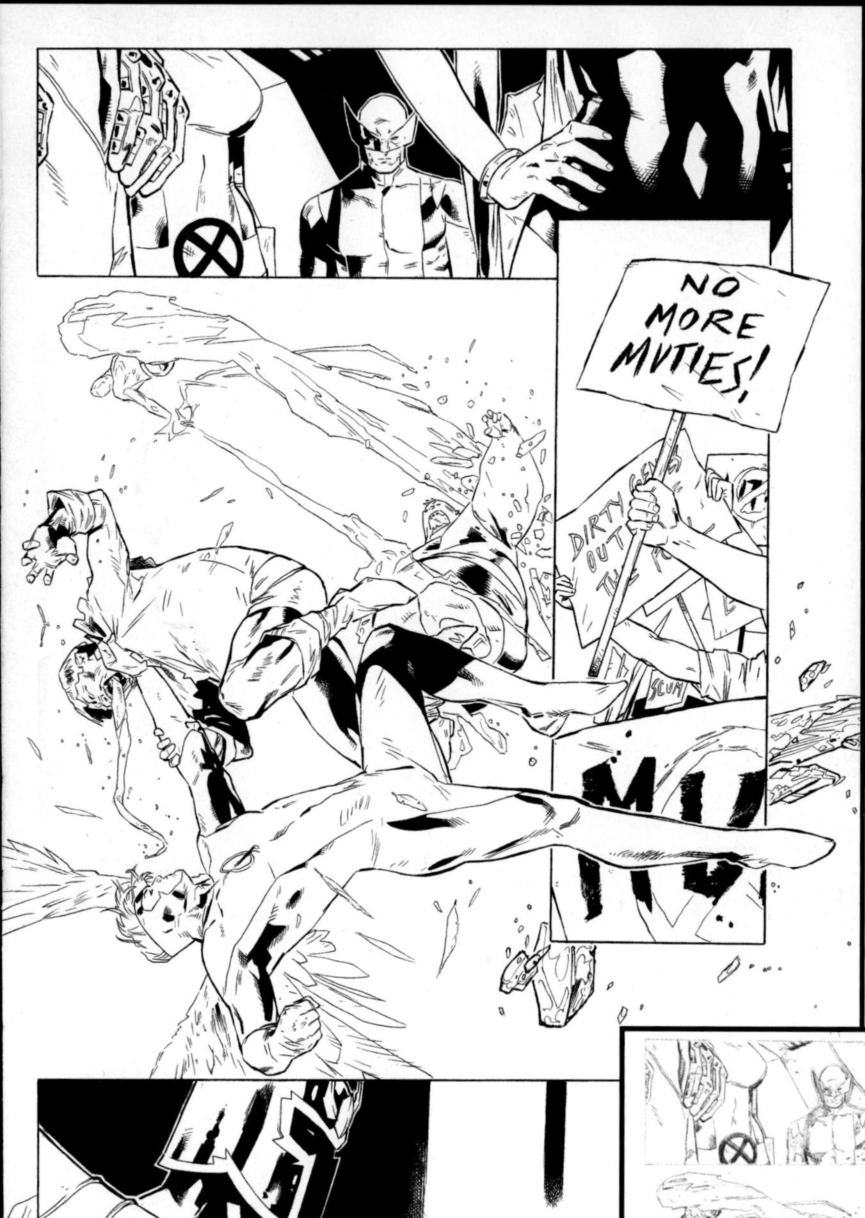
NO MORE MUTIES!
SCUM

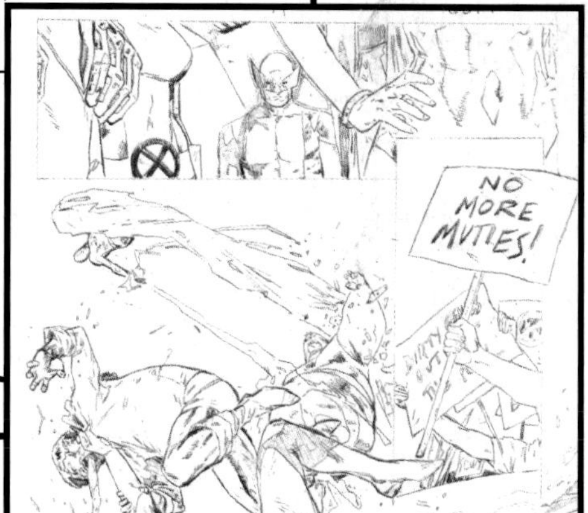
NO MORE MUTIES!

ISSUE #4 PAGE 19 PENCILS & INKS